JOURNAL FOR THE STUDY OF THE OLD TESTAMENT
SUPPLEMENT SERIES

46

Editors
David J A Clines
Philip R Davies

JSOT Press
Sheffield

THE BOOK OF THE JUDGES

An Integrated Reading

Barry G. Webb

Journal for the Study of the Old Testament
Supplement Series 46

For Alison

Copyright © 1987 Sheffield Academic Press

Published by JSOT Press
JSOT Press is an imprint of
Sheffield Academic Press Ltd
The University of Sheffield
343 Fulwood Road
Sheffield S10 3BP
England

Typeset by Sheffield Academic Press
and
printed in Great Britain
by Billing & Sons Ltd
Worcester

British Library Cataloguing in Publication Data

Webb, Barry G.
    The book of the Judges : an integrated
    reading.— (Journal for the study of the
    Old Testament supplement series, ISSN 0309-
    0787; 46).
    1. Bible. O.T. Judges—Criticism,
    interpretation, etc.
    I. Title   II. Series
    222'.3206   BS1305.2

ISBN 1-85075-034-3
ISBN 1-85075-035-1 Pbk

CONTENTS

ACKNOWLEDGMENTS

The present work is a revision of a PhD thesis based on work carried out in the Department of Biblical Studies of the University of Sheffield, and submitted in February, 1985.

My thanks are due, first of all, to my supervisors, David Clines and David Gunn, for being so generous with their time, and for the constant stimulation and encouragement they provided during my research, and to Melinda Fowl and others, for being such efficient and uncomplaining typists. A more general word of thanks is due to all the members of the Department of Biblical Studies at Sheffield for the congenial and stimulating atmosphere created by their openness and helpfulness in so many ways.

Substantial financial assistance was provided by the Tyndale Fellowship for Biblical and Theological Research, and this was supplemented by contributions from the Australian Fellowship of Evangelical Students, from the Brisbane and Sydney branches of the Christian Brethren Research Fellowship, from Burwood Brethren Assembly, and from a band of faithful friends and supporters from Moore Theological College.

All these, and a host of others, whether they knew it or not, were ministers of God to me. I am thankful to Him, and to them.

ABBREVIATIONS

ANE	Ancient Near East(ern)
BASOR	*Bulletin of the American Schools of Oriental Research*
BDB	F. Brown, S.R. Driver, and C.A. Briggs, eds., *A Hebrew and English Lexicon of the Old Testament* (Oxford: Clarendon, 1907 and reprints).
BH	*Biblia Hebraica* (3rd edition; ed. R. Kittel; Stuttgart: Württembergische Bibelanstalt, 1937)
BJRL	*Bulletin of the John Rylands University Library of Manchester*
CBQ	*Catholic Biblical Quarterly*
FRLANT	Forschungen zur Religion und Literatur des Alten und Neuen Testaments
G-K	*Gesenius' Hebrew Grammar*, edited by E. Kautzsch (2nd English edition; ed. A.E. Crowley, Oxford: Clarendon, 1910)
JBL	*Journal of Biblical Literature*
JNES	*Journal of Near Eastern Studies*
JSOT	*Journal for the Study of the Old Testament*
JTS	*Journal of Theological Studies*
OL	Old Latin version
PEQ	*Palestine Exploration Quarterly*
S^h	Syro-hexaplar version
VT	*Vetus Testamentum*
ZAW	*Zeitschrift für die alttestamentliche Wissenschaft*

NOTE ON THE TRANSLATION

In sections where the analysis of the text is particularly detailed (principally in Chapters 2 and 3) I display a translation of the Masoretic Text in lines for ease of reference in the discussion which follows. In general each line contains one complete idea, and this usually means that it contains one finite verb. Exceptions occur where two or more verbs are paired (as in 10.8a), where a subordinate clause completes the idea of the line (as in 10.14a), or where the text is corrupt (as in 10.11b). Also, appositional lists have been given separate lines (as in 10.6c and 9b). Direct speech is indented. The 'colometrical' principles I follow are the same as those used by J.P. Fokkelman in his *Narrative Art and Poetry in the Books of Samuel, a full interpretation based on stylistic and structural analyses, volume 1, King David (2 Sam. 9–20 and 1 Kings 1–2)* (Assen: Van Gorcum, 1981)—see the text on pp. 468-517, and the comments on pp. 8, 18—and which stem from M. Buber and F. Rosenzweig, *Die Schrift and ihre Verdeutschung* (Berlin, 1936).

I have not attempted to produce an original translation. In general the wording follows that of the RSV with 'Yahweh' substituted for 'the LORD'. Occasional further variations occur when a feature of the text to which I refer is not reflected in the RSV (as in 2.3a). The reasons for such deviations will, I hope, be apparent from the discussion provided.

PART I

Chapter 1

RATIONALE

1.00

This study is an exploration of the meaning of the book of Judges considered as a whole, and as distinct from what precedes and follows it in the canon. In this introductory chapter three converging lines of evidence are presented to justify the proposed study in principle. The chapter concludes with an exposition of the method which has been employed.

2.00

The first line of evidence is historical and relates to the antiquity and status of Judges as a distinct book.

2.01

In his treatise, *On The Confusion of Tongues*, in the course of an allegorical apology for the Tower of Babel story of Genesis 11, Philo compares it with the story of Gideon's punishment of the men of Penuel and destruction of their tower (Judg. 8.8-9, 17). Since for Philo both have the same allegorical significance he can appeal to the Penuel story for additional data to enable him to fill out his exposition of the Babel story. He does this particularly with reference to the allegorical significance of the tower:

> τὸν φιλαυτίας κλῆρον παραλαβόντες παῖδες παρὰ πατρὸς
> συναυξῆσαι γλίχονται μεχρις οὐρανοῦ, ἕως ἂν ἡ φιλάρετός τε καὶ
> μισοπόνηρος δίκη παρελθοῦσα καθέλῃ τας πόλεις, ἃς ἐπετείχισαν
> ψυχῇ τῇ ταλαίνῃ, και τὸν πύργον, οὗ τοὔνομα ἐν τῇ των
> κριμάτων[1] αναγραφομένῃ βίβλῳ δεδήλωται. ἔστι δὲ ὡς μὲν
> Ἑβραῖοι λέγουσι Φανουήλ, ὡς δὲ ἡμεῖς ἀποστροφὴ θεοῦ.

Having received from their father [Cain] self-love as their portion,
his children desire to add to it and raise it heaven high, until Justice
who loves virtue and hates evil passes by. She razes to the ground
the cities which they fortified to menace the unhappy soul, and the
tower whose name is explained in the recorded book of judgments.
That name is in the Hebrew tongue Penuel but in our own 'turning
from God'.[2]

The expression 'book of judgments' distinguishes the book to which
Philo is referring here from other books to which he refers elsewhere
in the same treatise. Thus, in his exposition of the expression 'sons of
men' in Gen. 11.5 he refers to 'the royal books':

> ἄγαμαι καὶ τῶν ἐν βασιλικαῖς βίβλοις ἱεροφαντηθέντων, καθ' ἃς οἱ
> πολλαῖς γενεαῖς ὕστερον ἀκμάσαντες καὶ βιώσαντες <ἂν>ὑπαιτίως
> υἱοὶ τοῦ τὸν θεὸν ὑμνήσαντος Δαβὶδ ἀναγράφονται, οὐ περιόντος
> οὐδ' οἱ πρόπαπποι τούτων ἦσαν ἴσως γεγενημένοι.

> I bow, too, in admiration before the mysteries revealed in the royal
> books where it does not offend us to find described as sons of God's
> psalmist David those who lived and flourished many generations
> afterwards, though in David's lifetime probably not even their
> great-grandparents had been born.[3]

The reference is apparently to the naming of David as the 'father' of
such worthies as Asa and Hezekiah in, for example, 1 Kgs 15.11 and
2 Kgs 18.3.

The method of citation employed here (reference to a named book
as the source) is not typical of Philo's general practice.[4] His reference
to the book containing the Penuel incident is of particular interest,
however, since it is the earliest extant reference to the book of Judges
as far as I have been able to determine. The book, of course, had a
long history prior to Philo's reference to it, but the documentation of
that history is all later than him.[5]

2.02

The wordings of the two oldest and best MSS of the Greek Judges
(κριταί) differ in so many details from the beginning to the end of the
book that Rahlfs, in his *Septuaginta* of 1935, found it necessary to
follow the precedent established by Ussher (1665)[6] and Lagarde
(1891)[7] and print the two texts in tandem. In Rahlfs' edition the A
text is at the top of each page and the B text at the bottom, with
separate critical notes for each. The textual phenomenon which is

exhibited visually in this way is unique to κριταί in the LXX corpus and has given rise to a vigorous debate, still ongoing, about the textual history of this book.

A review of the debate (to 1968) is given, with appropriate bibliography, in Jellicoe's *The Septuagint and Modern Study* and need not be repeated here.[8] In general the tide of opinion in this century has swung away from explanation in terms of two independent translations (favoured by, among others, Grabe 1705, Lagarde 1891, Rahlfs 1935, and Kahle 1959) towards explanation in terms of successive and more or less independent revisions of a common archetype, a hypothetical 'old Greek version' (favoured in various forms by Pretzl 1925, Billen 1942, Cooper 1948, Soisalon-Soininen 1952, and Bodine 1980), with B generally being regarded as representing an earlier form of the text than A.[9]

Common to all this work is the recognition that the phenomenon exhibited in Rahlfs's *Septuaginta* points to a textual history for κριταί which distinguishes it from the books which precede and follow it in the LXX corpus (Ἰησοῦς, Ῥούθ, Βασιλειῶν Α'). In addition, the mobility of Ῥούθ in the uncial MSS serves to underline not only its *own* separate identity, but, incidentally, that of κριταί as well: in Vaticanus (B) and Alexandrinus (A) Ῥούθ occurs between κριταί and Βασιλειῶν Α' A, but in Basilano (N) it occurs between Ἰησοῦς and κριταί.[10]

It is presumably to a form of this book that Philo refers in his comments on the Penuel incident, although his title for it is not the same as that by which it is identified in the uncials (i.e. κριταί) and his one verbatum quotation from it (Judg. 8.9) does not follow exactly either the A or B text but has elements in common with both.[11]

2.03

Josephus claims to have based his *Antiquities* on 'the sacred books' (αἱ ἱεραὶ βίβλοι)[12] of which, he tells us elsewhere[13] there are in all twenty-two, five of which deal with the period from creation to Moses, and thirteen of which deal with the period from Joshua to Artaxerxes I. He does not however give them individual titles nor indicate in the course of the *Antiquities* which of them he is utilizing at any given point. It is not surprising therefore that he does not name κριταί although he does use almost its entire contents in his account[14] of a quite distinct 'age of judges' which he defines in the following terms:

μετὰ δὲ τὴν ἐκείνου τελευτὴν ἔτεσι τοῖς πᾶσι δέκα καὶ πρὸς τούτοις ὀκτὼ τὸ πλῆθος αὐτῶν ἀναρχία κατέσχε. μετὰ ταῦτα δ᾽ εἰς τὴν προτέραν ἐπανῆλθον πολιτείαν τῷ κατὰ πόλεμον ἀρίστῳ δόξαντι γεγενῆσθαι καὶ κατ᾽ ἀνδρείαν περὶ των ὅλων δικάζειν ἐπιτρέποντες. καὶ διὰ τοῦτο τὸν χρόνον τοῦτον τῆς πολιτείας κριτῶν ἐκάλεσαν.

After his [Joshua's] death for full eighteen years the people continued in a state of anarchy: whereafter they returned to their former polity, entrusting supreme juridical authority to him who in battle and in bravery had proved himself the best; and that is why they called this period of their political life the age of judges.[15]

Interestingly, he does not locate the story of Ruth in this 'age of judges' but in the high priesthood of Eli[16] thus implicitly bracketing Ρούθ with Βασιλειῶν Α´ rather than with κριταί.

2.04
The differences between the A and B texts of κριταί, although extensive, are entirely differences of wording: both texts begin and end at the same point and contain the same subject-matter in the same order throughout, and both are in agreement in this respect with the MT of the same book.

2.05
There are only three references to the text of Judges (שפטים) in the Mishnah[17] but these are supplemented within the Talmud (that is, in the Gemara) by approximately two hundred further references.[18] In line with general practice in the Talmud most of these references are made without mention of the specific book which is their source. In a couple of cases, however, the book (ספר) of Judges as such does receive specific mention. Quotations below are from the English text of the Soncino editions.[19]

'Abodah Zarah 25a contains a discussion of the reference to the Book of Jashar in 2 Sam. 1.18, namely, 'he bade them teach the children of Judah [to handle] the bow, behold it is written in the Book of Jashar'. In the course of this discussion R. Samuel b. Naḥmani is quoted as having said:

It is the Book of Judges, which is here called the Book of Jashar, because it contains the verse, 'In those days there was no King in Israel; every man did that which was Jashar ['right'] in his own eyes'. And where is [Judah's skill in archery] referred to in it? 'That the generations of the Children of Israel might know, to teach them war'; now what kind of warfare requires teaching? Surely archery. But how do we know that this verse refers to Judah?—From the scriptural verse, 'Who shall go up for us first against the Canaanites, to fight against them? And the Lord said, Judah shall go up'.

The three citations in this quotation are from 21.25, the closing words of the book (cf. 17.6), from 3.2, and from 1.1-2, the opening words of the book, in that order. Other identifications for the Book of Jashar suggested in the discussion include 'the book of Deuteronomy' (R. Eleazar) and 'the Book of Abraham, Isaac and Jacob' (R. Johanan).

Judges is reckoned to be the second book in 'the Prophets': 'Our Rabbis taught: the order of the Prophets is Joshua, Judges, Samuel, Kings, Jeremiah, Ezekiel, Isaiah, and The Twelve' (*Baba Bathra* 14b). Later in the same paragraph Samuel is credited with its authorship: 'Samuel wrote his [own] book, and Judges and Ruth' (שמואל כתב ספרו ושפטים ורות).

The tractate *Soferim* provides an interesting insight into scribal practice involved in the transmission of the prophetic books:

> Between a book of the Prophets and another, one should not leave the same empty space as between two books of the Torah, but in each case the space must be that which has been prescribed for it. Furthermore, a book of the prophets must begin at the top (*Soferim* 111.2).

This tractate is generally reckoned to date from after the closure of the Babylonian Talmud proper and by some to be as late as the eighth century, but appeal is constantly made in it to what is established practice, with supporting 'quotations' from distinguished Rabbis as early as the first century CE. Whatever its date this tractate witnesses to the manner in which the distinctions between the various books of the Prophets, noted in the Talmud, were carefully preserved in subsequent transmission.

2.06

Such then is the entity with which this study is concerned. It is an objective reality, a received object for study and not one whose existence or parameters must be postulated before interpretation can begin. The close scrutiny to which I propose to subject it is justified in part, at least, by the institutional endorsement which has guaranteed its preservation and brought it within the purview of serious interpretation. It has the antiquity and status of a classic.

3.01

While it is clear that early authors and commentators recognized Judges as a book (βίβλος/ספר) with clearly defined limits and with its own distinctive subject-matter, it is not clear to what extent they recognized it as a literary unit with its own unique message, that is, as a conceptual unit.

The descriptive title used by Philo, 'the recorded book of judgments' (ἡ τῶν κριμάτων ἀναγραφομένη βίβλος), appears to identify judgment as the ideological focus of the book, and this is certainly in keeping with the theme of judgment on impiety which he is developing in *De Confusione* at that point. Such judgment is the allegorical meaning which Philo finds in the Penuel incident. But whether this is for him also the meaning of the book as a whole is impossible to determine because we do not know whether he coined the title himself or inherited it from others.

The standard titles κριταί/שפטים draw attention on the other hand, to the divinely energized agents of Yahweh's salvation—the 'judges'. In the Talmud however, as in Philo, the meaning or message of the book as such is never explicitly discussed. The rabbis use it as a source from which texts can be extracted for use in theological discussion, but in general, as we have seen, the book itself is not acknowledged as the source. It is significant only as part of a larger whole (the prophets, the scriptures) which is the true interpretive context for any of its parts, regardless of which 'book' they belong to. It is only on rare occasions when the requirements of a particular discussion demand it that the book as such receives mention at all.

It is Josephus who comes closest to treating the book of Judges as a meaningful whole. In line with his historiographical purpose he takes a more holistic approach to the book, utilizing most of its contents, as I have indicated. He does not use all its contents, however, and his omissions significantly alter the perspective, especially in relation to particular characters in the story. Gideon, for example, becomes 'a man of moderation and a model of every virtue' (V.vi. 6.230, Loeb trans.); all mention of involvement with the ephod cult at Ophrah is omitted. The internal arrangement of the book also is drastically modified in Josephus's account, the civil war of chapters 19–20 occurring before the advent of the first judge Othniel. Josephus does, by implication, offer an interpretation, however forced, of the book as a whole, but as I have indicated, attention is never drawn in the *Antiquities* to the separate books or to the breaks between them. The effect is to emphasize their continuity rather than their separateness, their meaningfulness as a *corpus* of sacred books (ἱεραὶ βίβλοι) rather than as distinct literary units.

3.02
That the stretch of material comprising our present book of Judges is part of a larger narrative and to that extent incomplete in itself is almost too obvious to warrant mention. Moreover, it is theoretically possible that the distribution of this larger narrative over a series of books was occasioned by the physical constraints imposed upon ancient writers by, for example, the length of ancient scrolls, so that the book divisions are simply divisions of convenience without any literary significance whatever.[20] Yet, as far as I am aware, it has never seriously been proposed that the book of Judges is, in fact, an entirely arbitrary unit of this kind, even by scholars who have had little or no interest in the separate books as such.

4.00
This brings us to the second line of evidence, which is historical-critical.

4.01
In his monumental study of 1943[21] Martin Noth argued that the division of the historical complex Deuteronomy—2 Kings into 'books' was a secondary development in the history of the tradition which partially obscured the more fundamental continuity—both literary and theological—of an original Deuteronomic History. In this original work Judg. 2.6ff. was the direct continuation of Josh. 23, Joshua's speech in that chapter marking the conclusion of the 'period of the conquest', and Judg. 2.6-11, 14-16, 18-19 being the Deuteronomist's introduction to 'the period of the judges' which in turn was formally concluded with Samuel's speech in 1 Sam. 12. Noth considered that Judg. 3.7-12.15 was composed by the Deuteronomist himself by combining a collection of stories about local tribal heroes with a short list of judge-figures (10.1-5; 12.7-15), Jephthah being the common factor. Judg. 13.1 was then followed directly by 1 Sam. 1.1ff.

Thus Judg. 2.6-11, 14-16, 18-19, 3.7-13.1 was the segment of this original Deuteronomic History from which the present book of Judges developed through a series of editorial revisions and expansions.

Noth argued that the 'deuteronomistically edited' passages, Josh. 24.1-28 and Judg. 2.1-5 were inserted secondarily after Josh. 23 and—later still—without any Deuteronomistic revision, 'the mass of old traditional fragments which form the present Judges 1'.[22] Finally the original introduction of chapter 2 was expanded, possibly in more than one stage, to give the present text of 2.11-3.6. The section 2.20-3.6 in particular clearly presupposed the existence of 1.21, 27ff.

Noth did not absolutely exclude the possibility that the Samson complex was part of the original Deuteronomic History but considered this unlikely on the grounds that it showed no signs of being worked on by the Deuteronomist, that Samson's name is conspicuous by its absence in 1 Sam. 12.11, 'a passage which clearly aims to be comprehensive (vv. 9-11)'[23], and that it was the Deuteronomist's usual practice to attach only one specified 'saviour' figure to each specified period of foreign rule, Samuel fulfilling this role in the context of the Philistine oppression announced in 13.1.

No comment was offered on the last five chapters of the book except that 'Judg. 17-21 was not part of the Dtr's work but was added later'.[24] In a subsequent article[25] Noth has discussed the background and purpose of the narrative in chapters 17-18 without direct reference to its context in the book. He does remark however that 'the entire story does not fit at all well into the Deuteronomistic conception of "the period of the Judges"'.[26] By arguing that the formula 'in those days there was no king . . .' is fully integrated into its narrative context in chapters 17-18 (17.6; 18.1) but merely redactional in chapters 19-21 (19.1; 21.25)[27] he implies that the narrative complex of chapters 19-21 was added redactionally and as a unit to the narrative of chapters 17-18.

4.02

The redactional history of the book of Judges, as such, was not a matter of primary concern to Noth, and his understanding of it must be gleaned from various asides in his treatment of related questions. Wolfgang Richter, however, in his *Die Bearbeitungen des 'Retterbuches' in der deuteronomischen Epoche* (1963)[28] has undertaken a much more systematic analysis of the question. He works within the broad parameters of Noth's thesis, but seeks to refine certain aspects of it, particularly those which have a direct bearing on the early redactional history of the book.

Richter considers that the 'Retterbuch', Noth's postulated collection of stories about local tribal heroes, had undergone at least one and probably two redactions before its incorporation into the Deuteronomic History. The work of the successive redactors is distinguished partly on stylistic grounds and partly in terms of their differing horizons of interest and the influences they manifest.

The first reviser of the 'Retterbuch', according to Richter, ignored its antimonarchial tendency and expressed his own theological concerns in the stereotyped editorial framework which he provided for the individual accounts of the heroes in chapters 3–8. In so doing he gave the periods of oppression a theological motivation (retribution) but was generally optimistic: Israel had known its rescuers who, under God, brought it peace (each successive episode ending with 'the land had rest'). His use of the formula, 'did what was evil in Yahweh's eyes', argues some dependence on Deut. 17.2, hence Richter's siglum Rdt_1, for this redactor, although no other deuteronomic influence is discernible. Richter suggests that this edition of the 'Retterbuch' served as a book of examples occasioned by the restoration of the popular army under Josiah.

To a second reviser Richter assigns the 'example' ('ein narratives Beispielstück') of Othniel in 3.7-11 (minus the numbers in 3.8, 11, the judge-formula of 3.10, and the death notice of 3.11). The theological interests of this reviser are expressed in the amplifications he provides to the framework patterns of his predecessor, particularly his detailing of the nature of Israel's sin (worship of foreign deities) and in his reference to Yahweh's anger at this (3.7b, 8a). Thus he sharpens Rdt_1's general theology of retribution into the more specific concept that the Yahweh cult brings victory while the cult of foreign gods brings defeat, an idea probably current in the Josianic reforms. Richter considers that the influence of Deut. 13 as well as 17.2ff. is apparent in his work and hence uses the siglum Rdt_2 for this redactor. Although hesitant about identifying him as a second hand, Richter feels on balance that this is justified and suggests that he may have been a Calebite (cf. 3.9).

Richter's third redactor, DtrG, is the equivalent of Noth's Deuteronomist. He introduces the 'minor judges' and revises the whole Retterbuch in the process to give the segment of the

Deuteronomic History which, on Noth's view, was the nucleus of the present book. He paints a very dark picture of Israel, particularly emphasizing its inveterate apostasy (see, in particular, 2.7, 10-12, 14-16, 18f., and 10.6-16) and thus reflects the tragedy of 587. Richter apparently considers, against Noth, that the Samson complex was included in DtrG's composition, since he notes how the mention of the gods of the Ammonites and the Philistines in 10.6 (which he attributes to DtrG) prepares the way for both 11-12 and 13-16.

Richter addresses himself only to that part of the book of Judges which, on his view, formed part of the original Deuteronomic History. The subsequent redactional expansion of this core into the present book has not so far received his attention in any published work. Neither Noth nor Richter consider to what extent the book in its final form is a coherent whole, but we may deduce from Noth's comments on chapters 1 and 17-18 in particular (see 4.01 above) that he, at least, saw the additions made subsequently to the work of the Deuteronomist as detracting from the redactional coherence of its core.

4.03

Some recent studies, however, have raised doubts about this rather negative assessment of the material which introduces and concludes the present book. Timo Veijola, in particular, has argued in a recent monograph[29] that chapters 17-21 in their present form are fully compatible with both the literary structure and theological concerns of the original Deuteronomic History and were in fact an integral part of it.[30]

Veijola is perhaps the best known exponent of a methodology which derives in the first instance from the work of Walter Dietrich[31] and ultimately from that of Rudolf Smend, whose article 'Das Gesetz und die Völker: ein Beitrag zur deuteronomistischen Redaktions-geschichte' (1971)[32] has proved to be the point of departure for a new and influential approach to the study of the Deuteronomistic History.

Smend considered that the Deuteronomist's introduction to the Judges period in the original Deuteronomistic History began in Judg. 2.10[33] and that in 2.17, 20-21, 23 this original introduction had been expanded by a systematic reviser of the Deuteronomic History whose overriding concern was with the law of Moses and with the effects of its observance or non-observance on Israel's relationships with the 'nations' (גוים) of Canaan. Smend also argued that this same redactor (DtrN), at the same time as his revision of the introduction in chapter 2 had inserted Judg. 1.1-2.5[34] (a pre-existing unit which he had not himself composed) since it was fully consistent with his own distinctive understanding of 'the conquest' and was perhaps even the source of it.[35] Smend found other clear examples of the work of DtrN in Josh. 1.7-9; 13.1; 23[36] and contended that further research would show that this redactor had effected a systematic revision of the entire Deuteronomistic History.[37]

4.04
The further work proposed by Smend was undertaken by Dietrich,[38] resulting in the now familiar analysis in terms of *two* major revisions—'prophetic' (DtrP) and 'nomistic' (DtrN)—of the work of the 'basic' Deuteronomist (DtrG),[39] an analysis which is accepted or even assumed in the work of an increasing number of European scholars.[40]

In two monographs Timo Veijola has analysed the varying perspectives on the monarchy in these successive redactions. In the first of these, *Die ewige Dynastie* (1975)[41] Veijola examines four groups of texts in which David and his dynasty are central[42] and concludes that the texts attributable to DtrG idealize David and his dynasty in contrast to the more critical and provisional attitudes displayed in DtrP and DtrN.[43] In his second monograph, *Das Königtum in der Beurteilung der deuteronomistischen Historiographie* (1977)[44] he extends his analysis to a second set of texts, this time from Judges and 1 Samuel, dealing with the emergence of kingship as an institution within Israel prior to David.[45] He seeks to show that, in general, the same distinctions between the views of DtrG, DtrP and DtrN respectively are evidenced in these texts also.[46] Judges 17-21 is one of the texts adduced in this second monograph in support of that part of his thesis relating to the basic Deuteronomist (DtrG).

Veijola argues that the 'pro-monarchical notices' (königsfreundliche Notizen) of 17.6, 18.1a, 19.1a, 21.25 give kingship unqualified endorsement as a legitimate institution necessary for securing the realm against internal disorder, both cultic (17-18) and social (19-21)—a task beyond the competence (and specific brief) of the judges.[47] In particular, by following the account of the gross cultic irregularities practised by Micah (17.1-5) with the note that 'in those days there was no king in Israel; every man did what was right in his own eyes' (17.6) the redactor implicitly subordinates cultic matters to kingly jurisdiction, a concept which played an essential role in the basic Deuteronomic History of DtrG.[48] In particular Veijola finds the locus of the expression 'every man did what was right in his own eyes' (איש הישר בעיניו יעשה, 17.6; 21.25) in the cult-centralization legislation of Deut. 12.8-12, verses which, with Smend, he attributes specifically to DtrG.[49]

He contends that the chapters have undergone extensive deuteronomic revision discernible (apart from the 'pro-monarchical notices') in 17.5, 76b, 13; 18.1b, 19, 30, 31b; 19.1b, 30; 20.4, 27b-28a. These redactional elements are identified as deuteronomic partly on the basis of characteristic terminology and style, and partly on the basis of the social/theological concerns they evince. For example Veijola argues that the redactionally produced characterization of the Levites in both 17-18 and 19-21 as unpropertied sojourners (גרים) dependent on the hospitality and support of their fellow Israelites (17.7b; 19.1; 20.4) reflects the deuteronomic legislation concerning 'the Levite within your gates (Deut. 12.12; 18.19; 14.27, 29; 16.11, 14; 26.11, 12, 13).[51] It also adds depth to the picture of cultic and social disorder in the two narratives. The formula 'from the day that the people of Israel came up out of the land of Egypt until this day' (למיום לעלות בני ישראל מארץ מצרים עד היום הזה, 19.30) is one of the more obvious examples of deuteronomic language to which he draws attention in these redactional passages (cf. Deut. 9.7, 1 Sam. 8.8; 2 Sam. 7.6; 1 Kgs 8.16; 2 Kgs 21.15; Jer. 7.25, 11.7).[52] Finally Veijola argues that these chapters are an integral part of a final 'cycle' of apostasy-punishment-deliverance which conforms to DtrG's conception of the 'Judges period' and in fact brings it to a close. Thus after the death of the judge Samson (16.30-31) Israel again does evil in the sight of the LORD (chs. 17-21) and suffers a humiliating defeat at the hands of the Philistines (1 Sam. 4), after which Samuel, the last judge is raised up as a deliverer (1 Sam. 7, esp. vv. 8-15).[53]

The impact of Veijola's work is already apparent in Alberto Soggin's recently published commentary on Judges.[54] In his introduction to chapters 17-21 Soggin comments that 'the arguments put forward by Veijola in favour of a Dtr edition [of chs. 17-21] ... are weighty ones, which open up a new period in the study of these chapters' (p. 263). Noth, Richter, Smend, and Veijola are all major scholars whose work may fairly be regarded as representing the main lines of development of redaction-critical study relevant to the

Judges material. The work of Smend and Veijola taken together suggests that the opening and closing sections of the book are much more closely integrated, redactionally and conceptually, into its central section than was recognized by Noth and Richter. However they continue to consider Judges 1 and 17–21 primarily in relation to the structure of the Deuteronomic History with its 'periods' as conceived by Noth, and only secondarily as the beginning and end of the extant book of Judges. I conclude this brief redaction-critical survey by looking at the work of two scholars who, while still working within the broad parameters of Noth's thesis, have addressed the final form of the *book* as such much more directly. I refer to Robert Boling and A. Graeme Auld.

4.05

The main lines of Boling's understanding of the redactional history of Judges are well known and a detailed review would be superfluous here.[55] I wish to indicate here simply the substantial areas of agreement between Boling and the major works reviewed above and to indicate where Boling's distinctive contribution lies, particularly with reference to the opening and closing segments of the book.

Boling agrees with Noth that the author of the original Deuteronomic History combined stories of 'saviours' with archival notes about the so-called 'minor judges' and contributed introductory material in chapter 2.[56] He agrees with Richter, however, that the stories of the 'saviours' had already been formed into an edited cycle ('the pragmatic edition') before they came into the hands of the Deuteronomic historian.[57] Boling's distinctive contributions come in his treatment of the *later* redactional history of the book. Here his analysis is strongly determined by his acceptance of F.M. Cross's thesis that there were two major editions of the Deuteronomic History, the first seventh century and ideologically supportive of Josiah's reforms (the 'Deuteronomic' edition) and the second sixth century and exilic (the 'Deuteronomistic' edition) transforming the work into a sermon on history addressed to the Judean exiles.[58]

To the 'Deuteronomic edition' of Judges Boling assigns the whole of 2.5–18.31, which thus begins with the Yahweh angel indicting Israel at Bochim (= Bethel)[59] and ends with a polemic against the shrine at Dan. Centrally located between these two limits is Abimelech's disastrous reign and destruction of Shechem in ch. 9. Boling comments:

It is difficult to avoid the conclusion that the historian has deliberately arranged his presentation so that the period of the Judges begins, centres, and ends with accounts that devalue possible competitors to the Jerusalem Temple, thus endeavouring to legitimate King Josiah's policies in the late seventh century.[60]

Boling attributes chapters 1 and 19–21 to a sixth-century updating which produced 'the final or Deuteronomistic edition' of the book.[61]

Boling's sensitivity to the literary structure of the final product is apparent in his following comment on chapter 1:

> The final (exilic) redactor of the introduction was . . . supplementing the critical perspective of the seventh century Deuteronomic Historian when he built into the interim between Joshua's death and Othniel's rescue of the nation (3:7-11) this prelude to the era, a little-known period which he indicated unfolded from an eagerly united beginning to a scattered and indecisive conclusion. *Compare the movement within the body of the book from Othniel in the south (3:7-11) to the Danite traditions in chs 13-18.*[62] [My italics]

Boling and Smend both see chapter 1 as being added as part of a major revision of the Deuteronomic History, and although Boling assigns ch. 1 and 2.1-5 to separate redactional stages, he does agree with Smend that 1.1-2.5 is a logical unity (ch. 1 now documents the charge made in ch. 2.1-5). However Boling's observation about the correspondence between the schematic arrangement of the material in chapter 1 and the plan of the central section of the book counts strongly against Smend's notion that 1.1-2.5 was added as an old pre-formed unit.

Boling's basic position vis-à-vis Smend receives independent corroboration in an article by Graeme Auld published in the same year as Boling's commentary.[63] Auld argues that Judges 1.1-2.5 is 'a deliberately contrived introduction to the "book" of Judges',[64] basing his case on an examination of the links between Judges 1 and material elsewhere in the Old Testament (especially Joshua) and an analysis of the structure and development of the passage as a whole. He concludes that it is

> a late prefatory note to the book of Judges which supplements, corrects and explains the treatment by the Deuteronomistic History of the period of the Judges. Part of it suggests that the troubled history of the northern tribes, about which the body of the book is largely concerned, was due to the failures during their

settlement of Canaan. Part of it compensates for the scanty
mention of Judah in the rest of the book . . . It is not unlikely that
this new preface is contemporaneous with the division of the
Deuteronomistic History into the now familiar separate books.[65]

I shall return to Auld in a moment.

In relation to the closing chapters of the book Boling anticipates a
major aspect of the work of Veijola in finding a link between the
portrayal of the Levites in chapters 17-21 and one of the major areas
of concern of Deuteronomy and the Deuteronomic historians.[66]
Chapters 17-18 depict 'the easy exploitation and corruption of a
promising young Levite at secondary shrines' and chapters 19-21
portray 'an outrage which was touched off by a failure of Yahwist
"hospitality" toward another Levite'.[67] Boling differs from Veijola in
assigning chs. 19-21 to a Deuteronomistic *revision* of the basic
history,[68] but is in agreement with him in proposing an exilic
provenance for them.[69] Evidence for the exilic dating of chs. 19-21 is
found in the prominence which they give to Judah and Benjamin,[70]
and to the old general assembly (עדה/קהל), an institution largely
suppressed during the monarchy, only to blossom again as the post-
monarchical 'congregation'.[71] Similar arguments for the setting and
function of Judges 19-21 in its final form have recently been
proposed in a major monograph by H. Jüngling.[72]

Boling's most distinctive contribution is his thesis that chs. 1 and
19-21 now provide the entire book with 'a tragicomic' framework:

> In its final form the Book of Judges begins with Israel scattered and
> ineffective by the close of chapter 1. It ends with a very delicate,
> persistent ideal—*Israel*, reunited in the wake of a tragic civil war—
> in an account that swarms with incongruities . . .'[73]

It is with this survival of 'Israel' in spite of all the vicissitudes and
absurdities of the Judges period that the Deuteronomistic editor
consoles the exiles, who live in a period when, once again, there is 'no
king in Israel'.

Graeme Auld, in reviewing Boling's *Judges*, takes issue with him
on points of detail, particularly in relation to Boling's use of the term
'Deuteronomistic'.[74] For Auld 1.1-2.5 and chs. 17-21 are 'post-
Deuteronomistic'. He does agree with Boling, however, in recognizing
a strong affinity between the opening and closing sections of the
book: the close verbal parallels between 1.1-2 and 20.18 and the
prominence which both oracles give to Judah he finds particularly

striking.[75] He concludes by attributing 'the outer framework of our book of Judges' (1.1–2.5, chs. 17–21) to 'a post-Deuteronomistic Judean editor'.[76]

Both Boling and Auld are in substantial agreement with Noth and Richter as to the earlier redactional history of Judges. What they attempt to do is to achieve a more precise description of the final stages of its redactional history. Boling's work in particular represents an application to Judges of F.M. Cross's work on the Deuteronomic History—a refinement of Noth's thesis which has commanded widespread acceptance, particularly in American scholarship.[77] The area of agreement between Boling and Auld therefore represents a development or refinement of earlier major studies.

Taken together the work of Boling and Auld suggests that the final editing of the book of Judges has in effect redefined the 'Judges period' so that its limits now correspond to those of the *book* of Judges, which in its final form is a rounded literary unit; a transitional period then begins with the birth of Samuel in 1 Samuel 1. It will be argued at the appropriate point in this dissertation that this is a more adequate description of the literary structure of the text than Veijola's proposal of a final cycle of the judges period extending from Judges 17 to 1 Samuel 7.

4.06

In summary, then, the redactional unity of the central section of Judges has long been recognized, and insofar as historical-critical scholars have addressed themselves to the *final* stages of the book's redaction, early skepticism about Judges being a literary unit in its own right has been seriously challenged.

5.00

The third line of evidence relates to evidence of literary design in the book as we now have it.

5.01

While the diachronic approach, particularly in the form of redaction criticism, has been the dominant mode in critical study of the Judges material, there have in recent years been an increasing number of synchronic studies. The most thorough of these have been of selected narrative units considered without reference to their function in the book as a whole, as, for example in J. Cheryl Exum's work on the

Samson narrative[78] or in D.F. Murray's analysis of the Deborah-Barak story.[79] In addition, however, several contributions have appeared suggesting that the book as a whole in its final form is a literary unit susceptible to such analysis.

5.02

In a short article published in 1967 J.P.U. Lilley called for 'a fresh appraisal of Judges as a literary work starting from the assumptions of authorship rather than of redaction'.[80] He was reacting against what he saw as 'an inherent bias towards fragmentation' in the then standard commentaries of Moore and Burney and the source-critical studies of Eissfeldt and Simpson— a bias which meant that they never really came to terms with the task of interpreting the text which presents itself to the reader.[81] The adoption of a working hypothesis to the effect that 'a person, properly called the "author" cast the book in its present mould, having conceived in his own mind the general idea and plan' would not, he argued, exclude in principle the possibility of later additions or editing, or still less deny the possibility of identifying sources, but would commit the interpreter to looking, at least initially, for maximum rather than minimum unity of plan.[82] Any formulation of authorial *purpose* would have to emerge from a consideration of the objective and formal character-istics of the text as a whole, and would take account of the fact that 'an author may conceivably have more than one purpose, not all equally in view in any one paragraph or section'.[83]

In the body of his paper Lilley presents a preliminary analysis of the book from this point of view in order to demonstrate (a) that there is sufficient *prima facie* evidence of overall design to justify the type of reappraisal he has proposed and (b) that such a reappraisal, even in a very preliminary form, illuminates aspects of the text which are either ignored or obscured by diachronic analysis.

The analysis itself appears much less remarkable now than it must have done against the backdrop of Moore and Burney, Eissfeldt and Simpson sixteen years ago, but certain aspects of it are still worthy of note. Lilley draws attention to 2.1-5 as providing the logical link between the two halves of the introduction (1.1-2.5 and 2.6-3.6) as well as constituting 'the first of a series of confrontations between the Lord and his people which are definitely part of the author's scheme'.[84] In the central section of the book (3.7-16.31) he notices 'the gradual departure from stereotyped formulae' in line with the progressive deterioration in Israel's condition as indicated in the successive narrative units. Thus the pattern of 3.7–16.31 is not merely repetitive or cyclic, but is a downward spiral—a progressive exploration of a theme for which the groundwork has been laid in 1.1–3.6. The deterioration continues until the land no longer recovers its peace (from Abimelech onwards), enemies are no longer repulsed and there is scarcely any more will to resist (the Samson episode) and until finally, in the closing chapters of the book 'civil war has added its special horrors to the tale of depression' (p. 101). Chapters 17–21 as a whole display the spiritual and moral failure underlying the nation's political misfortunes, and, with their refrain ('In those days there was no king in Israel; every man did what was right in his own eyes') serve both to sum up one distinct phase in Israel's history and to point forward to the next.

Lilley concludes that the main structure of the book is not adequately explained in terms of a 'pragmatic principle' (apostasy brings judgment, repentance deliverance) and that 'although the breaking of the covenant is present as a motif (2.1ff.; and implicitly in 6.8ff.; 8.23; 10.15) it is not dominant and does not of itself provide the dramatic interest to call forth and sustain historical writing of this calibre' (p. 102). This dramatic interest is provided by the selection and arrangement of the narrative units. The meaning of the work emerges from the form, content, and development of the whole and cannot be stated adequately in terms of any 'editor's scheme' which is less than this (pp. 99, 102).

5.03

In 1974 in an essay called simply, 'The Book of Judges',[85] Kenneth Gros Louis noted that certain parts of the book had figured prominently in Western literature and other art forms, especially the Samson story and to a lesser extent those of Gideon, Jephthah, and Deborah (p. 141). However, while the literary potential of some of the stories had been recognized, that of the book as a whole had been largely overlooked:

> Artists and readers have turned admiringly to the individual stories, culled from them, reworked them, without paying much attention to the ways in which the stories might fit together, without, in other words, considering all of Judges as a literary work with its own themes and structure' (p. 141).[86]

The paper does not in fact offer any analysis of the structure of the book *as a whole* (there is no mention of the Othniel episode of 3.7-11, the 'minor judges', or chapters 17-21), and in this respect the conclusions reached about 'what ultimately unifies *Judges*' (p. 162— my emphasis) go beyond the evidence presented. What it does offer however is evidence that the stories of the major judges from Ehud to Samson constitute a unified and structured sequence in which a number of related themes are progressively developed.

There is nothing new in the author's observation that the pattern of decline and recovery foreshadowed in 2.11-21 is 'the dominant unifying pattern' which gives 'surface unity' to the stories, and suggests 'a theory of history'. He is more sensitive than most, however, to the profoundly *personal* issues involved in this pattern. In 2.11-19 where the full dimensions of the pattern are expounded, Israel repeatedly 'plays the harlot' and Yahweh is both 'angered' and 'moved to pity'. Thus while the alternation between glory and misery 'suggests a certain futility' it is not mere repetition without meaning, 'for God repeatedly comes to Israel's aid and his actions indicate a profound concern and affection for Israel. That affection is perhaps another unifying element of Judges' (p. 144). All this finds narrative realization in the individual episodes, which are unified at a deeper level by a network of repeating motifs:

> There is a remarkable coherence to these narratives; incidents and elements of each re-echo in all of the others (p. 157).

The author argues that at this deeper level preparation for these major episodes is already made in two narratives embedded in chapter 1, a chapter which is otherwise annalistic in character. The narratives in question are the story of Achsah (vv. 11-15) and the story of the taking of Bethel (vv. 22-26).[87] The shrewdness and opportunism of the woman Achsah will be reflected in the activities of the major judges generally, and her mastery of the male heroes Othniel and Caleb in the similar mastery exercised by Deborah and Jael, the 'certain woman' of 9.53, Jephthah's daughter (11.53) and Delilah. The Bethel narrative of vv. 22-26 adds to shrewdness and opportunism the motif of 'treachery', a major motif in the Ehud story and one which also figures prominently in those of Deborah/Barak (Jael), Gideon/Abimelech, and Samson. Gros Louis comments that these two brief narratives in chapter 1 'prepare us well for the stories of the greater judges' (p. 145) and 'are important in setting the tone for the whole book' (p. 144).

Within the major episodes themselves the author finds further common elements, especially the way in which God's saving activity, and the course of events, again and again reverse the expectations of both the characters and the reader. The unlikely nature of each of the chosen deliverers is a particular aspect of this general feature. It is argued that through the repetition of these motifs from episode to episode certain sub-themes are developed, especially 'the value of every kind of man' (p. 161), and 'the paradoxical nature of human experience' (p. 162). This development is seen as reaching its climax in the Samson story, where all of the dominant motifs are present, and most receive their most sustained and elaborate development (pp. 157-62).

Gros Louis thus finds literary coherence in Judges 1-16 both at the level of overall structure and at the level of narrative texture. The various themes and subthemes are woven together into a literary whole.

5.04

Robert Polzin's *Moses and the Deuteronomist* is a projected 'literary study of the Deuteronomic History' of which only the first volume, on Deut.-Judges, has so far appeared (pub. 1980).[88] It is an experiment in the application to a biblical 'work' (the Deuteronomic History in its final form) of the critical techniques of modern-day Russian formalism.[89] The 'composition' of the text is analysed primarily in terms of the shifts of 'perspective' or 'point of view' on the various 'planes' of the text: phraseological, temporal, spatial, psychological and ideological. Perspective on the ideological plane— the deepest plane—is approached through an analysis of perspective on the more superficial planes.[90]

From the point of view of 'composition' in this sense Judges is regarded by Polzin as a distinct literary unit within the larger whole because of what he sees as its more radical ideological perspective vis-à-vis Deuteronomy and Joshua:

> The evaluative gaze of the Deuteronomist, so intent upon the principles of divine justice in the Book of Deuteronomy, then measurably softened by the actual account of God's merciful giving of the land in the Book of Joshua, now confronts the awesome fact of God's continued compassion on Israel in spite of their weakness ... The Book of Judges is a major turning point in the narrative because it self-consciously reveals the weaknesses and

limitations of all ideologies, however necessary and unavoidable they may be (pp. 161-62).

For Polzin this radical perspective is not only a distinguishing but a unifying factor in Judges since he finds it in evidence in every major segment of the book.[91]

Questions about literary structure which play a central role in more traditional literary criticism (e.g. about how the plot is constructed) and in Rhetorical Criticism (questions of balance, repetition, symmetry and closure) play a secondary but important role in Polzin's analysis. Because they deal with phenomena which are not primary data in terms of his chosen methodology, Polzin generally deals with such questions implicitly rather than explicitly, but it is clear that even in this 'secondary' sense Polzin regards Judges as a distinct literary unit. For example:

a. He notes that the opening chapters of Judges do not simply *continue* the Joshua narrative but 'recapitulate' certain of its contents in order to bring into sharp relief the failure of Israel to complete the conquest (and the reasons for this failure) before going on in the rest of the book to narrate the consequences which flowed from this failure (pp. 147-48).[92]

b. He is sensitive, as Gros Louis was, to the dense network of interlocking motifs which unify the narrative units at a deeper level than the repeating surface pattern. This is everywhere evident in the analysis and the following example could be multiplied many times over:

> . . . we find in the Ehud story intimations of a theme that will grow in importance in the book, until it reaches an imposing climax in the story of Samson: the characterization of a judge who carries out, either symbolically or effectively, the LORD's designs in an apparently unknowing fashion (p. 160).

c. A more comprehensive design is implied by his comments on chs. 19–21. The inquiry and response in 20.18 are 'in deliberate contrast' to those of 1.1-2 (p. 202) and the war of occupation with which the book begins (Israel v. the Canaanites) and the civil war with which it closes (Israel v. Benjamin) are seen as a literary bracket which is functional in terms of the book's theme (cf. Boling above).[93]

5.05

One final contribution requires mention at this stage, namely, 'The Composition of the Book of Judges', an article by D.W. Gooding, published in 1982.[94] The author produces an argument from design to support the proposition that 'whatever the sources used, the work of compiling them into their present form was the work of one unifying mind' (p. 72). In the introductory section of the paper he argues that the 'reigning theory' that Judges is the product of 'a multiplicity of redactors' is already rendered suspect by the numerous disagreements, in detail and substance, among its leading proponents—disagreements which Gooding details at some length (pp. 70-72).[95]

The point of departure for Gooding's own analysis is a basic structural observation on which he finds there *is* general agreement among critical scholars, namely, that Judges consists of three major parts: 1.1-3.6, introductory material; 3.7-16.31, the stories of the judges; and 17.1-21.25, an epilogue consisting of two stories, both involving a Levite (p. 72). The introduction also, by general agreement, consists of two distinct segments (1.1-2.5, 2.6-3.6) each introduced by a reference to the death of Joshua. Taking the formula 'Israel did/continued to do what was evil in Yahweh's sight' as a major structural marker, Gooding divides the central section of the book into seven major segments, with the minor notices as supplementary notes to the major episodes to which they are attached.[96] On this reckoning the Gideon episode stands at the structural centre of the book, and Gooding argues that it has a symmetrical design as follows (p. 74):

a.	his fight against idolatry	6.1-32
b.	his fight against the enemy	6.33-7.25
b'.	his fight against his own nationals	8.1-21
a'.	his lapse into idolatry	8.22-32

In this symmetrical pattern the second item in each pair of elements (a-a', b-b') represents a serious decline in or worse example of the situation depicted in the first element. That is, it is 'a symmetry which calls attention to decline' (p. 75), and this is its thematic significance. It is Gooding's contention that the entire book consists of paired elements which stand in the same kind of relationship to each other within a comprehensive symmetrical pattern, as follows:

A B   C D E F E′ D′ C′   B′ A′
Introduction | Epilogue
                           Gideon
                          a b b′ a′

A and A′ are paired for the same reasons as in the contributions of other scholars referred to above. The basis on which the other elements are paired may be briefly summarized as follows:

B   Israel forsakes Yahweh and serves other gods
B′   Idolatry is rampant. Levites service idolatrous shrines.
     Dan conquers Laish and establishes idolatry.
C   Othniel's Israelite wife the secret of his success (cf. 1.11-15; 3.6)
C′   Samson's foreign women the secret of his downfall
D   Ehud—takes message to a foreign king—slays Moabites at the fords
     of the Jordan
D′   Jephthah—sends messages to a foreign king—slays Ephraimites at
     the fords of the Jordan
E   Jael slays Sisera and ends the war
E′   'A certain woman' slays Abimelech and ends the war

The features on which the symmetry depends are for the most part significant motifs in the respective stories. Whether or not they are 'essential and leading features', as the author claims (p. 79 n. 22) is a question on which I hope my own analysis may shed some light.

The theme of decline which Gooding finds *implicit* in the symmetry he finds to be *explicit* in the introduction (2.19)—further evidence of 'one unifying mind'. Finally, he sees the Gideon episode which is formally at the centre of the book, as a major turning point in its narrative development, for with Gideon's turning his hand against his compatriots and his manufacture of the idolatrous ephod, *the judges themselves* become involved by their own actions in the more general pattern of decline. It is a development which Gooding sees continued through the Abimelech, Jephthah, and Samson episodes (pp. 74-75).

5.06
All of these synchronic studies of Judges are modest in scope and are not characterized by the kind of systematic attention to detail normally expected in major studies.[97] However, the data presented and the provisional conclusions reached do, in my judgment, constitute sufficiently strong *prima facie* evidence of overall literary

design in Judges to justify a more detailed literary analysis of the book in its final form.

6.00
Before proceeding with the analysis itself, however, it is necessary to make explicit the major guiding principles of the method to be employed.

6.01
The method first of all takes account of the fact that the literary unit to be studied is a *narrative* text. Everything in the text is encapsulated, as it were, within the narrative form. Thus, for example, the hymnic material of chapter 5 is bound into the narrative form of the text by the words which introduce it, 'Then Deborah and Barak the son of Ahinoam sang *on that day* . . ' (5.1). Likewise although the text is clearly a piece of religious instruction, this instruction is at no point separable from the narrative form of the text. Even such an explicitly theological statement as 'Israel did what was evil in the sight of Yahweh' is not an abstract proposition about evil or the character of God but is a narrated event: one character in the story (Israel) did something which another character in the story (God) disapproved of. If there is an identifiable point of view in the work on any religious or moral issue this emerges through the internal dynamics of the story and is not stated directly.

6.02
The method takes account, secondly, of the fact that the narrative contained in the book of Judges is more properly to be described as history-as-plot rather than as history-as-chronicle. That is, if the subject matter is 'what happened in the life of Israel between the death of Joshua and the birth of Samuel', this is presented not as a mere succession of events,[98] but rather as *plot* in which events are causally related to one another. Hence the narrative meaning of the text (its meaning as *story*) is taken to consist in the interaction of persons and events within the unfolding plot. The relationship between these persons and events and the historical realities which they represent is an issue which lies beyond the purview of the present study, which is an inquiry into the 'narrative meaning' of the text in the sense just described.

6.03

In keeping with this focus on narrative meaning the dramatic structure of the text, its plot, is taken to be its *essential* structure, that which constitutes it as a narrative and functions as the primary carrier of its meaning. Hence other structures, whether surface structures (as in Rhetorical Criticism) or deep structures (as in Literary Structuralism) are considered only in so far as they can be shown to illuminate narrative developments within the unfolding plot.

Insofar as Rhetorical Criticism in practice focuses on 'the literary unit in its precise and unique formulation'[99] its methodology is well adapted to the study of narrative meaning. As applied to a narrative text it calls attention to the precise manner in which the story is told. The formal features of the text to which it customarily draws attention are, as surface structures, *ipso facto* aspects of plot structure, though not for that reason all equally significant in terms of narrative meaning.

Structuralist methodologies bear a more tangential relationship to the pursuit of narrative meaning.

Vladimir Propp's primary interest was in the history of the folktale, and in particular the Russian folktale.[100] By reducing each particular tale to a sequence of deep-lying plot functions he was able to display the basic structure of the genre and to distinguish 'pure' forms from 'corrupted' forms of the tale. The basic thrust of his methodology is well summarized in his own words as follows:

> Rejecting all local, secondary formations, and leaving only the fundamental forms, we shall obtain that one tale with respect to which all fairy tales will appear as variants.[101]

A different narrative genre, myth, featured in the work of Claude Lévi-Strauss.[102] He saw myth as a means by which the representatives of a particular culture resolved or at least coped with the irreducible oppositions (life/death, exogamy/endogamy, agriculture/warfare etc.) endemic in the culture. His mapping of the deep structures of particular myths in terms of binary opposition and progressive mediation was in the interest of displaying this sociological function of the genre.

The narratives studied by Propp and Lévi-Strauss respectively were essentially oral productions preserved in written form. The application of their respective methodologies to more distinctively 'literary' texts was greatly facilitated by the synthesis achieved in the work of A.J. Greimas.[103] Greimas proposed that all narratives could be seen as realizations of the same underlying scheme consisting of six 'actantial' roles (analagous to Propp's plot functions) arranged in a grid of binary oppositions (cf. Lévi-Strauss). With Greimas the focus shifts from the study of genre-history or genre-function to the study of how narratives produce meaning. In this respect the literary structuralism of Greimas is analogous to the linguistic structuralism of Ferdinand de Saussure.[104] Structuralist studies of biblical narrative genres (e.g. parable)[105] and of particular biblical narratives[106] reflect the respective influences of Saussure, Propp and Lévi-Strauss in varying proportions, and most are strongly influenced by Greimas.

Structuralism has clearly played a major role in the current resurgence of interest in the study of biblical narratives in their final form, particularly in its separation between historical perspectives and narrative analysis, and in its focus upon the potential meaningfulness of 'oppositions' within a narrative text. I am aware that in both these areas it has influenced my own perception of the task of narrative interpretation. Nevertheless structuralist methodologies in general regard the 'told' story of a narrative text as an epiphenomenon of underlying codes which are the 'real' carriers of meaning. Consequently phenomena which are of the essence of the story as told (e.g. character development or disintegration, changes of pace, tone, or point of view, and the building and relaxation of tensions) are not phenomena with which structuralist methodology deals[107] although it may indirectly contribute to our understanding of them. Hence I have not adopted a structuralist model for my own method in the present study although I reserve the right to make use of insights derived from structuralist studies where appropriate. I have made use of the techniques of Rhetorical Criticism within the guidelines laid down above.

6.04

The book of Judges is here studied as a narrative whole, without prejudice to which parts are earlier and which later, for two reasons: a *prima facie* case exists that the book is a literary unit susceptible of such analysis, and, only such a mode of analysis respects the connectedness of the text as story and hence makes the investigation of its narrative meaning possible. In this sense the method employed is synchronic as opposed to diachronic. Interaction with diachronic studies of the same text is envisaged at two levels. First, it is recognized that studies in the diachronic mode have produced some valuable insights about the literary structure of the finished product, and these insights will be utilized where appropriate. It is hoped, secondly, that the synchronic analysis presented here will help to facilitate finer discrimination between tensions which are arguably meaningful in terms of the narrative developments taking place in the text, and those which are not. Diachronic studies at their best have been sensitive to this distinction (though not generally in a systematic way) while at their worst have shown no such sensitivity at all.[108]

6.05

The reappraisal of Judges offered in this study does not attempt to demonstrate unity of authorship or claim to have discovered what the person or persons responsible for the final form of Judges meant by the book as a whole. The author of a narrative work may not be aware of all that it means, especially if he has not created it *ex nihilo*, but taken existing materials, or even an existing narrative, and modified them (or it) to make the work what it now is.[109] What the reappraisal does seek to do is to understand the work as an integrated whole. What it seeks to demonstrate is that the work in its final form is a more meaningful narrative work than has generally been recognized.

6.06

Much more could be said about method, but I conclude with a short list of the kinds of questions which I brought to the text:

(a) How is the work organized? What are the identifiable breaks in the text (changes in setting, chronology, or subject)? Are there echoes of language, imagery, or scene which suggest significant parallels or contrasts between various parts of the work? Where repetition occurs is there any variation within the repetition? Are there any unexpected turning points in the plot and where do the crises occur?

(b) How are the characters portrayed? Do they develop or remain static? On which character of characters does the spotlight fall? Which characters are present throughout the work and which come and go? Are the characters portrayed sympathetically, with detachment, or unsympathetically? Are we invited to question their motives? What kinds of relationships exist among the characters, and how do these relationships change? Do the characters express views or attitudes which are contrary to ones expressed elsewhere in the story, either by other characters or by the narrator himself?

(c) Is the subject matter treated humorously, seriously, dispassionately, ironically? If there is irony, at whose expense is it? Where different points of view are expressed, which find wider endorsement in the work and which are implicitly rejected? Do ideas recur and are they developed in the course of the work? Do any of them stand out as major concerns (themes) of the work? Does the work have one all-embracing theme or a number of related themes?

The number of questions could be multiplied almost indefinitely but I hope that these will be sufficient to indicate the general orientation to the work with which I began this reappraisal. The text, of course, had many questions of its own to address to me. What follows is an account of the dialogue which ensued and the fresh understanding of the book which emerged.

Chapter 2

SOUNDING, 10.6–12.7

I begin this presentation of the results of my research with an analysis of the Jephthah story. This is not where my study of the text of Judges began; it began where the reader must begin, at chapter one. However, it was my encounter with the story of Jephthah, more, perhaps, than with any other part of the work, which helped to shape my understanding of the book as a whole.[1] The analysis of this particular story, presented here, will serve as both a point of departure and a point of reference for the wider analysis which follows.

1.00
Jephthah is introduced into the narrative of the book of Judges at 11.1 with the statement, 'Now Jephthah the Gildeadite was a 'mighty warrior' (גבור חיל). The notice of his death and burial at 12.7 marks his exit. He figures prominently in all that happens between these two limits. This segment of text contains within itself all the information which is necessary to make it comprehensible as a complete story. One does not even have to go outside this segment of text to find the situation which forms the background to the story since this is neatly summarized in 11.4: 'the Ammonites made war against Israel'.

1.01
The literary structure of the central section of Judges leaves us in no doubt, however, that the story of Jephthah in its finished form begins not at 11.1 but at 10.6, with the formula 'the Israelites continued to do[2] what was evil in Yahweh's sight' (cf. 3.12; 4.1; 13.1). Among other things the following analysis will attempt to show that, in terms of

both literary structure and theme, the material which precedes the introduction of Jephthah himself in 11.1 is closely integrated into the main body of the narrative.

2.00

A network of causation, sometimes explicit, sometimes implicit, links persons and events within this larger narrative. Thus Israel's apostasy (10.6) leads, via Yahweh's intervention (10.7), to its subjugation by Ammon (10.8-9). This has two consequences, the first religious (Israel returns to Yahweh, 10.10-16) and the second political (Jephthah is elevated in Gilead, 11.4-11). Israel's relationship with Ammon moves from complication, through increasing tension, to climax (11.32a) and, again via Yahweh's intervention (11.32b) to resolution (11.33). But this resolution gives rise to two further complications and crises, the first domestic (Jephthah and his daughter, 11.34-39) and the second political (Jephthah and the Ephraimites, 12.1-6). The successive resolution of these two crises brings the narrative to its conclusion. That is, the subject matter (what happened to Israel in the lifetime of Jephthah) is conceptualized as plot, and the basic plot structure of the narrative in its finished form is clearly recognizable. In the close reading which now follows I refine considerably this basic analysis of plot-structure and at the same time to move into an analysis of the story's thematics.

3.00

10.6-16 contains an exposition of the crisis out of which the plot is generated. It is a crisis with a double focus, one religious (Israel has provoked Yahweh to anger by forsaking him and serving other gods, vv. 6-7) and one political (Israel is faced with virtual annihilation at the hands of Ammon, 10.9).

The religious crisis is apparently resolved in 10.16, where Israel puts away its foreign gods and returns to the worship of Yahweh:

v. 6   they served (עבד) the baalim . . .
         they abandoned Yahweh
         and did not serve (עבד) him

v. 16   they put away the foreign gods
         and served (עבד) Yahweh.

Thus the situation announced in 10.6 is formally reversed in v. 16 and vv. 6 and 16 frame the intervening material.

At 10.17 the narrative moves into an entirely new phase (see below).[3] The military/political crisis now becomes the overt focus of interest and sustains the forward momentum of the story until it in turn is resolved at 11.33b.

We shall call 10.6-16 Episode 1 of the Jephthah Story.[4] The text is as follows[5]:

10.6-16

6   And the people of Israel continued to do what was evil in the
        sight of Yahweh,
b   and served the Baals and the Ashtaroth,
c   the gods of Syria, the gods of Sidon, the gods of Moab, the
        gods of the Ammonites, and the gods of the
        Philistines;
d   and they forsook Yahweh,
e   and did not serve him.
7   And the anger of Yahweh was kindled against Israel,
b   and he sold them into the hand of the Philistines and into the
        hand of the Ammonites,
8   And they crushed and oppressed the children of Israel that
        eighteenth year—
b   all the people of Israel that were beyond the Jordan in the
        land of the Amorites, which is in Gilead.
9   And the Ammorites crossed the Jordan to fight also against
        Judah and against Benjamin and against the house
        of Ephraim;
b   so that Israel was sorely distressed.
10   And the people of Israel cried to Yahweh, saying,
b   We have sinned against thee,
c   because we have forsaken our God
d   and have served the Baals.
11   And Yahweh said to the people of Israel,
b   Did I not deliver you from the Egyptians and from the
            Amorites, and from the Ammonites and from the
            Philistines?
12   The Sidonians also, and the Amalekites, and the
            Maonites oppressed you;
b   and you cried to me,
c   and I delivered you out of their hand.
13   Yet you have forsaken me
b   and served other gods;
c   therefore I will deliver you no more.

14   Go and cry to the gods whom you have chosen;
b   let them deliver you in the time of your distress.
15   And the people of Israel said to Yahweh,
b   We have sinned;
c   do to us whatever seems good to thee;
d   only deliver us, we pray thee, this day.
16   So they put away the foreign gods from among them
b   and served Yahweh,
c   and he became indignant over the misery of Israel.

While the political crisis which came to a head in 'that eighteenth year'[6] (8a, detailed in 8b-9b) is clearly the seed from which larger political and military developments will emerge later in the story its function within this first episode is to trigger off the 'cry' to Yahweh in 10a which leads directly into the dialogue of vv. 10-15. Both participants in the dialogue refer back specifically to what has been reported in the first part of the episode (10c recalls 6d, 10d recalls 6b; 13a recalls 6d, 13b recalls 6b, 14a recalls 6bc, and 15d reflects the critical situation reported in vv. 8-9).

It is clear therefore that the essential drama of Episode 1 is enacted in the dialogue between Israel and Yahweh in vv. 10-15. What precedes is 'off-stage' as it were, and preparatory for the confrontation which takes place in this dialogue.

In a manner quite unparalleled in the preceding judge-narratives, the formula of 10a ('the Israelites cried out to Yahweh, cf. 3.9, 15; 4.3; 6.7) is supplemented by a detailing of the precise form which the cry took in this instance.[7] It consists of the following elements:

A.	*Confession* 'We have sinned...'	10b, and again in 15b.
B.	*Submission* to the will of Yahweh as judge and overlord. 'Do to us whatever is good in your sight'	15c

This is to be read in conjunction with 6a as a disavowal of any rights vis-à-vis Yahweh. Israel has done what is *evil*, in Yahweh's sight; it is now for Yahweh to do what is *good*, , in his sight, that is, to dispose of Israel as he sees fit. Cf. the submission of the Gibeonites to Joshua in Josh. 9.24-25.

C.   *Appeal* for immediate aid. 'Only deliver us this   15d
       day'

The cry is accompanied by

D.   *Acts indicative of renewed loyalty to Yahweh.*
       Removal of foreign gods and return to the   16a
       worship of Yahweh.

Yahweh does not hear Israel out and then respond but interjects at
an early stage. The divine speech is marked formally as an
interjection by the way in which the cry is resumed (by 'we have
sinned' in 15b) from the point at which it was interrupted (10b-d).
Yahweh anticipates the appeal (C) and rejects it even before it is
made.

The angry tone of the speech is expressed particularly in the irony
of 14a: 'Go, cry (זעק) to the gods you have chosen.' These words
reject the religious nuance which the Israelites have given to זעק by
their confession (10ab). Yahweh recognizes the purely utilitarian
nature of their 'cry' and confronts them with it: Israel cries to
Yahweh rather than to others only because they judge him to be
more useful to them in the present circumstances ('your time of
trouble', 14b). He speaks as one who knows that he has been used in
this way in the past (12b-13b) and is determined not to be so used
again (13c). That is, although the cry here has the accoutrements of
repentance, it is not accepted at its face value by Yahweh.

It is generally held[8] that all this changes in v. 16; that the putting
away of the offending foreign gods gives proof of the genuineness of
Israel's repentance and that Yahweh's response in 16c involves an
implicit recognition of this. Thus, for example,

Richter: 'V. 16 schliesst gut an V. 15 an: Die Israeliten besiegeln
             ihre Reue durch die Tat' (*Die Bearbeitungen des
             'Retterbuches'*, p. 23).
Boling: 'Lip service would not suffice. They had to put behind
             them the cause of their guilt and fear (see 6.7-10)—
             other gods' (*Judges*, p. 193).

On this reading of the text the scenario here is parallel in substance
to that reflected in such passages as:

Jonah 3.10   When God saw what they [the Ninevites] did, how
             they turned from their evil way, God repented of the
             evil which he had said he would do to them; and he
             did not do it.

or

Jer. 26.10	Did not he [Hezekiah] fear Yahweh and entreat the favour of Yahweh, and did not Yahweh repent of the evil which he had pronounced against him?

Cf. also Exod. 32.14; Jer. 18.7-8; 26.3; Joel 2.13-14; Amos 7.3-6. But there are at least two problems with such a reading: it does not take sufficient account of the content of Yahweh's speech in 11b-14b, nor of the precise terms in which his response is described in 16c.

Yahweh's words in 12b-13c clearly imply that the putting away of foreign gods is part of the routine with which he has become all too familiar from previous experience. His complaint is not that Israel has failed in the past to back up its cry by putting away its other gods, but rather that on each previous occasion, after deliverance has been granted, Israel has abandoned him for these gods again (13b, cf. the refrain of 3.12, 4.1, 6.1). Hence his refusal to deliver Israel any more (13c). In short Yahweh's interjection anticipates the putting away of the foreign gods as an expected accompaniment of the appeal for help, and rejects both. In view of this the precise terms in which his final response is described in 16c require close scrutiny.

The two key terms in 16c are the verb קצר, and the noun עמל. Neither of them occurs in Jonah 3.10 or the similar texts cited above, which characteristically use instead either נחם or שוב with הרע: God 'repents' of 'the evil'. That is, so far as terminology is concerned, these other passages are like one another but unlike Judg. 10.16.

The Old Testament usage of קצר may be summarized briefly as follows: literally, 'to cut short, to reap'; metaphorically 'to be powerless or ineffective', but only in the stock rhetorical question 'Is Yahweh's hand/spirit shortened?' (Isa. 50.2; 59.1.; Num. 11.32; Mic. 2.7); in all other cases it is expressive of frustration, loss of patience, anger:

Num. 21.4-5	The people *became exasperated* (קצר) because of the way[9] and spoke against Moses.
Job 21.4-5	Why should I not *be impatient* (קצר)? Look at me and be appalled.
Zech. 11.8-9	But I *lost patience* (קצר) with them, and they detested me. So I said, 'I will not be your shepherd. What is to die, let it die.'

Interestingly, the only other occurrence in the Old Testament is at Judg. 16.16 where it refers to Delilah's nagging:

When she pressed him hard with her words day after day and urged him he *became exasperated* (קצר) to the point of death, and he told her all his mind.

Hence when used of a personal response to a situation קצר normally expresses frustration, impatience, exasperation, anger—inability to tolerate the situation any longer.

The noun עמל is commonly used in the Old Testament to refer to labour experienced as hardship, or more generally, to hardship of any kind (e.g. Gen. 41.51; Deut. 26.7; Job 3.10; 5.6, 7; 7.3; 11.16; Pss. 25.18; 55.10; 73.5, 16; Prov. 31.7; Isa. 53.11; Jer. 20.18). As such it is an entirely appropriate term to sum up the condition of Israel described in vv. 8-9. It is apparently this which exasperates Yahweh in 16c. Comparison with Jonah 3.10 throws the special character of our present text into sharp relief: not, 'God *repented* when he saw *what they did*, how they turned from their evil way,' but 'Yahweh *could no longer tolerate* their *misery*' (my emphasis).

A closer parallel with the Samson–Delilah situation in particular is suggested in a recent proposal by Robert Polzin, namely that עמל in 16c refers to Israel's efforts to persuade Yahweh to help them. Hence his translation, 'he grew annoyed [or impatient] with the troubled efforts of Israel'.[10] (The parenthesis is Polzin's).

The semantic range of עמל is certainly wider than 'trouble, hardship' and the like. The neutral sense, 'hard work, effort', is clearly attested, though characteristically late (frequently in Ecclesiastes, and cf. the cognate verb in Ps. 127.1; Prov. 16.26; Jonah 4.10). As an ethical term it is widely used of 'mischief' either conceived or carried out against someone, but this is hardly applicable here. Polzin has tried to exploit the wider semantic possibilities of עמל, but the special meaning he gives it in 16c is unattested elsewhere and cannot carry conviction in a context where the most commonly attested meaning of the term is so clearly applicable. עמל may reasonably be taken to *include* Israel's importunity (since this is an aspect of its miserable condition) but not to refer specifically to it as Polzin suggests.

The comparison with the Samson–Delilah episode is nevertheless illuminating. In 16.16 Samson becomes exasperated *and* relents— gives Delilah what she wants. But the verb קצר does not of itself carry the meaning 'to relent, to yield'—this is expressed by the words which follow. Other, quite different responses may follow the exasperation denoted by קצר as is clear from Num. 21.4-5, Job 21.4-5 and Zech. 11.8-9 above.

The full construction, 'A became exasperated (קצר) with/because of X and did Y' is exhibited by Num. 21.4-5 and Zech. 11.8-9. In Judg. 16.16 the second element, 'because of X', is replaced by a circumstantial clause *preceding* the verb ('when she pressed him with her words. . .'). Verse 16c of our present text contains the first two elements of the pattern but not the third: Yahweh (A)[11] became exasperated (קצר) with the misery of Israel (בעמל ישראל, i.e. 'with X'). The action which flows from the exasperation in this case is not specified. We may perhaps infer from the cause of the exasperation (Israel's misery) that Yahweh, like Samson, will relent. But that is an inference for which we must seek confirmation in the ensuing narrative. The text at this point specifies only his irritation, his annoyance, his exasperation.

To summarize, then, the drama of Episode 1 is produced by the interplay of three different conflicts: the conflict between Israel and Ammon, the conflict between Israel and Yahweh, and the conflict within Yahweh himself. The conflict between Israel and Ammon brings to a head the conflict between Israel and Yahweh which comes to expression in the dialogue of vv. 10-16. It is here that the essential drama of the episode takes place. Israel appeals to Yahweh; Yahweh responds by confronting Israel. The angry tone of the divine speech, plus the emotive terms used in 7a and 16c invite us to reflect on the emotional conflict within Yahweh. He is angered by Israel's apostasy (7a) yet unable to accept their repentance. He is aware that even if it is real it is temporary—it will not last. He is affronted by Israel's attempt to use him and hotly rebuffs their appeal, but finds their continued misery unendurable (16c).

The depth and dramatic intensity of the episode is largely lost when it is levelled through in terms of a human/divine repentance scenario. A much closer parallel to the present text is to be found in Hosea 5.15-6.6, although that, too, has its own unique tone and dramatic content.

4.00
At 10.17 sq.[12] we are transported to the battle zone where the Ammonites are about to launch a major new offensive and the Israelites are taking desperate counsel with one another.

10.17-18

17 Then the Ammonites were called to arms,
b   and they encamped in Gilead;

c   and the people of Israel came together,
d   and they encamped at Mizpah.
18   And the people, the captains of Gilead, said to one
     another,
b   Who is the man that will begin to fight against the
         Ammonites?
c   He shall be head over all the inhabitants of Gilead.

The parallelism of v. 17 (AB // A'B') mirrors stylistically the
confrontation between the two sides, but the subtle difference of
nuance between ויצעקו, 'were called [to arms]' (17a), and ויאספו,
'assembled' (17c)[13] already hints at the theme which is developed in
the direct speech of v. 18: Israel is without effective leadership and
hence extremely vulnerable in the face of this new threat.

Furthermore Yahweh has retired into the background. In this
respect the present scene presents an ominous contrast to the
corresponding scene of the preceding Gideon narrative. There Israel
is indicted by a prophet (6.7-10), but this indictment is followed
immediately by the appearance of Yahweh's angel to commission
Gideon (6.11 sq.). Here, after a much more heated indictment, this
time by Yahweh himself, no such intervention is apparent.

The expression בני ישראל (Israelites) now assumes a more particular
and limited sense than it had in 10.6-16.[14] Now it is used of the
assembled Israelite men-at-arms (17c). But it is Gilead which is
immediately threatened (17b) and the captains of the Gileadite
contingent (18a)[15] who are singled out from the larger company to be
the principal actors in the scene. Thus in contrast to the dialogue of
Episode 1 the direct speech in this scene is given a specific locale
(Mizpah[16] 17d) and the human characters are presented with greater
definition.

This is no orderly assembly called and presided over by a
competent leader. The captains do not speak with one voice and have
no strategy to put forward. They do not even address their men but
speak confusedly 'each to his neighbour' (18a, cf. the townsmen of
Ophrah in 6.29). The question they ask (18b) recalls the very similar
question with which the book of Judges opens (1.1), but how different
the circumstances! There the Israelites, united and on the offensive
against the Canaanites, address the question to Yahweh. Here,
confused and on the defensive, the captains of Gilead address it to
one another and there is little sign of any effective Israelite unity (an
issue which will surface explicitly later in the narrative). The

captains, as they see it, have been left to their own resources, and none of them wants the job. They are prepared to offer inducement to anyone who will do it for them (18c—see below) but no one suitable is at hand. All is now set for the introduction for Jephthah as a גבור חיל (mighty warrior) in 11.1.

4.01

The forward momentum of the story is briefly arrested while we are introduced to Jephthah and told a little of his personal history.

11.1-3

1   Now Jephthah the Gileadite was a mighty warrior,
b   but he was the son of a harlot.
c   Gilead was the father of Jephthah
2   And Gilead's wife also bore him sons;
b   and when his wife's sons grew up,
c   they thrust Jephthah out,
d   and said to him,
e   You shall not inherit in our father's house;
f   for you are the son of another woman.
3   Then Jephthah fled from his brothers,
b   and dwelt in the land of Tob;
c   and worthless fellows gathered around Jephthah,
d   and went out with him.

This flashback is formally set off from the main stream of the narrative by the disjunctive, 'Now Jephthah (ויפתח)' of 1a. He is a Gildeadite (1a, c)[17] but the son of a prostitute (1b) and an outcast from his clan, disinherited by his 'legitimate' brothers (v. 2).[18] He flees, and becomes an exile in 'the land of Tob (טוב)' (3b)—which is ironically, for Jephthah, the place of alienation, rejection, disinheritance[19]—where other social misfits[20] gather round him and 'go out' with him (3d). We are left to draw the natural conclusion— Jephthah and his men sustain themselves by plunder. But socially undesirable though he may be, Jephthah is a seasoned fighter, and a natural leader, with men (and presumably equipment) at his disposal.

And so this unit presents us with a paradox: the outcast with no social status is in fact a גבור חיל in a double sense, a warrior and a man with considerable resources at his command.[21] The early mention of his prowess (1a) sets him in stark contrast to the 'captains' of 10.17-18 and at the same time hints that fear of domination may have been the unexpressed motive behind his expulsion.[22]

4.02
We are returned to the main story line with the news, in 11.4, that the Ammonites have now launched their threatened offensive:

11.4-11

4   After a time the Ammonites made war against Israel.
5   And when the Ammonites made war against Israel,
b   the elders of Gilead went to bring Jephthah from the land of
            Tob;
6   and they said to Jephthah,
b   Come and be our leader,
c   that we may fight with the Ammonites.
7   But Jephthah said to the elders of Gilead,
b   Did you not hate me,
c   and drive me out of my father's house?
d   Why have you come to me now
e   when you are in trouble?
8   And the elders of Gilead said to Jephthah,
b   That is why we have turned to you now,
c   that you may go with us
d   and fight with the Ammonites,
e   and be our head over all the inhabitants of Gilead.
9   Jephthah said to the elders of Gilead,
b   If you bring me home again to fight with Ammonites,
c   and Yahweh gives them over to me,
d   I will be your head.
10   And the elders of Gilead said to Jephthah,
b   Yahweh will be witness between us;
c   we will surely do as you say.
11   So Jephthah went with the elders of Gilead,
b   and the people made him head and leader over them;
c   and Jephthah spoke all his words before Yahweh at Mizpah.

With the ineffectiveness of the 'captains' so clearly established, and with the military situation now critical (5a) the 'elders of Gilead (זקני גלעד)' take matters into their own hands (5b). The words are well chosen at this point to convey the confidence with which the elders set out: they go to 'fetch (לקח)' Jephthah from the land of Tob.

On meeting Jephthah they come straight to the point: 'Come, be our leader (קצין), and we will fight the Ammonites' (6bc). 'Be our קצין' appears to refer here specifically to taking command of the men in the field—assuming responsibility for the conduct of the war.[23] Perhaps the elders assume that the outcast will be flattered and jump at the chance of such rapid advancement. But they underestimate his shrewdness and opportunism. He is not as amenable as they expect. He angrily rejects their appeal, charging them with responsibility for his earlier expulsion (v. 7).[24] Desperate, the elders propose new terms, and this time their tone is much more deferential: 'We have returned to you that you may come with us and fight the Ammonites and be our head (ראש) over all the inhabitants of Gilead' (8b-e). The change from קצין to ראש, the reversed order (from 'be קצין and fight' to 'fight and be ראש') and the full description, 'ראש *over all the inhabitants of Gilead*' (my emphasis) all indicate that something more permanent, wide-ranging and prestigious is now on offer, namely, 'tribal chief' or the like.[25] This is the offer that was originally proposed by the captains (10.18c); the elders had apparently hoped to secure Jephthah's services for less.

This revised offer brings Jephthah to the point of bargaining (9b-d):

> If you (אתם) cause me (אותי) to return to fight the Ammonites
> and if Yahweh gives them over to me
> Then I (אנכי) will be over you (לכם) as head (לראש).

This formulation of the bargain is Jephthah's own, and it is shrewd. He had used personal pronouns emphatically in his earlier rebuttal of the elders: 'Didn't you (אתם) hate me (אותי)?' Now he uses them again, this time in a chiastic pattern to make it explicit that what is involved is a transfer of power from the elders to himself. לראש stands emphatically in the final position. Further, Jephthah draws out the implications of the order, 'come-fight-be head' in 8b-e. This did not specifically lay down victory as a condition, but Jephthah is realist enough to recognize that only victory will create the conditions in which the offer of ראש will be implemented. By invoking Yahweh, however, he elevates victory to the status of divine endorsement of himself and so further enhances his own authority vis-à-vis the elders. Thus Yahweh re-enters the story obliquely, neither speaking, nor acting, nor being addressed directly, but, on the lips of Jephthah, as a trump card in the negotiations, and, on the lips of the elders (10a) as a presence, a silent witness of all that takes place.

The elders acquiesce completely in the terms as Jephthah has now formulated them: 'We will surely do according to *your word* (כדברך)' (10c, my emphasis). Satisfied, Jephthah returns with them to Mizpah where he is received with such enthusiasm by the military (understandably relieved!) that they ('the people', cf. 10.18a) make him both ראש and קצין on the spot! (11b). The Gileadites appear to be as uncoordinated in the conduct of their internal politics as they are in the conduct of the war![26] A more solemn, ceremonial ratification of the terms already agreed between Jephthah and the elders is indicated in 11c, however, where 'his words' refers back to 9b-d via 'your word' in 10c, and where 'before Yahweh' is in fulfilment of 10b, 'let Yahweh be witness between us'. Jephthah has undoubted popular support, but his appointment as 'head of all the inhabitants of Gilead' will become effective only if he wins the war.

Thus the question that was asked at Mizpah in 10.18 is answered by Jephthah's arrival there in 11.11, and 10.18–11.11 constitutes one complete movement in the narrative. We shall call it Episode II.

4.03
The dialogue of vv. 5-10 is the heart of this episode—its dramatic centre—just as the dialogue of 10.10-15 was the heart of Episode I. Interest centres on the appeal to Jephthah and his response to it.

In 8b the elders say that they have 'returned (שוב)' to Jephthah. This can hardly be taken in its simple literal sense here since it is Jephthah, not the elders who has literally gone away and who literally returns (3a, 11a). Rather, it is used metaphorically of a change of mind or attitude in relation to Jephthah. Jephthah has just accused them of hating him and driving him out and asked why they have 'come to' him (בוא אל) now that they are in trouble (7b-e). The elders reply that they have 'returned to' him (שוב אל). Their tone is deferential as we have seen and their words carefully chosen to win Jephthah over.[27] They adopt the language of repentance.[28]

This change of mind in the elders is of course politically motivated. Their relationships with Jephthah are conducted on a strictly business basis; hard-nosed negotiation is the essence of the game they play, and in this they find that Jephthah is more than a match for them. Their 'repentance' nevertheless bears a remarkable resemblance to the repentance of Israel in Episode I. It arises out of the same situation (inability to cope with the Ammonites without help from the one they have rejected), it has the same object (to

obtain the help of the one they have rejected), it meets with a similar
initial rebuttal, and it is pressed with some kind of importunity. The
Israelites end up by acknowledging Yahweh as their unrivalled God
(10.16a-b); the Gileadites end up by making Jephthah their head and
commander (11.11b).

Where the two episodes differ sharply is in the *final* response given
by Yahweh and Jephthah respectively. Yahweh can no longer tolerate
the misery of Israel; Jephthah manifests only self-interest. There is
something deeply satisfying, it is true, in Jephthah's mastery over the
other characters in the episode—none of them inspires sympathy.
The captains are caricature leaders; Jephthah's brothers and the
elders are joint perpetrators of an injustice for which their present
humiliation is a fitting punishment. Jephthah's triumph follows the
rags-to-riches pattern of classical comedy.[29] And we cannot help but
be impressed by the skill he displays as a negotiator. Yet for all this
the episode displays an aspect of his personality which we will later
have cause to reflect upon more deeply, namely, the calculating way
in which he goes about achieving his personal ambitions. The
implicit contrast between Jephthah and Yahweh draws dramatic
force from the fact that we are not allowed to forget that Yahweh
stands in the background as a silent witness of all that takes place
(10b, 11c).

4.04

To summarize then, while Episode I provided us with one perspective
on Israel's repentance (Yahweh's reaction to it) this episode provides
us with a second, namely, its similarity to the 'repentance' of the
elders. These two perspectives are complementary; they reinforce
one another rather than cancel one another out. In addition, Episode
II introduces us to Jephthah, tells us a little of his personal history,
and draws attention to two aspects of his character: his skill as a
negotiator, and his calculating self-interest. Finally it raises implicitly
the question of how the relationship between Jephthah and Yahweh
will develop.

5.00

A new movement begins in 11.12. In line with ancient precedent (see
vv. 17-21) Jephthah sends messengers[30] with a brief verbal challenge
to the enemy king: 'What is at issue between us that you have come
to fight against my land?' (v. 12). The tone is not conciliatory, and

these are not the words of a man who is desperate for peace (see further below). The answer is equally uncompromising. To the charge that the Ammonites have come to fight against '*my land*', the king counters that 'Israel, on coming from Egypt, took away *my land*' (v. 13—my emphasis). This at once broadens the debate by bringing 'Israel' into the picture and introducing an historical argument. The onus is now on Jephthah to show that his cause is just.

The messengers are despatched again (v. 14), this time with a long and detailed defence of Israel's title to the disputed territory which, as recognized by both parties, is bordered by the Arnon to the south, the Jabbok to the north, and the Jordan to the west (cf. v. 13 with v. 22). Significantly, however, Jephthah's opponent recognizes no eastern boundary; he evidently considers that the territory in question is part of Ammon, which properly extends to the Jordan (v. 13). Jephthah specifies the eastern border rather vaguely and provocatively as 'the wilderness' (v. 22, contrast Num. 21.24). By consigning Ammon implicitly to the wilderness in this way he hints at the likely economic motive behind its westward expansion into the more fertile lowlands adjacent to the Jordan.[31] At the same time his words contain the veiled threat of a counter offensive that might deprive Ammon of the marginal arable lands it currently possesses.[32] For reasons which will become apparent below, however, it is the southern border, the Arnon, which is more conspicuous in Jepthah's 'defence' (see vv. 18, 26).

Central to Jephthah's argument is his claim that when Israel came from Egypt the territory now under dispute was ruled by one 'Sihon, king of the Amorites' (v. 19) and that Yahweh gave it to Israel because of Sihon's refusal to give Israel passage (vv. 19-23). (Preparation for this claim is made as early as 10.8b in Episode I where Gilead is referred to as 'the land of the Amorite'.) The argument is summed up *in principle* in the parallel members of v. 24:

> Is it not [right] that whatever your god Chemosh gives
>   you to possess, you should possess
> And that everything that Yahweh our god has given to
>   us to possess, we should possess?

What is referred to in the second half of the verse is clearly Israel's rightful title to 'the land of the Amorite'. What is acknowledged in the first half of the verse is that Ammon has similarly legitimate title to *other territory* in the region.

The words 'your god Chemosh' are rather startling in view of the
consistent distinction in the Old Testament between Milcom/Molech
as god of Ammon and Chemosh as god of *Moab*.[33] What is clear from
the content of Jephthah's argument as a whole, however, is that he
recognizes his opponent as legitimate ruler of *both* Ammon *and*
Moab. Thus to his opponent's charge that Israel took away '*my* land'
(v. 13) Jephthah replies that it took away 'neither the land of Moab
nor the land of the Ammonites' (v. 15). In vv. 25-26 Jephthah
addresses his opponent as successor to the kings of Moab (including
Balak ben Zippor) whose example he should follow by recognizing
the land north of the Arnon as Israelite and refraining from war. The
natural inference is that Jephthah recognizes Ammon's title to 'the
land of Moab' as being as legitimate as Israel's title to 'the land of the
Amorite'. He argues that the ancient border between these two
territories should be respected.[34]

Thus behind the present expansion of Ammon into Gilead lies a
prior expansion of Ammon into Moab.[35] No explanation is given, but
if one arrives at the Jephthah story via the earlier chapters of the
book it is a development which is easily envisaged. The Ammonites
were last mentioned in 3.13 as temporary allies of Moab. The
subsequent demise of Eglon and his forces (3.29) provides precisely
the kind of power vacuum in the region that would make Ammonite
expansion likely. (Israel was clearly not in an expansionist phase.)

Jephthah concludes by asserting that not he, but his opponent is in
the wrong and by appealing to 'Yahweh the judge' to decide 'this day'
between the disputants:

27a I (אוכי) have not committed any crime against you (לך)
  b but you (אתה) do me (אתי) wrong by making war on me.
  c Let Yahweh the judge
     judge today between the Israelites and the Ammonites.

The paired oppositions between the emphatic pronouns in a and b
represent stylistically the diplomatic deadlock which has now been
reached: claim stands against counterclaim, and accusation against
counteraccusation. In the background the two armies confront each
other. A higher authority must now decide, and Jephthah's appeal to
Yahweh to decide 'today' is in effect a declaration of war. Jephthah
has no intention of restoring Gilead 'peacefully (בשלום)' as his
opponent has demanded (v. 13). The issue will be settled on the
battlefield.

The Ammonite makes no further reply. The account of the negotiations is formally terminated by the narrator's report, 'the king of the Ammonites did not heed the words of Jephthah which he sent to him' (v. 28), forming a closure with v. 12. A new movement begins in v. 29. We shall call 11.12-28 Episode III of the Jephthah narrative.

5.01
Once again interest centres in a dialogue and again the dialogue takes the form of a confrontation—there is conflict between the participants. This time the dialogue occupies virtually the entire episode, but one of the participants remains nameless[36] and off-stage, as it were. Only one personality comes under scrutiny in this episode, and that is Jephthah.

From 'Jephthah the Gileadite' in Episode II he becomes here 'Jephthah the Israelite statesman'. It is a rather abrupt transition, but not wholly unexpected, nor without preparation in the preceding narrative. In Episode II he was made head and commander of Gilead (11.11) and it was clearly with the defence of Gilead that those who appointed him were primariy concerned. But the question of 10.18b was asked in the context of an assembly of the 'Israelites' (10.17c) and from the moment of his introduction there has always been a presumption that he was destined for greater things. (Notice how 11.4, immediately after the introduction of Jephthah, keeps the wider perspective of Episode 1 before us.) In the present episode the king's broadening of the debate in v. 13 implicitly recognizes Jephthah as a leader and spokesman for 'Israel'. Jephthah responds by drawing extensively in his reply on Israel's national traditions as the following parallels make clear:[37]

v. 17	//	Num. 20.14, 17, 2;	
v. 18	//	Num. 21.4, 10-13	
v. 19	//	Num. 21.21, 22	Cf. Deut. 1-3
v. 20	//	Num. 21.23	
v. 21	//	Num. 21.24	

In particular, his references to the sending of 'messengers' to the kings of Edom and Moab (v. 17) and to the king of the Amorites (v. 19) sets his own diplomacy in the context of ancient 'Israelite' precedent (he speaks of 'Israel' having sent messengers)—a connection which alerts the reader to the similarities between the diplomacy of Jephthah and that of Moses.[38]

The dialogue this time is conducted at a distance and clothed for the most part in the formal and restrained language of diplomatic convention. On the whole reason predominates over passion, and it is not surprising, therefore, if in 'Jephthah the statesman' we feel that we have lost touch to some extent with 'Jephthah the Gileadite' of Episode II. Nevertheless, within the constraints that situation and convention impose it is apparent that the two have certain clear traits of character and behaviour in common. The one sharp interrogative sentence which constitutes Jephthah's first message in v. 12 is in the same style as his opening questions to the elders in 11.7, whom he likewise considered his enemies. But the Ammonite King is an enemy of an entirely different order who presents a much greater challenge to Jephthah's skill with words, and his second message takes account of this fact.

The conclusion to the diplomatic exchange ('the King... refused to heed the words of Jephthah') can be properly assessed only in terms of Jephthah's apparent objectives as indicated by the tone and content of his diplomacy. If he has been suing for peace, he has obviously failed, but this does not appear to be the case. Israel is in no position to negotiate acceptable terms of peace (10.8-9) and this is implicitly recognized in Episode II where the characters (the captains, the elders, and Jephthah) speak only of fighting (10.18; 11.6, 8, 9). Accordingly Jephthah's tone is uncompromising throughout. His second message is in the style of a prophetic lawsuit in which 'Thus says Jephthah' (v. 15) corresponds to the standard formula, 'Thus says Yahweh'.[39] Jephthah has gone on the diplomatic offensive—a very bold move in the circumstances! He presents Israel's case (in a legal sense)[40] against the Ammonites, and the entire argument in his second message is aimed at establishing the conclusion reached in v. 27a, namely, that Ammon, not Israel, is the guilty party in the present dispute. His message ends, as I have said, with a virtual declaration of war (v. 27b). Jephthah is already resolved to fight before he despatches this second message.

Jephthah's statesman-like behaviour is the sort of action which could be expected to gain him prestige in the eyes of his fellow Israelites, to boost his own morale (and theirs),[41] and to secure a brief respite—possibly a very valuable one—before the battle is joined. But Jephthah is hardly so naive as to suppose that his powerful enemy will be intimidated by a threat of force from enfeebled Israel, or that he will accept the arguments presented and desist on moral grounds. Jephthah, as we already know from Episode II, is not a naive person.

It is apparent from his appeal to 'Yahweh the judge' in v. 27b that from Jephthah's point of view his diplomacy functions on two levels: first, in relation to the Ammonite (from whom he cannot expect a favourable response) and second in relation to Yahweh who, as judge, is witness to the proceedings and in whose hands the fate of the disputants finally rests. Jephthah's long 'speech' is both a message to the Ammonite and evidence laid before Yahweh the judge. It is from the *latter* quarter that Jephthah hopes for a favourable response; indeed, he has staked everything on obtaining it (11.19).

Such a response from Yahweh will, of course, serve Jephthah's personal interests (11.9) and those of his fellow-Gileadites as well as those of Israel as a whole. But Jephthah now speaks as a spokesman for 'Israel', and invokes the historic relationship between Yahweh, Israel, and the land in question:

v. 21 'Yahweh, the god of Israel' gave Sihon and his land to 'Israel'

v. 23 'Yahweh, the god of Israel' dispossessed the Amorites before 'his people Israel'

v. 24 Yahweh is 'our god'—'we' will possess all that he has given 'us' to possess.

(Contrast the plain 'Yahweh' of 11.9 where the national interests as such are not directly on view.) This language is determined in part by the requirements of the argument vis-à-vis the Ammonite, which turns on technical questions of sovereignty (v. 24). But at the same time it implies that in the present dispute Yahweh's interests and those of Israel coincide, so that Jephthah, as spokesman for Israel, has a special claim on Yahweh's help.[42] In the war of words he can beat the Ammonite on his own, but to beat him on the battlefield he needs the assistance of Yahweh.

In general Episode III builds upon the earlier impression of Jephthah as a master with words. 'The words of Jephthah' in the final sentence of this episode (11.28) resonates with 'all his words' in the final sentence of the previous one to indicate that 'the words of Jephthah' is indeed a *Leitmotiv* binding the two episodes together and establishing the essential continuity between 'Jephthah the Gileadite' and 'Jephthah, Israelite statesman'.

Episode III, then, shows us something of Jephthah's potential for greatness. He is capable of transcending the Gileadite sphere and assuming responsibility for the affairs of Israel as a whole. But in the light of Episode II we know that in doing so *in this particular instance* he is at the same time pursuing his own personal political ambitions (11.9). Whether he is capable of any *disinterested* concern for Israel's welfare is a question which remains unanswered.

Jepthah's climactic appeal to 'Yahweh the judge' is part of a more general tension-building function of the episode. Episode III keeps the prospect of a final do-or-die military clash with the Ammonites steadily in prospect, but at the same time delays its arrival by Jephthah's long speech which slows down the forward momentum of the story. Throughout the episode Yahweh remains in the background (though Jephthah now refers to him more and more)—his personal attitude to Jephthah still undisclosed. As we come to the end of the episode, however, and Jephthah appeals to Yahweh to decide the issue 'this day' (v. 27) it is clear that the climax of the narrative is at hand. Yahweh's intervention is imminent, and when it comes it will be decisive for all concerned, as Jephthah himself clearly recognizes.

6.00
The fourth episode extends from 11.29 to 11.40. Again the essential drama is focussed in a dialogue, this time between Jephthah and his daughter (vv. 35-38).

With the coming of Yahweh's spirit upon Jephthah in 29a the two principal characters of the narrative are at last brought into direct contact with one another, and the story begins to move rapidly towards its climax (note the threefold repetition of the verb עבר in 29b, c, d):

11.29-33

29 Then the Spirit of Yahweh came upon Jephthah,
  b and he passed through (עבר) Gilead and Manasseh,
  c and passed on (עבר) to Mizpah of Gilead,
  d and from Mizpah of Gilead he passed on (עבר) to the Ammonites.
30 And Jephthah made a vow to Yahweh, and said,
  b   If thou wilt give the Ammonites into my hand,
31   then whoever/whatever comes forth from the doors of my house to meet me when I return victorious from the Ammonites, shall be Yahweh's,
  b   and I will offer him/it up for a burnt offering.

32   So Jephthah crossed over (עבר) to the Ammonites to fight
       against them;
b   and Yahweh gave them into his hand.
33   And he smote them from Aroer to the neighborhood of
       Minnith, twenty cities, and as far as Abelkeramim,
       with a very great slaughter.
b   So the Ammonites were subdued before the people of
       Israel.

The coming of the Spirit initiates a sequence which is familiar
from the career of the first judge as presented in 3.7-10:

Othniel 3.10		*Jephthah* 11.29-32
The Spirit of Yahweh came upon (ותהי על) him	A	The Spirit of Yahweh came upon (ותהי על) Jephthah.
(and he judged Israel)		(see comments below on 29b-d)
and he went out (יצא) to war (למלחמה)	B	and he advanced (צבר) towards the Ammonites to fight against them (להלחם בם) (32a)
and Yahweh gave (נתן) C-R King of Aram into his hand	C	and Yahweh gave (נתן) them into his hand

A similar sequence underlies the intervening narratives concerning
Ehud, Barak, and Gideon, though Yahweh's spirit is not mentioned
in every case. Gideon is invested (לבש) with Yahweh's spirit (6.34);
Ehud is simply 'raised up' by Yahweh (3.15, cf. Othniel 3.9); Barak is
summoned by Yahweh's word through Deborah (4.6). The action of
Yahweh in A establishes divine sanction for events B and C which
follow, and predicts their successful outcome.

Jephthah does not go out to confront the Ammonites at once. He
first moves across (עבר) Gilead and Manasseh[43] (29b) before
retracing his steps (עבר) to Mizpah (29c, cf. 11.11) and then
advancing directly (עבר) against the Ammonites from there (29d,
32a).[44] Jephthah's 'tour' of Gilead and Manasseh is presumably
connected in some way with his preparations for the battle. It
occupies the same position in the A→ B→ C sequence as Gideon's
call-up of volunteers from Manasseh, Asher, Zebulun and Naphtali

in 6.34-35, and Othniel's 'judging' of Israel in 3.10 (see diagram above). In this latter case the verb שפט (to judge) is brought into the closest possible association with Othniel's role as 'saviour (מושיע)' of Israel (3.9), that is, his conduct of the war. Moreover the order—'the Spirit came ... he judged ... he went out to war ...—supports the view taken by Boling[45] (following Richter[46]) that שפט here has particular reference to the 'mobilization' of Israel for holy war.[47] Such mobilization had a religious aspect (calling Israel back to an undivided loyalty to Yahweh) and a military aspect (assembling a fighting force). Compare Samuel's 'judging' (שפט) of Israel in the context of the Philistine crisis of 1 Sam. 7 (esp. vv. 5-6).[48]

In the case of Jephthah Israel has already reaffirmed its loyalty to Yahweh (though not necessarily to Yahweh's satisfaction) in the assembly of 10.10-16, and an army of sorts, composed of 'Israelites' (בני ישראל), has already taken up a forward position at Mizpah (10.17). But prior to Jephthah's appointment morale has been very low (10.17-18). We may reasonably surmise, in these circumstances, that the purpose of Jephthah's 'tour' of 29bc is to show himself as leader and to call up reinforcements (cf. 12.2). It may even be that one purpose of his negotiations with the enemy was to buy himself sufficient time to do this (the vague ותהי, literally 'And [the Spirit of Yahweh] came ...' of 29a does not of itself demand strict chronological sequence without a specific time adjunct, 'after these things' or the like). But this is conjecture. What is clear from the text is that the fourfold repetition of עבר in 29b-32a establishes the link between Jephthah's endowment with Yahweh's Spirit (29a) and his Yahweh-given victory (32b). His 'passing through', 'passing on' and 'crossing over' are in fact segments of one movement of which Yahweh's Spirit is the motive force.

This movement is interrupted, however, by Jephthah's making of a vow in vv. 30-31. The vow is clearly marked as an interruption by the way in which the final words of 29d are resumed in 32a, after the vow has been made, thus:

29d   from Mizpah of Gilead *he passed on* (עבר) *to the Ammonites*

[the vow]

32a   So *Jephthah crossed over* (עבר) *to the Ammonites* to fight
against them.

This interruption initiates a sequence of events, unique to the Jephthah story, and terminating formally in v. 39b, which forms an inclusio with v. 30a:

v. 30a   Jephthah *vowed* a *vow* to Yahweh
v. 39b   he did to her [according to] the *vow* which he *vowed*.

Once the vow is introduced it takes over, as it were, dominating the episode and subordinating to itself material which would otherwise have been climactic in its own right. Thus the climax of the first sequence, the victory over the Ammonites, receives only summary treatment (32b-33), its chief interest being that it creates the conditions in which Jephthah will be obliged to fulfil his vow. These two sequences, which between them span the episode, may be represented as follows:

A. Jephthah's   leads to   His victory
   endowment   ➞   over Ammon
   with the Spirit

B.   Jephthah's   His victory   leads to   The fulfilment
                vow   +   over Ammon   ➞   of the vow
                (v. 30)   (v. 39)

Two things are apparent from this outline of the literary structure of the episode. First, while the victory is *causally* related to Jephthah's endowment with the Spirit it is only *incidentally* related to the vow. Second, as the inclusio between v. 30a and v. 39b suggests, the vow and its fulfilment is the axis along which the tension, and hence the dramatic interest, of the episode is built and resolved. While Yahweh's involvement in sequence A is quite explicitly stated (vv. 29a, 32b) his involvement, if at all, in sequence B is never explicitly referred to. That is, while divine determinism operates in sequence A it is not clear whether or not it operates in sequence B.

For the first time Jephthah addresses Yahweh directly (30a). The opening words of his vow, 'If you will indeed give the Ammonites into my hand' (30b), echo the key condition in his bargain with the elders, 'If... Yahweh gives them up before me' (11.9c), and in so doing brings Jephthah's personal stake in the outcome of the war directly into focus again. Publicly and officially (Episode III) Jephthah has spoken only of the interests of Israel; privately his mind works on his own interests. Publicly he has argued that Israel is the innocent party and expressed confidence that Yahweh's judgment will be in Israel's favour; privately he remembers that he himself has been the innocent party in a dispute (11.1-3) and found his rights[49] disregarded by those who should have protected them (11.7).[50] The emphatic infinitive (נָתוֹן, —if you will *indeed* give) expresses his insecurity—will Yahweh, after all, reject him too? Jephthah has everything to lose if the battle goes against him, not least his life (see 12.3), but also his position in his clan and tribe, and that clearly means a great deal to him. Formerly an outcast, he is now 'head and commander of all the inhabitants of Gilead'. But if he loses the war the whole cycle of rejection will begin again. If Yahweh rejects Jephthah now, so too will Jephthah's people—again.

Ironically, after resting his case confidently with Yahweh the judge (11.27), Jephthah now slips a bribe under the table:

31a   whoever/whatever comes forth from the doors of my house
        to meet me when I return victorious from the Ammonites
        shall be Yahweh's
31b   and I will offer him/it up as a burnt offering.

As the elders once offered inducement to Jephthah so Jephthah now offers inducement to Yahweh. Jephthah is now the suppliant, but even in this role his words exhibit all the shrewdness which we have come to expect of him. The vow is quite specific in pledging a burnt offering (31b) but more circumspect in nominating the victim. In fact it does not specify any particular victim but only the *means* by which the victim will be identified. This immediately introduces a high degree of dramatic tension into the episode—Who or what will the victim turn out to be? The language is ambiguous,[51] but more applicable to a human being than to an animal, especially the phrase לִקְרָאתִי, 'to meet me'.[52] The gravity of the situation, too, suggests that human rather than animal sacrifice is being contemplated.[53] The vow puts all the occupants of Jepthah's house at risk, but Jephthah will offer only what is forced from him. Like the elders he will not (metaphorically) offer 'רֹאשׁ' if he can get by with 'קָצִין'. He is willing to take his chances. The vow is not impulsive; it is shrewd and calculating—entirely in keeping with Jephthah's character as we have come to know it.

The deep irony of the situation is that *we* know that the rejection which Jephthah so much fears is a phantom. Yahweh's spirit has already come upon him; the divine judge has already decided to save Israel by his hand. But this is information which is given to us, the readers. Jephthah himself shows no awareness of it. Nor is this contradicted by the fact that in v. 29 he has already begun to move at the impulse of Yahweh's spirit. The last major judge-narrative, that of Gideon, has illustrated two quite different kinds of activity by

Yahweh in relation to his chosen instrument. On the one hand is the visual and verbal activity of Yahweh's angel (6.11-24), Yahweh's speaking to Gideon directly (7.2,4,9), and the dream report and its interpretation which he allows Gideon to overhear (7.13-14). All of this is addressed to Gideon's consciousness. It affects his behaviour *indirectly*, through his consciousness. On the other hand, as a separate event, is the intervention of Yahweh's Spirit, which affects his behaviour *directly* at a particular point (6.34-35). Jephthah has received no visitation, as Gideon, nor any prophetic word, as Barak (4.6-7). His words, 'If you will indeed give the Ammonites into my hand', recall his own words to the elders (11.9), not a promise he has received from Yahweh (contrast Gideon, 6.36). No dialogue has taken place between himself and Yahweh; the only communication of this kind which has attended his enlistment has been with men (Episode III). From Jephthah's point of view Yahweh is still aloof and uncommitted. Jephthah has already become Yahweh's instrument without being aware of it (cf. Samson in 13.25-14.4). We watch from a vantage point he does not share as he takes extreme measures to secure divine help which has already been granted to him.[54]

6.01
Jephthah's victory over the Ammonites brings him, predictably, to the threshold of his home:

11.34-40

34 Then Jephthah came to his home at Mizpah;
 b   and behold, his daughter came out to meet him with timbrels
      and with dances;
 c   she was his only child;
 d   beside her he had neither son nor daughter.
35 And when he saw her,
 b   he rent his clothes, and said,
 c   Alas, my daughter! you have brought me very low,
 d   and you have become the cause of great trouble to me;
 e   for I have opened my mouth to Yahweh,
 f   and I cannot turn back.
36 And she said to him,
 b   My father, if you have opened your mouth to Yahweh,
 c   do to me according to what has gone forth from your
         mouth,

d	now that Yahweh has avenged you on your enemies, on the Ammonites.
37	And she said to her father,
b	Let this thing be done for me;
c	let me alone two months,
d	that I may go and wander on the mountains
e	and bewail my virginity, I and my companions.
38	And he said,
b	Go.
c	And he sent her away for two months,
d	and she departed, she and her companions,
e	and bewailed her virginity upon the mountains.
39	And at the end of two months, she returned to her father,
b	who did with her according to the vow which he had made.
c	She had never known a man.
d	And it became a custom in Israel
40	That the daughters of Israel went year by year
b	to lament the daughter of Jephthah the Gileadite
c	four days in the year.

Verse 34a, with ביתו, 'his house', standing emphatically at the end of the line recalls the words of the vow (31a) and evokes keen anticipation. In 34b יצאת (lit. *coming* out) and לקראתו (to meet him) again echo the language of the vow (31a) and the use of הנה (Behold!) with the participle gives an awful immediacy to the scene which now unfolds. We are transported to the scene of the action and witness it directly as it takes place: 'See, his daughter, coming out to meet him'.

Again the narrative is heavy with irony, this time with a particular poignancy because of the innocence of the daughter. She knows not what she does. She 'comes out' 'to meet him'—thus fulfilling the vow—with timbrels (בתפים) and dancing (ובמחלות) to celebrate a joyful occasion in the traditional way: her father has returned 'in peace (בשלום)' (31a). However, unlike the women who went out after Miriam to celebrate Yahweh's victory at the sea in the same way (Exod. 15.19-21) or those who likewise celebrate David's victories in later times (1 Sam. 8.6-7), she comes out alone, and it is her solitariness which is given terrible emphasis in 34cd: 'only she, alone; beside her he had neither son nor daughter'. The words underline both the isolation of the child (she and no other is to be the sacrifice) and the plight of the parent (the vow will render him childless, his personal שלום is shattered). The full horror of the situation is clear to us before the characters themselves confront it.

When he does see her (35a) Jephthah tears his clothes and cries out in anguish (35bc). There is no need for us to dismiss this as mere histrionics. He had risked his daughter, it is true, but hoped to avoid the necessity which now confronts him. Then he was in a state of intense anxiety; now he is in the flush of victory. Face to face with her, he finds that he values her more, much more, after the battle than he had before. But for all that it is not for his daughter that he mourns (others will do that); Jephthah mourns for himself:

35c   Ahh, my daughter, you have indeed laid me low (כרע־כרע)[55]
35d   You (את) have become the cause of my calamity (עכר)[56]

He calls her 'my daughter' but offers her no solace[57], only accusation. The emphatic pronoun את, and the play on the roots כרע and עכר underline both the reproach and the self-absorption which his words express. At the moment of recognition and disclosure Jephthah thinks only of himself.[58] He refers to the vow only indirectly:

35e   I have opened my mouth to Yahweh
35f   And I cannot turn back

It is partly an admission of responsibility (I have opened my mouth) and partly a denial of responsibility (I cannot turn back). At best we can give Jephthah only our qualified sympathy.

It is otherwise with his daughter. When she speaks she echoes her father's words:

36b   My father, you have opened your mouth to Yahweh.

As the remainder of her speech shows she repeats these words not in counter-recrimination but as a way of grasping their significance, coming to terms with them, and steadying herself for a dignified response. Her next words show that she has fully grasped the dreadful logic of the situation:

36c   Do (עשה) to me whatever has gone forth from your mouth,
36d   For Yahweh has done (עשה) for you deliverance from your
       enemies.

She asks only for two months to bewail her virginity with her female friends (she will find her solace there, 37b-f). Her father has only one word for her—'Go' (38b). It is the last word he speaks in the episode. From now on only the narrator is heard.

At the end of two months she returns to her father; her submission is complete. The time has come, and there is no word from heaven to stay Jephthah's hand.[59] So now, quickly, without judgment, the narrator tells the deed. Only the narrator refers to the vow directly, by its name, but even here there is reticence: not, 'he offered her up as a burnt offering,' but, 'he did (עשה) to her his vow which he vowed (נדרו אשר נדר)'.[60] The terminology of this climactic sentence echoes that of both 30a (נדר—the father's making of the vow) and 36cd (עשה—the daughter's submission to it).[61]

In terms of the literary structure of the episode, what follows in 39c-40c is a postscript; the climax of the episode has already been reached and passed with the closure effected by 39b.[62] Yet in terms of subject-matter it is closely related to vv. 37-38. The corresponding elements are as follows:

vv. 37-38	vv. 39c-40c
two months	yearly, four days in the year
she went (הלך)	they go/used to go (הלך)
she and her companions	the daughters of Israel
bewail (בכה)	commemorate (תנה)
my virginity/her virginity	she had never known a man
	It became a custom/tradition (חק) in Israel

For the most part the 'before' (vv. 37-38) and the 'after' (vv. 39c-40c) are related as particular to general. The daughter (and her companions) go (38d) for one four-month period; the Israelite women go (40a) year by year, four days each year. That is, it becomes a tradition/custom in Israel (39d).[63] The daughter and her companions 'weep' (37e, 38e) before the sacrifice; after it the Israelite women 'commemorate' (40b). Compare 5.11 where תנה is used of 'rehearsing' the righteous deeds of Yahweh that is, keeping the memory of them alive by repetition.[64] Though the rehearsing of 11.40b probably *involved* weeping/mourning[65] it is in itself a more specialized term than בכה.[66] Thus the חק of 39d is depicted in v. 40 as an activity which honoured the memory of Jephthah's daughter.[67] A striking parallel is to be found in 2 Chron. 35.25:

> Jeremiah composed laments for Josiah, and to this day all the men and women singers commemorate Josiah in the laments. These became a tradition (חק) in Israel.

This postscript shifts the focus from the vow to the victim and in so doing draws our sympathy even more firmly away from the father and towards the daughter. We are reminded of her virginity (39c). It was her virginity which she had asked leave to bewail upon the mountains before her death (37c-e). This was the bitterest thing of all for Jephthah's daughter: not to die, but to die young, unfulfilled, childless. For she, too, was rendered childless by the vow. Cut off, with no child to succeed or remember her she may well have been numbered among the unremembered, among 'those who have perished as though they had not lived' (Sir. 44.9).[68] Indeed, she remains nameless in the narrative. But, we are told, there *were* those who remembered: the daughters (בנות) of Israel went out year after year, and it was the daughter (בת) of Jephthah whose memory they honoured (40b,c).

Through all of this Yahweh remains silent. The only actions which are explicitly attributed to him are those directly related to the relieving of Israel's distress by saving them from the Ammonites (11.29a, 32b).

The closing reference to 'Jephthah *the Gileadite*' (40b) recalls the first mention of him in 11.1a (Now Jephthah the Gileadite . . .). It reminds us of Jephthah's origins and prepares us for a development which will take place in the final episode of the narrative which now follows.

7.00

Episode IV has explored the private and domestic consequences that flowed (via the vow) from Jephthah's victory over the Ammonites. With the change of scene and the introduction of the Ephraimites in 12.1 we are returned to the public and political sphere. The fifth and final episode of the narrative, 12.1-7, will explore the political consequences that flowed from that victory.

The victory has confirmed Jephthah as head and commander of the Gileadites. But if his authority is now accepted in the eastern sector of Israel, this is clearly not so in the west. With the external threat removed, intertribal jealousies flare up again (cf. 8.1-4):

12.1-4b

1   The men of Ephraim were called to arms,
b   and they crossed to Zaphon
c   and said to Jephthah,
d   Why did you cross over to fight against the Ammonites,

e   and did not call us to go with you?
f   We will burn your house over you with fire.
2   And Jephthah said to them,
b   I and my people had a great feud with the Ammonites
c   and when I called you
d   you did not deliver me from their hand.
3   And when I saw that you would not deliver me,
b   I took my life in my hand,
c   and crossed over against the Ammonites,
d   and Yahweh gave them into my hand;
e   why then have you come up to me this day,
f   to fight against me?
4   Then Jephthah gathered all the men of Gilead
b   and fought with Ephraim.

The Ephraimites behave much as the Ammonites had done: they mobilize for war (צעק 1a, cf. 10.17) and cross over into Gilead to confront Jephthah there (1ab, cf. 10.17).[69] The issues are different, of course. The stated grievance this time is not about land but about Jephthah's leadership. The Ephraimites demand an explanation from him as to why he did not summon them to help in the war with the Ammonites (1de). They are clearly not prepared to recognize any leader of 'Israel' who acts independently of Ephraim. Their wounded sense of self-importance is focussed nicely in the emphatic pronoun at the beginning of 1e: ' . . . and *us* (ולנו) you did not call . . .' Their show of arms, together with their threat to burn Jephthah's house over his head (1f) is plainly intended to either intimidate him[70] or provoke him into a fight. It is a powerful challenge to Jephthah's credibility as a leader.

According to 8.1-3 Gideon earlier faced a similar challenge from the same quarter. But in his case the challenge was less intense. The Ephraimites at that time did not mobilize specifically for the purpose of confronting Gideon. Indeed they had mobilized at his request (7.24) and had further recognized his leadership by bringing him the heads of the two Midianite princes they had captured and slain (7.25). Their complaint was that Gideon had not summoned them earlier (8.1). Their 'contending sharply' with Gideon (ויריבון אתו בחזקה, 8.1) may have involved threats but this is not explicitly stated.[71] Gideon's personal circumstances, too, were different. He had not completed the war with the Midianites, at least to his own satisfaction (8.4-5), and could not risk fighting on two fronts. Hence he appeased them with flattery and avoided a military confrontation with them (8.2-3). In Jephthah's case at least two months have elapsed since the decisive defeat of the Ammonites (11.37-39) and he has no pressing business to distract him from the matter in hand.

Jephthah takes the same basic approach to the Ephraimites as he had to the Ammonites. He resorts to diplomacy in the first instance, rebuffing the charge they have brought against him and giving his own account of the circumstances leading up to the present confrontation (2a-3a; cf. 11.15-22). He refers to Yahweh's involvement in these antecedent circumstances (it was Yahweh who gave the Ammonites into his hand, 3d; cf. 11.21),[72] and ends with a rhetorical question implying that he is in the right and that the Ephraimites are wrong to make war on him as they have done (3ef; cf. 11.27a). The Ephraimites, like the Ammonites, make no reply, whereupon Jephthah takes to the field and wins a resounding victory (vv. 4-6; cf. 11.29-33). The summary notice of v. 7 makes the political consequences clear: the tribes west of the Jordan are brought to heel and Jephthah judges *Israel* for six years. In times of crisis, whether external or internal, Jephthah emerges as a strong, effective leader. Something of the potential for greatness foreshadowed in Episode 3 is realized in this final episode.

But there is another perspective on Jephthah in this final episode which emerges on closer examination. The Ephraimites take issue with Jephthah personally (1d-f). Jephthah responds by declaring his solidarity with his own tribal group, 'I was a ריב man,[73] *I and my people*, with the Ammonites . . .' (2b, my emphasis). This at once sets the particular point at issue in the broader context of Ephraimite-Gileadite relations and prepares the way for an escalation of the conflict into a full-scale intertribal war. The diplomacy which follows lacks the same quality of high moral seriousness as that which characterized Jephthah's diplomacy with the king of Ammon. Jephthah's claim that he *did* summon the Ephraimites (2e) is rendered dubious by the lack of any confirmation of it in the preceding narrative. There is no solemn appeal here to Yahweh the judge to decide the issue. Jephthah mentions Yahweh only to enhance his own authority vis-à-vis the Ephraimites (3d, cf. his similar tactic in dealing with the elders in Episode II, 11.9c). If he argues that he is in the right it is not, in this case, to establish an entitlement to divine help but solely to score a psychological advantage over his opponents. Jephthah is still the same skilful practitioner with words, but he appears more eager for the fight on this occasion, and more confident.

His solidarity with his own people takes concrete form in 4a: 'Jephthah gathered *all the men of Gilead* to fight with Ephraim' (my emphasis). At this point Jephthah recedes into the background (he is mentioned no more in the battle report of vv. 4-6) and the broad deep-seated intertribal animosities come explicitly to the fore as the *real* cause of the war:

4c　　The men of Gilead smote Ephraim
4d　　*because they said*
4e　　*You are fugitives of Ephraim* (פליטי אפרים) *you Gileadites*
4f　　*in the midst of Ephraim and Manasseh* (my emphasis).

The diplomacy of vv. 1-3 was superficially like that between Jephthah and the Ammonites, but with significant differences. The same applies to the report of the battle, only here the contrasts are more striking than the similarities. This time there is no mention of divine charisma, nor does Yahweh give the victory. Indeed, as far as we know Yahweh is not involved in any way. This battle is not presented as a holy war, but with wry humour as a rather squalid tit-for-tat tribal feud. The Gileadites answer the taunt of the Ephraimites ('you are fugitives of Ephraim', 4e) by putting them to inglorious rout and thereby making them the *true* 'fugitives of Ephraim', (v. 5)—פליטי אפרים again. The pronunciation test of vv. 5-6 adds a further sardonic touch to the scene. The tactic of seizing the fords of the Jordan (v. 5), previously used to such effect by Israelites against Moabites (3.27-30) and by Israelites against Midianites (7.24-28) is now used by Israelites against Israelites. The slaughter is prodigious (v. 6). This intertribal feud under Jephthah is part of a thematic development (progressive internal disintegration) which reaches its climax in the civil war involving the whole of Israel at the end of the book (chs. 19-21).

It is difficult to see what else Jephthah could have done in the circumstances, and it may well be that his conduct served the interests of Israel as a whole better than any other available option. But the narrator does not allow us the luxury of any simple categorization of him as 'worthy' or 'wicked'. He is strong, decisive, capable, but at the same time thoroughly parochial—a Gileadite first and foremost, and thoroughly enmeshed in the destructive intertribal jealousies of the period. There is no magnanimity about him; if he serves the national interest he does so incidentally. From being a figure of almost Mosaic bearing in Episode III he modulates here into a tribal chief, drawing upon the loyalty he can command from his own people to settle old scores, consolidate his position, and extend his sphere of influence. Holy war gives way to power politics. Yahweh apparently takes no further interest in him. It was only as a temporary deliverer that he had Yahweh's endorsement (11.29, 32).

This final episode, then, brings together two contrasting perspectives on Jephthah which had been juxtaposed earlier in the narrative: 'Jephthah the Gileadite' (Episode II) and 'Jephthah the Israelite statesman' (Episode III). The summary notice of v. 7 provides the final comment on this dual perspective:

> *Jephthah judged Israel* for six years
> and *Jephthah the Gileadite* died
> and was buried in his own city in Gilead[74] (my emphasis).

8.00 *Conclusions: The Meaning of the Jephthah Story*

We are now in a position to stand back, as it were, to try to grasp the narrative as a whole, and to reflect on its meaning in the light of the foregoing analysis.

The turning point in Israel's relationships with the Ammonites comes at 10.32-33. Everything prior to that point anticipates the battle which takes place there, and everything that follows harks back to it in some way. Episode IV, in which this turning point occurs is, on any reckoning, the climactic episode of the narrative. In terms of Yahweh's long-awaited and decisive intervention, in terms of the profound way in which the personality of Jephthah is explored through his dealings with Yahweh on the one hand, and his daughter on the other, and in terms of the dramatic intensity which is generated, this episode is the heart of the narrative as a whole. Yet, as we have seen, the victory over the Ammonites is not the climax of this episode. The centre of dramatic interest is displaced, by the vow, to the dialogue between Jephthah and his daughter which *follows* the victory.

What is true of this episode is true of each of the five episodes of which the narrative is composed. The Israel/Ammonite conflict is the link connecting all the episodes, but within each episode it provides the occasion, the background, for a dialogue, and it is in the dialogue that the real dramatic interest of each episode is centred, thus:

Episode	Dialogue
1. 10.6-16	Israel vs. Yahweh, vv. 10-16
2. 10.17-11.11	The elders vs. Jephthah, 11.5-11
3. 11.12-28	Jephthah vs. the Ammonite King, 11.12-28
4. 11.29-38	Jephthah vs. his daughter, vv. 34-38
5. 12.1-7	Jephthah vs. the Ephraimites, vv. 1-4a

It follows that if the story has a major theme, these dialogues are likely to bear very directly upon it.

To return to the fourth, climactic episode—the dialogue here, between Jephthah and his daughter, concerns Jephthah's *vow* and its implications. The vow is not referred to directly by either party, but both allude to it circumspectly using the same expression:

first Jephthah—

35e   I have opened my mouth to Yahweh

(פציתי פי אל יהוה)

then his daughter—

36b   You have opened your mouth to Yahweh

(פצית את פיך אל יהוה)

The expression is striking enough in itself, involving both alliteration (p-p) and assonance (ī-ī), and its repetition at this crucial point in the narrative throws it into special prominence. It gains thematic significance from the *Leitmotiv*, 'the words of Jephthah', which links the previous two episodes. His negotiations with the elders, his diplomacy with the king of Ammon, and his vow have amply displayed Jephthah's facility with words. Jephthah, we know, is *good* at opening his mouth (how ironical that his name should be יפתח 'he opens'). What has precipitated the crisis with his daughter is that he has opened his mouth to *Yahweh*, that is, he has tried to conduct his relationship with God in the same way that he has conducted his relationships with men. He has debased religion (a vow, an offering) into politics. It is the sequence of dialogues in episodes 2-4 which gives the point its dramatic force. The same point is made by the 'parallel' dialogues of episodes 1 and 2: Israel has debased repentance into negotiation.

This then, I propose, is the major theme of the narrative in its finished form. It is about the tendency to accommodate religion to political norms. It shows this happening at both the national and the personal level. It shows us Yahweh's reaction to it, and how (in one particular case at least) it brought tragedy in its wake. The literary pattern of the story—five episodes each featuring a dialogue— reinforces the theme by throwing these dialogues (the primary carriers of the theme) into prominence and into association with one another. That is, meaning and form are combined in an artistic mode of expression, and the narrative in its final form has the character of a literary composition or 'work'.

As for literary works in general, in contrast, say, to pieces of political propaganda or religious tracts, the meaning cannot be stated adequately in terms of a monotheme. The story also has something to say about the nature of Yahweh's involvement with Israel, and this also is part of its meaning. It portrays that involvement as deeply personal and emotional rather than as merely formal and legal; as not, in the final analysis, governed by abstract principles of reward and punishment, justice and retribution. Yahweh saves Israel under protest. He is angry at Israel's apostasy and affronted by its 'repentance'. Yet he cannot tolerate its continued misery; he cannot simply leave it to its fate. He intervenes briefly to relieve Israel of the Ammonite yoke. But he does not intervene to relieve Jephthah's anguish, or to spare his daughter. He uses Jephthah to deliver Israel, but he never really approves of him. His silence is the other side of his anger.[75]

In its penetrating study of the man, Jephthah, the story has something to say about the human condition, and this also is part of its meaning. Jephthah is a capable man—capable with words, capable in battle, a strong decisive personality, and a leader of men. He has potential for true greatness. But he has a background, a personal history, which helps us to understand his limitations even if we cannot condone them. He is insecure, and he is self-centred. He can never fully engage with anyone's interests but his own. This is the hardness in the man and the reason why he can never be great. It is to this insecurity and self-interest that his daughter is sacrificed; Jephthah cannot be a father. For the same reason he cannot be a Moses. 'Jephthah the Gileadite, head and commander of all the inhabitants of Gilead' is as high as Jephthah can rise. He may judge Israel, but he can never care about it as Yahweh does.

So one could go on. The meaning cannot finally be abstracted from the story. The narrative itself is the only formulation of the meaning which contains all its aspects. The purpose of the kind of analysis I have offered here is first, to highlight some of the more conspicuous aspects of that meaning and second (and more fundamental) to draw attention to the literary character of the work so that the reader may orient himself to it appropriately and so be able to appreciate its meaning more fully for himself.

9.00 *Guidelines for a similar analysis of the book as a whole*
The thesis which I wish to advance in the balance of this study is that the book of Judges as a whole is likewise a coherent literary work with thematic focus on the one hand and richness of meaning on the other. Before proceeding it would be as well at this point to make explicit some of the findings of the present chapter regarding the literary character of the Jephthah story. This will provide at least some initial orientation to the task which lies ahead.

a. *Coherence.* The Jephthah story was found to be a coherent literary unit on at least four levels:
(i) Subject-matter: All the material in the story is related in some way to one particular crisis in Israel's relationships with the Ammonites.
(ii) Plot: It has a beginning, middle and end which contribute to the build-up and release of dramatic tension. This is the basic compositional structure which gives it coherence as a story.
(iii) Characterization: The character of Jephthah (central to four out of the five episodes) is presented with a consistency which enables us to recognize him as the same personality throughout. The same is true of Yahweh but he is not explicitly present in the action to nearly the same extent.
(iv) Theme: The story has thematic focus, that is (in this particular case) one major theme which is distinguishable from other levels of meaning.

b. *Intelligibility as a self-contained unit.* This is closely related to its coherence. The narrative in its final form is intelligible to a high degree as a self-contained unit. However certain aspects of it were found to gain added significance when read in the light of material which precedes the story in its canonical context. In some cases this proved to be crucial for the analysis. I refer particularly to the sequence initiated by the spirit of Yahweh coming upon Jephthah, and to the very limited nature of Yahweh's (explicit) involvement with Jephthah in contrast to the degree of his involvement in the careers of Othniel–Gideon.

c. *Narrative art.* I refer here to the literary means by which meaning at various levels is realized:
(i) Formal structure. I refer particularly to the division of the

narrative into five episodes, each featuring a dialogue. This is a pattern superimposed upon the basic plot structure of the narrative and is one of the principal means by which thematic focus is achieved. All of the episodes are characterized by the initiation, building up, and conclusion of an action, and in this sense they are 'natural' divisions within the larger story. They are given added definition in most cases by the use of the literary device of *inclusio*.

(ii) Paralleling of situations. Closely related to c(i) is the paralleling of actions in order to exploit fully the *kind* of situation involved. Thus

Israel's appeal to Yahweh	//	The elders' appeal to Jephthah
The bargain between the elders and Jephthah	//	The bargain (vow) between Jephthah and Yahweh
Jephthah's diplomacy with the Ammonite	//	Jephthah's diplomacy with the Ephraimites
The war with the Ammonites (holy war)	//	The war with the Ephraimites (tribal feud)

These 'same-but-different' parallels play a major role in the realization of the major theme. They also contribute significantly to the coherence of the narrative, and, as an aspect of this, to the portrayal of the character of Jephthah. They serve to highlight both the constants in his personality and the shifts in his *modus operandi* as circumstances change.

(iii) Repetition of key words/motifs. Key words are repeated to frame episodes, to highlight cause and effect (especially in Episode IV), to draw attention to a *Leitmotiv* ('the words of Jephthah'; 'Jephthah the Gileadite'), or to distil out the essence of a situation ('I have opened my mouth to Yahweh'—Episode IV; 'fugitives of Ephraim'—Episode V).

(iv) Authorial restraint. Meaning is conveyed throughout by implicit, indirect means: through narrated events, through irony, and above all through dialogue. We are left to infer motivation from behaviour, and the contrasting perspectives in which the major characters are set—Jephthah, Yahweh, Israel (Episode 1)— generate a strong sense of the complexity and ambivalence of their responses to situations and their relationships with one another.[76] For this reason the text is highly resistant to any simplistic, reductionist form of interpretation.

Certain of these findings appear to offer immediate promise of wider applicability within the book, especially c(i), the thematic significance of an episodic structure superimposed on a basic storyline, c(ii), paralleling of situation in order to exploit fully the significance of the *kind* of situation involved, and c(iii), repetition of key words and motifs (cf. the review of preliminary studies in sections 5.01–5.06 of Chapter 1 above). Further, the Jephthah narrative has been at the centre of scholarly discussion regarding the sources of the book, its redactional history, and related historical questions about the period to which the book refers.[77] We are now in a position to test the hypothesis that results achieved here are typical rather than a-typical by reading the whole book in its final form in the light of questions which have been raised by close study of what is, on any reckoning, one major segment of it.

PART II

Chapter 3

OVERTURE, 1.1–3.6

As 10.6-16 precedes the introduction of Jephthah in the Jephthah
narrative, so 1.1–3.6 precedes the introduction of the first judge in
the book as a whole. Two questions immediately arise: Is 1.1–3.6 a
coherent unit, and how, if at all, is it integrated into the rest of the
book? Because 1.1–3.6 incorporates a large number of distinct
traditionary units, each with its own special set of exegetical
problems, I have found it necessary in the first instance to treat each
of these small units in succession (in sections 1.01–1.24). The larger
significance of the detailed observations made in this initial survey
may not always be apparent at the time they are made, but will, I
trust, become clear in the light of sections 1.25–2.03 at the end of the
chapter.

1.00 *The Coherence of 1.1–3.6*

1.01
The opening words, 'Now after the death of Joshua . . .', indicate
both the continuity and discontinuity of the present narrative with
something that has preceded. To the extent that the present narrative
assumes the reader's familiarity with another narrative (in this case
the story of Joshua's career and death) it makes itself dependent on
that other narrative for its own intelligibility. To the extent that it
repeats material from that other narrative, changes it, or adds to it, it
makes itself independent of it.[1] The Joshua story with which the
reader is assumed to be familiar in Judg. 1.1 is itself set off from what
we may for convenience call the Moses story by the opening words of
the book of Joshua: 'Now after the death of Moses . . .' Joshua has, of
course, figured in the biblical story prior to this point, but only in

Moses' shadow. It is only after the death of Moses that Joshua
becomes the central (human) character. The book of Joshua is, in
this sense, his story in its finished, canonical form. It is set off from
the Moses story, and reaches its own conclusion in the death of
Joshua himself. A major new narrative development is announced by
the opening words of the book of Judges. They set the narrative
which is now to be unfolded in the context of a broad narrative
tradition with which the reader is assumed to be familiar. They do
not of themselves imply direct literary continuity with or dependence
upon what has gone before. Such obviously independent works as
Ruth and Ezekiel begin, like Judges, with ויהי followed by a temporal
clause (and cf. the ויהי which opens the book of Jonah).

These opening words are fully integrated (in terms of narrative
sequence) into what immediately follows, and do not stand apart
from it as a general heading as is sometimes alleged.[2] They firmly
locate the exchange between Yahweh and Israel in vv. 1-2, and the
events which flow from it, as happening *after* Joshua's death.

1.02

1.1-2

1 After the death of Joshua
b The people of Israel inquired of Yahweh,
c   Who shall go up first for us against the Canaanites,
d   to fight against them?
2 Yahweh said,
b   Judah shall go up;
c   behold, I have given the land[3] into his hand.

The dialogue between Israel and Yahweh in 1b-2c presupposes that
part of the Joshua story which refers to the 'remaining nations (גוים)'
and Yahweh's promise to dispossess them after Joshua's death; that
is, to Joshua's valedictory in Joshua 23 (esp. vv. 4-5). After the death
of their great military leader, the Israelites (still full of enthusiasm to
continue the struggle) seek guidance directly from Yahweh concerning
the further conduct of the war. The inquiry of 1cd envisages a series
of campaigns by individual tribes, or groups of tribes. The question
is, Who will go first (בתחלה)?[4] But the concept of a united Israel
remains. Whoever goes first will do so 'for us (לנו)', that is, for Israel.
It will be the first symbolic blow which will open a new phase in the
struggle between 'Israel' and 'the Canaanite'. In his reply Yahweh

gives this honour to Judah (2bc). The effect of this brief dialogue, and in particular of the victory oracle of 2c, is to suggest that the struggle has entered its last phase and will soon be brought to a successful conclusion.

1.03

1.3

A   Now Judah said to Simeon his brother

  B   'Go up with me into my allotted territory (גרל)

    X   and let us fight the Canaanite!

  B'   and I also will go with you into your allotted territory (גרל)

A'   So Simeon went with him.

This tightly constructed unit intervenes between the oracle of bc, 'Judah shall go up . . .' and its implementation in 4a, 'And Judah went up . . .' Judah 'speaks' to 'his brother' (3a). The categories are personal and fraternal, and these opening words of the unit set the agreement between the two tribes in the context of the tradition (reflected in Gen. 29.31-35) that they were descended from full blood brothers.[5] In this sense the alliance is a 'natural' one. Judah's actual words, however, reflect a much more immediate and practical concern.[6] They take for granted the situation described in Josh. 13-19, according to which Joshua allocated land to the various tribes by lot (גרל), and especially Josh. 19.1-9 according to which Simeon's allotted territory falls within that of Judah. In these circumstances the practical advantages of Judah's proposal are obvious. If Judah's words evince a keen eye for the practicalities of the situation, they do not, on the other hand, betray any lack of enthusiasm for the task. The members of the unit are arranged concentrically around the exhortation, 'Let us fight the Canaanite!' (3c). Simeon goes with Judah (3e).

The Judah-Simeon pact receives explicit mention again in v. 17, where Judah goes 'with Simeon his brother' to fight the Canaanite in Zephath/Hormah (in Simeon's allotted territory according to Josh. 19.4).[7] They 'strike' (נכה) its inhabitants and 'utterly destroy' (חרם) the city.[8] These two verses frame the intervening material, in which Simeon falls into the background and attention is focused on the exploits of Judah.

1.04

Judah's campaigns in vv. 4-16 (+ 17) are divided into two major movements, the first 'up', beginning in 4a 'And Judah went up (עלה)',[9] and spanning vv. 4-8, and the second 'down', beginning in 9a 'And afterwards the Judahites went down (ירד)', and spanning vv. 9-17. The downward movement is further divided programmatically into three stages by 9b: the hill country, the Negeb, and the foothills.[10] Only highlights are given for each of the two major movements. In the upward movement the campaigns against Bezeq and Jerusalem are featured; in the downward movement those against Hebron, Debir, and Zephath/Hormah. Verse 18 with its reference to the plain עמק (cf. v. 18 with v. 19b) stands outside both the frame provided by vv. 3 and 17 and the threefold schema for the downward movement announced in 9b (extending only to the foothills שפלה). It is best regarded as the first item in an appendix extending from v. 18 to v. 21, in which the extent and limitations of Judah's achievement are summarized. A completely new movement begins in v. 22: 'The house of Joseph went up ...'

1.05

And Simeon went with him [i.e. with Judah]	3e
And Judah went up	4a
And Yahweh gave the Canaanite and the Perizite into their hand	4b

It is not clear whether the plural in 4b (*their* hand) and the plural verbs which follow in vv. 4-6 refer distributively to יהודה (Judah, 4a) or to the allies, Simeon and Judah. In any case we must assume Simeon to be actively involved in the Bezeq campaign which is now described in vv. 4-7. The transition to the Jerusalem campaign (v. 8) is provided by 7ef, 8a: 'they brought him [the lord of Bezeq] to Jerusalem, and he died there, and the Judahites fought against Jerusalem ...'[11] בני יהודה (Judahites) now becomes the unambiguous subject of the plural verbs which follow in the balance of v. 8. The victories are attributed to Yahweh's help in fulfilment of the oracle (cf. 4b with 2c).

1.06

The victory at Bezeq is described in vv. 4-7 according to a traditional pattern of narration clearly attested elsewhere in the former prophets, especially in the books of Samuel (1 Sam. 4.10; 4.17; 13.1; 2 Sam. 2.17; 18.6-7). The elements of the pattern are as follows:

1   A brief statement that the battle was joined
2   A brief mention of the outcome (typically in terms of the flight/
     defeat of one side).
3   A mention of casualties (typically large) suffered by the defeated
     side
4   An account of the death of a person or persons of importance on
     the defeated side.[12]

In our present text the wording of elements 1 and 2 (4a, 4b) is such as
to link the victory firmly with the oracle of v. 2 as I have already
mentioned. Element 3 (4c) is entirely typical. Element 4 is much
more elaborate than in the typical instances of the pattern cited
above. A whole three-verse section (13 lines) is devoted to the
description of the capture, mutilation, and death of the lord of Bezeq.
The climax is reached in the direct speech of v. 7 (3 lines) in which
the enemy 'king', even with his limited perception of God (appropriately he speaks only of God [אלהים], not Yahweh [יהוה])[13]
acknowledges that he has suffered only what he deserved. All in all it
is reported as a glorious victory achieved with Yahweh's help. The
humiliation of the Canaanite ruler is dwelt upon with apparent
relish. The brutality is justified (from the victim's own mouth!) as
divine retribution.[14]

1.07
Judah met with similar success at Jerusalem according to v. 8, but
here only the briefest summary of the action is given, entirely in
stock expressions: they fight against it (ב לחם), capture it (לכד), strike
it with the sword (נכה לפי חרב), and set it on fire (שלח באש). In short,
they deal it a devastating blow in the same crusading spirit as
characterized Joshua's campaigns against Jericho, Ai, and Hazor (see
especially Josh. 6.24; 8.8, 19; 11.10-11 where the same stock
expressions are used).[15] The continued presence of the Jebusites is
accounted for by a note in the appendix to this Judah section (v. 21—
on which see further below).

1.08
The narration of the downward[16] phase of Judah's campaign opens
with another success in v. 10:

1.10

10   And Judah went against the Canaanites who dwelt in Hebron
b   (now the name of Hebron was formerly Kiriath-arba);

c   and they defeated Sheshai and Ahiman and Talmai.

The three names in line c connect the victory reported here with a specific Hebron tradition with which the reader is assumed to be familiar and according to which Sheshai, Ahiman, and Talmai were the 'sons' of Anak whose 'father' was Arba, '*the* great man among the Anakim'[17] (Josh. 14.15, cf. Josh. 15.14; 21.11; Num. 13.22). Thus line b, 'the name of Hebron was formerly city of Arba', provides the link between the general statement of line a (Judah went against the *Canaanites* who inhabit Hebron) and the particular statement of line c (they struck *Sheshai* etc.). The tradition adds time-depth to the three names of line c; they evidently signify not individuals but families of Anakites whose association with Hebron was believed to reach back beyond the Mosaic period (Num. 13.22).[18] The tradition also adds lustre to the Judahite victory reported here, for the stature and prowess of the Anakim were proverbial.[19] All that is clear from the one verb, נכה, in line c is that the Judahites 'defeated' the enemy.[20] But again, a note in the 'appendix' (v. 20) has something to add, on which see below.

1.09

1.11-15

11   From there they went against the inhabitants of Debir.
b   The name of Debir was formerly Kiriath-Sepher.[21]
12   And Caleb said,
b   He who attacks Kiriath-sepher and takes it,
c   I will give him Achsah my daughter as wife.
13   And Othniel the son of Kenaz, Caleb's younger brother,
             took it;
b   and he gave him Achsah his daughter as wife.
14   And when she came to him,
b   she urged him to ask her father for a field;
c   and she alighted from her ass,
d   and Caleb said to her,
e   What do you wish?
15   She said to him,
b   Give me a present;
c   Since you have set me in the land of the Negeb,
d   give me also springs of water.
e   And Caleb gave her the upper springs and the lower springs.

With Judah's advance to Debir (11a)[22] the text moves into a more expansive narrative style. Individual characters[23] are singled out for our attention—Caleb, Othniel, and Achsah—and they achieve a degree of personal identity through their actions and (in the case of Caleb and Achsah) through their speech. Caleb here acts in his traditional role as a 'leader (נשׂיא)' of Judah (Num. 13.1-2, 6; 34.18; cf. Josh. 14.6[24]). Othniel, of the same clan as Caleb and linked in close family ties with him (13a)[25] is also a champion of Judah so that the victory at Debir is both their personal triumph and, at the same time, yet another success for Judah.

Verses 11-15 in fact constitute a complete mini-narrative with its own characters and plot, in which a drama is enacted on a different level from that being played out between Judah and the Canaanites in vv. 3-19 as a whole. The plot of vv. 11-15 concerns a father, a daughter, and an aspiring suitor. The issues are essentially personal and domestic. The successful military action, so important in the larger narrative, is reported with extreme brevity: 'Othniel . . . took it [Debir]' (13a). Within vv. 11-15 the taking of Debir is of interest primarily because of the way it affects the relationships between Caleb, Othniel and Achsah.[26]

From the moment of her entry in person (14a) Achsah ceases to be a passive object acted upon by the two men. She seizes the opportunity to get something which neither her father nor her husband had considered.[27] Her father had already given the 'the land of the Negeb' (ארץ הנגב) as her dowry (15c); she greatly enhances its value by negotiating successfully for adequate water rights (15de).

All three characters in this vignette will assume greater significance in the larger narrative which is yet to unfold. Othniel will reappear as the first judge (3.7-11). In the light of 2.7 Caleb will appear as a representative of 'the elders who outlived Joshua' and in whose days Israel still served Yahweh. On the other hand his promise to give Achsah to whoever would take Debir for him (12bc)[28] will find a grotesque and tragic parallel in Jephthah's vow (11.30-31). Achsah's practical shrewdness and resourcefulness in seizing the initiative from both Othniel and Caleb[29]—the two male heroes of the story—introduces a motif which will recur at crucial points in 3.6–16.31, particularly at 4.17-22 (Jael), 9.53-54 (the 'certain woman' of Thebez) and 16.14-21 (Delilah). Othniel's marriage to Achsah will also assume greater significance in the light of 3.6, on which see further below.

1.10

1.16

16   And the descendants of the Kenite, Moses' father-in-law,
      went up with the people of Judah from the city of
      palms into the wilderness of Judah, which lies in
      the Negeb near Arad;
b   and they went and settled with the people (חעם).

From the hill-country the Judahites now move down into the Negeb
(or more precisely the Negeb of Arad', 16a).[30] This move has been
anticipated both by the programme of 9c ('the hill country and the
Negeb') and by Caleb's granting of 'the land of the Negeb' to his
daughter in 15c—confirming the direction of Judahite expansion. As
the Judahites now continue their advance into the Negeb the focus of
the narrative shifts from Kenizzites (11-15) to Kenites (16).[31]

Verse 16 has a number of textual uncertainties[32] with the result
that certain details remain obscure. Some things are clear however.
The opening words, 'The descendants of the Kenite, Moses' father-
in-law', set the present report against a background of tradition with
which the reader is assumed to be familiar, and since it is specifically
alluded to, we may expect this background to enhance our understanding of the foreground of the text in some way. I shall return to
this in a moment. Further, these Kenites *benefit* from Judah's
penetration into the Negeb: they enter the Negeb with Judah (16a)
and settle there (16b). The very different consequences for the
Canaanite inhabitants of the Negeb are reported in the next verse
(17).[33]

The benefit enjoyed by the Kenites is particularly illuminated by
the background attested in Num. 10.29-32. There Moses prevails
upon[34] a leading member of this same clan[35] to accompany Israel as a
guide, promising that

> as Yahweh does good to us
> so we will do good for you (v. 32).

The benefit enjoyed in Judg. 1.16 is the fulfilment of the promise of
Moses.

One particular uncertainty in the text calls for special comment at
this point, however, since (intentionally or not) it foreshadows an
important development which will take place in the ensuing
narrative. What are we to make of the vague חעם with which the

verse ends? Most scholars emend to [לקין]העמ 'the Amalekites' following Budde and Moore (cf. 1 Sam. 15.6).[36] Budde also considered עמו 'possible':[37] the Kenites who have accompanied Israel/Judah are reunited with 'their own people'.[38] Kaufmann suggests העם ערד 'the people of Arad'—'they have got for themselves a new heritage on the border of the wilderness'.[39] Whether העם is left to stand or one of the suggested emendations is adoped, the text still leaves us in uncertainty regarding what form the relationship of the Kenites to Israel will assume in the future. The Kenizzites of vv. 11-15 were shown as thoroughly integrated into Judah; the Kenites of v. 16 are seen as having a much more tenuous connection and their long-term loyalties remain in doubt. We are thereby prepared for the ambivalent role Kenites will play when they reappear in chapter 4 (vv. 11, 17ff.).

The disjunctive syntax of 16a invites us to read עלו as a pluperfect: 'Now the Kenites... had gone up from the city of palms with Judah...' Thus, by implication this note identifies the point from which Judah 'went up' (עלה; cf. 1c, 2b, 3b, 4a) as 'the city of palms'— that is, Jericho (Deut. 34.3).[40] A retracing of Judah's steps in Judges 1 leads us northwards to the same general locality, and 2.1 seems to envisage Gilgal, near Jericho,[41] as the site at which the Israelites had assembled to inquire of Yahweh in 1.1. (See my comments in section 1.17 below regarding the 'going up' of the messenger of Yahweh in 2.1a.)

1.11

1.18-19

18   Judah also took Gaza with its territory, and Ashkelon with
        its territory, and Ekron with its territory.
19   And Yahweh was with Judah,
 b   and he took possession of the hill country
 c   but he could not drive out, the inhabitants of the plain,
 d   because they had chariots of iron.

The first item of the 'appendix' (see section 1.04 above) summarizes Judah's achievements. Two notes on their efforts to occupy the coastal plain (18 + 19cd) frame a central statement about their success in the hill-country (19ab). The retrospective reference to Yahweh in 19a ('Yahweh was with Judah') is the counterpart of the oracle of v. 2, giving the following symmetrical arrangement of major compositional elements in vv. 2-19:

A	*Prospect*: Yahweh's promise to give Judah victory	v. 2
B	The Judah-Simeon alliance	v. 3
X	Judah's successful campaign	up vv. 4-8 down vv. 9-16
B'	The Judah-Simeon alliance	v. 17
C'	*Retrospect*: Yahweh was with Judah	v. 19.

But the qualification provided by 18 + 19cd is a major one, and the first disquieting admission,[42] that everything did not go according to plan: Judah 'captured (לכד)'[43] Gaza, Ashkelon and Ekron and their environs (v. 18) but 'was unable to dispossess (לא להוריש)'[44] the inhabitants of the plain 'because they had chariots of iron' (19cd). That is, despite initial successes there by Judah, the plain (עמק) remained in the possession of its Canaanite[45] inhabitants. We are left to wonder *why* iron chariots should have proven so decisive (19d) if Yahweh was indeed with Judah (19a). It is not a circumstance we could have anticipated,[46] and there is something profoundly unsatisfying about the simple juxtaposition of 19ab and 19cd. This is not explanation-without-remainder,[47] but paradox, and we are left to wonder what, precisely, it signifies. It is the beginning of a much more mixed picture of Israel's military exploits in the remainder of the chapter.

1.12

1.20-21

20   And they gave Hebron to Caleb,
b   as Moses had said;
c   and he drove out from it the three sons of Anak.
21   But the people of Benjamin did not drive out the Jebusites
     who dwelt in Jerusalem;
b   so the Jebusites have dwelt with the people of Benjamin in
     Jerusalem to this day.

Two further notes complete the appendix to this part of the chapter. Like those of 18 and 19cd they are a pair, the first positive and the second negative. But this second pair deal with two distinct locations (Hebron/Jerusalem) and two distinct protagonists (Caleb/the Benjaminites). Both are supplementary notes to victories reported in vv. 3-17, the first at Jerusalem (v. 8), on the upward phase of Judah's campaign, and the second at Hebron (v. 10), on the downward phase.

The supplementary notes reverse the order: first Hebron (v. 20), then Jerusalem (v. 21). 'As Moses said . . .' (20b) explicitly locates the note of v. 20 in the context of the tradition according to which Hebron had been promised to Caleb as his special inheritance (Josh. 14.6-15, esp. v. 9). The second note (v. 21) assumes that Jerusalem was in the territory allotted to Benjamin, as in Josh. 18.28 (cf. Josh. 15.8 according to which Judah's northern border passed just south of Jerusalem).[48] The two notes are concerned with the occupation (ירש) of these two sites after the victories reported in vv. 8 and 10.

They are a *contrasting* pair; the contrast is focused in the inverted syntax of 21a and the repetition of ירש;

	A	B
20c	he [Caleb] drove out (ירש) from there [Hebron]	

C
the three sons of Anak

C′
21a but the Jebusite, the inhabitant of Jerusalem,

	B′		A′
	they did not drive out (ירש)—the Benjaminites.		

Whereas Caleb follows up Judah's successful strike (נכה) against Hebron (v. 10) by driving out (ירש) the Anakite inhabitants (v. 20)[49] the Benjaminites fail to do the same at Jerusalem (vv. 8, 22). The contrast made by the juxtaposition of the two notes sets the failure of the Benjaminites in a particularly bad light. A contrast with the corresponding (negative) note in the first half of the appendix adds further weight to the indictment: while the Judahites 'could not' drive out the inhabitants of the plain (19c), the Benjaminites 'did not' drive out the inhabitants of Jerusalem (21a); worse, the Jebusites 'lived with the Benjaminites in Jerusalem to this day'[50] (21b, my emphasis). It is the harbinger of a more general state of affairs which emerges in the second half of the chapter (vv. 27-33).

1.13

1.22-26

22	The house of Joseph also went up against Bethel;
b	and Yahweh was with them.
23	And the house of Joseph sent to spy out Bethel,
b	(Now the name of the city was formerly Luz).

24 And the spies saw a man coming out of the city,
b and they said to him,
c Pray, show us the way into the city
d and we will deal loyally (חסד) with you.
25 And he showed them the way into the city;
b and they smote the city with the edge of the sword,
c but they let the man and all his family go.
26 And the man went to the land of the Hittites
b and built a city,
c and called its name Luz;
d that is its name to this day.

At 22a we have passed beyond the limits of the 'Judah section' (vv. 3-21) and stand at the beginning of a major new structural unit. This is signalled by the introduction of the expression 'the house of Joseph'. It is used twice in quick succession (22a, 23a) and then dropped until it reappears in v. 35. These references frame the intervening material, which deals with the wars of the northern tribes.[51] Verse 36 stands outside this frame as an appendix. In terms of literary structure this 'Joseph section' is parallel to the 'Judah section' of vv. 3-21:

	Judah (south)		*Joseph* (north)
v. 3	The Judah/Simeon alliance	v. 22	The house of Joseph
	Wars of 'Judah', including Calebites/Kenizzites.		Wars of the house of Joseph, including (in addition to Manasseh and Ephraim) Zebulun, Asher, Naphtali, Dan.
v. 17	The Judah/Simeon alliance	v. 35	The house of Joseph
vv. 18-21	Appendix	v. 36	Appendix

The words גם הם in v. 22a, together with the verb עלה draw attention to the parallel structure at the very outset of the Joseph section: 'the house of Joseph went up, *they also*' (my emphasis; cf. 4a, 'Judah went up').[52]

But if 22a is the beginning of a new structural unit, it is also the beginning of a new *movement* in the narrative. The 'Judah' and 'Joseph' sections are linked in a narrative chronology which is schematically linear: Judah 'first' (בתחלה, 1c), then Joseph. The forward momentum of the narrative, sustained throughout 4a-19b, is checked in 19cd, momentarily recovers in v. 20, and is lost again in v. 21.[53] If the Judah section is considered as a 'movement', it falters and stops in the 'appendix' (vv. 18-21). With 22a ('Now the house of Joseph went up . . .') momentum is regained. The narrative begins to surge forward once more, and our expectations are at once raised by 22b, 'and Yahweh was with them'—echoing 19a.[54] The Joseph section begins, like the Judah section, with a notable victory (cf. vv. 22-26 with vv. 4-7).

At the same time as there is a change of momentum in vv. 22sqq., there is also a change of style. Summary reporting (vv. 16-21) gives way, once again, to a more expansive narrative style.[55] Traditional motifs appear (the sending out of spies, leniency to an informer, the secret entrance to the city), together with direct speech (24cd) and a simple plot. From the point of view of plot, the Bethel story of vv. 22-26 is a complete, if simple, story in its own right—a mini-narrative. Only the גם הם of 22a explicitly connects it to the larger narrative in which it is located. In what follows I first consider the details of this mini-narrative before moving outwards again to examine how it functions within the larger narrative of which it is a part.

In the light of 22ab we expect the destruction of Bethel to be the climax of this 'Bethel story'. It is this to which our expectations, and hence our interest, are initially directed. Before this climax is reached, however, a complication is introduced into the plot which means that the story will not be completed by the expected victory. If achieved, the victory will lead to something else:

| show us the way into the city | 24c |
| and we will deal loyally (הסד) with you | 24d |

Thus a new focus of interest is established and the plot now consists of two interwoven strands which cannot be resolved simultaneously. The plot must now have a two-phase resolution. The first strand reaches its resolution in the destruction of Bethel (25b); the second in the discharge of the הסד-obligation (25c). But at this point the plot takes a surprising turn: the discharge of the הסד-obligation leads to the building of a 'new Luz' (26a-d). Only in retrospect do we see the anticipatory function of 'Luz' in 23b.

The victory is reported briefly as follows:

| 22a | The house of Joseph also went up against Bethel |
| 22b | and Yahweh was with them . . . |

25c   and they smote the city with the edge of the sword.

The direct speech, the traditional narrative motifs (spies, informer, secret entrance) and the unexpected twists in the plot (and hence the dramatic interest of the story) are all located in the *second* strand of the plot. It is this strand of the plot which makes vv. 22-26 what they are, a story, rather than a merely conventional announcement of victory. We conclude therefore that the true climax of the story is arrived at by following strand 2 to its resolution (25c) and surprising consequence (26). This is a story about an agreement made with a Canaanite, and not only, or even essentially about the conquest of Canaanite city.[56]

The released informer builds a city and names it Luz. He raises up a new Luz as a memorial to the city which he betrayed (cf. 26c with 23b). Is it an act of penance, or of defiance, or of simple nostalgia? The text does not tell us. What is clear is that the informer has not become an Israelite. He remains a 'Luz-ite', that is a Canaanite, at heart. Precisely what, in geographical/political terms, is signified by 'the land of the Hittites' in v. 26 is not certain.[57] Clearly the man retires to a safe distance—beyond the limits of Israelite settlement. But he does not go away into oblivion. He (re)builds something which is within the sphere of awareness—and contact—of future generations of Israelites: 'Luz, that is its name to this day' (26c, d).[58] It is not just a man and his family that survive to flourish again (25c), but Canaanite culture in a very tangible form—a city.

We must now return vv. 22-26 to their context in Judges 1 and ask how they function there. Here 22a provides us with our cue, especially by means of the verb עלה (to go up)and the words גם הם (they also). We are invited by the way in which the text is structured to compare the Bethel campaign of vv. 22-26 with the Bezeq campaign of vv. 4-7. Both result in victory. In 4b the victory is attributed directly to Yahweh's intervention: 'Yahweh gave the Canaanites and the Perizzites into their hand'. The corresponding statement in 22b ('Yahweh was with them') creates an *expectation* of God-given victory, but does not explicitly connect Yahweh and the victory in the way that 4b does. The focus of interest in vv. 22-26 is upon the *strategy* used to capture Bethel: spies, use of an informer, an agreement, a secret entrance (giving the attackers the advantage of surprise). In both stories one Canaanite in particular is singled out for close attention: the 'lord of Bezeq' in vv. 4-7, and the unnamed informer of vv. 22-26. The lord of Bezeq is shown as wholly within the power of the Judahites: they find him (5a), fight against him (5b), pursue him (6b), seize him (6c), mutilate him (6d) and take him to Jerusalem (7e). He survives the attack on Bezeq only long enough to acknowledge the 'justice' of what he has suffered at the hands of his captors (7a-d)—then he dies (7f). A quite different relationship develops between the Josephites and the informer in vv. 22-26: they see him (24a), speak to him (24b), make an agreement with him (24cd), he helps them (25a), and they release him and all his family (25c); he builds a new Luz (26). The radically new feature in vv. 22-26 is the pledge to deal loyally (חסד) with a Canaanite on certain conditions.

To return briefly to 22b ('Yahweh was with them'), it is noteworthy that unlike the similar expression in 19a this is not a summary remark at the end of the story. It is not brought forward at the end as an explanation for why things turned out as they did: 'so, you see, Yahweh was with them' (cf. Josh. 6.27!). Rather it raises expectations (of another Bezeq-type victory) which are in part fulfilled and in part confounded, and we are left to ponder precisely how Yahweh was involved and to what extent he approved or disapproved of the strategy involved. A more adequate appreciation of the function of vv. 22-26 in their context must wait upon a careful reading of the ensuing narrative (especially vv. 27-33 and 2.1-5).

1.14 *Excursus*
a. *1.22-26 in the light of the Jacob/Bethel tradition(s)*
1.22-26 takes on additional significance (though not a different significance) when read against the background of the Jacob/Bethel tradition(s) attested in Gen. 28 and 35 (cf. 48.3). A number of details in the text evoke this background: 'the house of Joseph went up (עלה) to Bethel' (cf. Gen. 35.1); 'the name of the city was formerly Luz' (cf. Gen. 28.19; 35.6-7; 48.3); 'he built a city and called its name Luz' (contrast Gen. 28.18-19; 34.7). When read against this background the Bethel of Judges 1 appears as a place which Yahweh has already claimed (as a site sacred to himself) by a theophany (Gen. 28), and a place which Jacob has already claimed for Yahweh by raising a מצבה (pillar) (Gen. 28), building an altar (Gen. 35), and calling it Beth-el, and claimed for 'Israel' by burying his dead there (Gen. 35.38). Luz has already been exposed, leached, purged of its Canaanite identity.[59] Canaanite Luz has no right to exist; all that remains is for its physical 'remains' to be obliterated. This is what we expect to occur as the house

of Joseph go up to Bethel in 22a—Yahweh with them (22b). What in effect happens is that Luz is not obliterated, but 'moved'.[60] The building and naming of the new Luz in v. 26 is an ironic inversion of Jacob's symbolic building and naming of Bethel in Genesis 28 and 35. The contest between 'Bethel' and 'Luz' (Israelite and Canaanite culture) is not decisively resolved in Judges 1 (see 2.1-5!).

b. *1.22-26 and the taking of Jericho in Joshua 2 and 6*[61]
The narrative of vv. 22-26 bears some fairly obvious resemblances to the story of the capture of Jericho in Joshua 2 and 6. I have given priority above to the comparison of vv. 22-26 (Bethel) with vv. 4-7 (Bezeq) since this 'parallel' is in the immediate context and arises directly out of the literary structure of Judges 1. The 'Jericho parallel' cannot be passed over without comment, however, firstly because it is so striking (at least superficially) and because the capture of Jericho is a highlight of the Joshua story which is presupposed in Judges 1 (see my comments above on 1.1a). The relevant points of similarity and difference may be summarized briefly as follows:

Bethel (Judges 1)		*Jericho* (Joshua 2 and 6)	
1. Yahweh was with them	22b	1. (See 11 below)	
2. They reconnoitre Bethel	23a	2. Joshua sends out spies	2.1a
3. The sentries meet a man	24a	3. The spies meet a harlot	2.1b
4. —		4. The harlot helps the spies	2.3-6
5. A חסד agreement is made with the man	24cd	5. A חסד agreement is made with the harlot	2.8-14
6. The man helps the attackers	25a	6. The harlot continues to help the spies	2.15-21
7. The city is taken—directly through the help of the man and indirectly through the help of Yahweh	25ab	7. The city is taken—directly through the help of Yahweh and indirectly through the help of the harlot	6.1-21
8. The man and all his family are spared	25c	8. The harlot and all her family are spared	6.22-25

9.	The man goes to 'the land of the Hittites'	26a	9.	The harlot dwells 'in the midst of Israel' 6.25
10.	The man builds a new Luz	26b-d	10.	'Cursed before Yahweh is the man who rises up and builds this city of Jericho.' 6.26
11.	(See 1 above)		11.	Yahweh was with Joshua 6.27

Both stories involve a חסד agreement with a collaborator (element 5). In the Jericho story the collaborator cooperates spontaneously and at great personal risk to herself (2.1-7). She then declares herself to be a believer in Yahweh as supreme god and asks in his name for a pledge of חסד ('swear to me by Yahweh', 2.8-12). She subsequently lives in the midst of Israel as one who has renounced her former Canaanite religion (6.25).[62] In the Bethel story the agreement is proposed by the attackers and it is the pledge of חסד which induces the man to co-operate.[63] He shows that he is still a Canaanite by building a new Luz (here the contrast with Josh. 6.26 is quite striking). In the Jericho story the Rahab strand of the plot, while prominent, is nevertheless secondary to that which deals with the spectacular victory described in 6.1-21. This is achieved by divinely revealed strategy and divine power. The statement 'Yahweh was with Joshua' comes as a summary statement at the end of the story and gives implicit endorsement to all that has taken place.

The victory at Bethel is in some obvious ways similar to that achieved at Jericho, but with some disquieting variations and shifts of emphasis. The comparison raises again the same questions about vv. 22-26 as emerged from the comparison with the Bezeq episode of vv. 4-7.

1.15

1.27-28 (+ 29-35)

27   Manasseh did not drive out the inhabitants of Bethshean and its villages, or Taanach and its villages, or the inhabitants of Dor and its villages, or the inhabitants of Ibleam and its villages, or the inhabitants of Megiddo and its villages;

b   for the Cannanite was determined to live in this land.

28   When Israel grew strong,
b   they put the Cannanites to tributary service,
c   but did not drive them out at all.

After the account of the united assault on Bethel there now follows a series of reports on the activities of the northern tribes taken individually: first the two Joseph tribes 'proper', Manasseh (vv. 27-28) and Ephraim (v. 29), then the Galilean tribes, Zebulun, Asher, Naphtali (vv. 30-33),[64] and finally Dan (vv. 34-35). In view of the broad south-north schema of the section, and of the chapter as a whole, the occurrence of Dan in the final position is somewhat unexpected.[65] I shall return to this below.

The momentum which was regained in vv. 22-26 is now immediately lost.[66] No further sacking of cities, killing or expulsion of Canaanites is reported; only arrangements by which Israelites and Canaanites co-exist. The note about Manasseh in vv. 27-28 begins and ends with the same statement: Manasseh 'did not drive out (לא הוריש)' the Canaanites in the cities listed. In v. 28c this is reinforced by the infinitive: 'did not drive them out at all'.[67] The explanation, in v. 27b, is cast in the most general terms: 'for the Canaanite was determined (יאל hiphil) to live in this land'. What appears to be envisaged is a stand-off situation in which the Canaanites make a determined stand and their assailants lack either the ability or the will (or both) to dislodge them. (Cf. v. 35 where the same verb is used.)[68] A compromise arrangement eventually emerges: the Canaanites remain in possession of their cities but render tributory service (מם)[69] to Israel (28ab). More of this in a moment.

The formula 'did not drive out' (לא הוריש) recurs in connection with Ephraim (29a), Zebulun (30a), Asher (31a) and Naphtali (33a). In the climactic Dan notice it is replaced by, '*the Amorites pressed* (לחץ) *the Danites* back to the hill country, for they did not permit them to go down to the plain' (34ab, my emphasis; cf. 19cd). The introduction of the verb לחץ is ominous, and in fact turns out to be a foretaste of things to come (cf. 2.18; 4.3; 6.9; 10.12). In the Ephraim notice לא הוריש is paired with a second expression which draws attention specifically to the co-existence of Ephraimites and Canaanites in the same locality: 'the Canaanite dwelt in his [Ephraim's] midst (בקרבו) in Gezer' (29b). This second expression also is repeated in subsequent notices, but with portentous variations as follows:

the Canaanite dwelt in his [Zebulun's] midst (בקרבו)   30b

Asher dwelt in the midst (בקרב) the Canaanites, the   32a
inhabitants of the land

He [Naphtali] dwelt in the midst of (בקרב) the Canaanites, the   33b
inhabitants of the land

This data is part of a carefully articulated double progression
spanning vv. 22-34 as follows:[70]

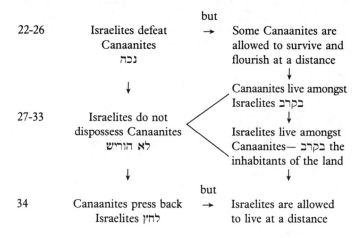

After the Bethel episode of vv. 22-26 the notices are simply
juxtaposed (note the disjunctive syntax). The 'progression' has no
chronological dimension; it is purely compositional and thematic. It
draws attention in a rather striking way to the *vulnerability* of the
northern tribes to counter-pressure from the Canaanites; some tribes
(those later in the list) more so than others.

But here we must return and pick up another thread, beginning
with the reference to 'tributary service (מס)' in 28ab. The compositional pattern which we have just observed (focusing on the
vulnerability of the tribes) is punctuated at certain points by
statements in which a state of vulnerability which has just been
described is reversed. There are four references in all to Canaanites
being subjected to מס, the first and last references being fuller than
the intervening two:

28a   but when Israel became strong (חזק)
b   it put the Canaanite to מס.

30c   and they [the Canaanites] became מס

33c   the inhabitants of Beth-shemesh and Beth-anath became מס
           to them [to Naphtali]

35b   but the hand of the house of Joseph bore down heavily
           (כבר)

c   and they [the Amorites] became מס.

In 28b the imposition of the מס in Manasseh's territory is attributed
not to Manasseh itself but to 'Israel' and then only after a period of
consolidation ('when Israel became strong'). A similar process is
envisaged in 35bc where it is the 'house of Joseph' which subjugates
certain Amorite cities (35a) within Dan's allotted territory. While a
process (involving the passage of time) is envisaged, the entire
process is viewed as having taken place in the past.

The past in which the events of Judges 1 are set is framed by the
death of Joshua (1.1) and the indictment of Israel by the 'messenger
of Yahweh' (2.1-5). Only twice is clear reference made to a later
period, in both cases by means of the formula 'to this day' (21b, 26d).
No such 'breaking of the frame' occurs in connection with the מס in
vv. 27-35.[71] It is often assumed that v. 28 refers to the pressing of
Canaanites into service in the early monarchy (1 Kgs 9.15-21, esp.
vv. 20-21).[72] The wording of v. 28 certainly admits of such an
interpretation, but the same can hardly be said of v. 35,[73] nor of v. 33.
The terms 'house of Joseph' and 'Israel' do not, of themselves,
involve any reference to the kingdom period, especially in view of the
way they are used earlier in the chapter ('house of Joseph' in vv. 22,
23, and 'Israel' in v. 1).[74] The use of forced labour in the monarchy
period in fact lies beyond the horizon of the present narrative.[75]
What is envisaged, rather, is joint action to achieve what was beyond
the capacity of the several tribes acting independently, namely, to
ensure that where Israelites and Canaanites lived in close proximity,
hegemony lay with the Israelites. The Deborah-Barak story will
show how fragile was this 'solution' to the vulnerability of the
northern tribes (4.2-3).

It can now be seen that the Bethel story of vv. 22-26 anticipates the
developments which take place in vv. 22-25 as a whole. It features,
not the victory itself, but the *arrangement* worked out between the
Josephites and the informer, whereby 'Israel' gains the advantage but
'the Canaanite' is allowed to exist and perpetuate his own culture,

albeit at a distance. The remainder of the Joseph section shows the vulnerability to which the northern tribes were exposed by their failure to dispossess certain Canaanites within their borders and the arrangement that finally emerged as a means of coping with this situation. Beginning with vv. 22-26 the focus shifts from conquest to co-existence. Verses 27-35 drive home the lesson of the 'anecdote' provided in vv. 22-26.[76]

1.16

1.36

And the border of the Amorites (האמרי) ran from the ascent of Akrabbim, from Sela and upward . . .

The obvious lexical link between this note and the Joseph section to which it is appended is האמרי (the Amorite[s], cf. vv. 34-35).[77] But the geographical place names, Akrabbim and Sela, appear to locate the 'border' referred to in the extreme south of Canaan and not between the Danites and the Amorites of the coastal plain as we might have expected (cf. Josh. 15.1-4; Num. 34.1-5).[78] Accordingly האמרי undergoes a semantic shift in v. 36, referring now either to Canaanites in general (as in Josh. 24.22: cf. Gen. 48.22) or to those associated with the southern hills bordering on the Negeb (as in Deut. 1.44). A consideration of the narrative function of the note may help us to decide between these two possibilities.

The note appears to be anachronistic in its narrative context. Has not Judah effectively disinherited the Amorites/Canaanites in the south? Would it not now be more appropriate to call this line the border of Judah or of Israel (as anticipated in Josh. 15.1-2 and Num. 34.1-3 respectively)? No, because by the time this note is introduced the focus of the narrative has shifted from conquest to co-existence. When the whole process of conquest and settlement has run its course, Israel dwells within 'the border of the Amorite'.[79] The Amorites/Canaanites are still 'the inhabitants of the land' among whom Israel dwells (see especially 32a, 33b). This note provides a final sardonic comment on the chapter as a whole, and on VV. 22-35 in particular. Formally it is parallel to the notes appended to the Judah section.[80]

1.17

2.1-5

1   Now the messenger of Yahweh went up from Gilgal to
        Bochim.
b   And he said,
c   I brought you up from Egypt,
d   and brought you into the land which I swore to give to your
                fathers.
e   I said,
f   I will never break my covenant with you,
2   and you shall make no covenant with the inhabitants
                    of this land;
b   you shall break down their altars.
c   But you have not obeyed my voice.
d   What is this you have done?
3   And I also said,
b   I will not drive them out before you;
c   but they shall become [thorns] in your sides,
d   and their gods shall be a snare to you.
4   When the messenger of Yahweh spoke these words to all the
                people of Israel,
b   The people lifted up their voices and wept.
5   And they called the name of that place Bochim,
b   and they sacrificed there to Yahweh.

Compositionally this unit belongs with what precedes it; thematically
it provides the transition from what precedes to what follows. It is
also the first of a series of three confrontations between Yahweh and
Israel which extend from here into the very centre of the book:

2.1-5   The messenger of Yahweh[81] confronts Israel.

6.7-10   A prophet, sent by Yahweh, confronts Israel.

10.10-16   Yahweh himself confronts Israel.

The first clue to the compositional relationship of 2.1-5 with the
material of the preceding chapter is the reappearance of the verb עלה
(to go up) as the opening word of this unit. This verb has occurred in
chapter 1 at 1c, 2b, 3b, 4a, 16a, 22a. Its use in 2.1a corresponds
formally to its use in 1.4a ('Judah went up') and 1.22a ('the house of
Joseph went up'). It does not occur at all in 2.6-3.6, the balance of
this introductory section of the book. It is a keyword in a
compositional sense rather than a thematic sense; it does not itself

enunciate the theme of 1.1–2.5, but by both its frequency and its distribution it helps to unify this extended segment of text and to define the several units of which it is composed,[82] thus:

A$_1$	1.1-2	The assembled Israelites ask Yahweh, 'Who will go up . . . ?'
B$_1$	1.3-21	Judah goes up.
B$_2$	1.22-36	Joseph goes up.
A$_2$	2.1-5	The messenger of Yahweh goes up to indict the assembled Israelites.

In the all-Israel assembly (A$_1$) which opens this larger unit the activity of B$_1$B$_2$ is anticipated; in the all-Israel assembly (A$_2$) which closes the unit, the activity of B$_1$B$_2$ is reviewed and evaluated.

'Bochim' in 2.1a is anachronistic in terms of the narrative's own chronology, for the weeping does not begin until 4b, and 'the place' is not named Bochim (weeping) until 5a.[83] The introduction of the name in v. 1, however, anticipates its explanation in v. 5 and these two verses function as a literary frame for the unit. 'Gilgal' in 1a is simply dropped into the narrative without comment. But it is a word pregnant with connotations in a narrative which presupposes, as this one does, our familiarity with the exploits of Joshua and his generation (1.1a; cf. 2.6-10). Gilgal is the point from which the messenger of Yahweh goes up, and so, perhaps the point from which all the 'goings up' of chapter one have originated (cf. 1.16a).[84] The same kind of twist is given to עלה in 2.1 as is given to הבה in Gen. 11.7. There Yahweh 'goes-to' to give his verdict on the 'goings-to' of the builders in vv. 3-4. Here Yahweh, in the person of his messenger, 'goes-up' to give his verdict on the 'goings-up' of the Israelites in chapter 1.[85] The recurring עלה of chapter 1 raised expectations high; but to what an unexpected end those expectations have now come: Israel weeping under the stinging rebuke of Yahweh's messenger! Or, to put the same issue in slightly different terms, to what a pass Israel has come 'after the death of Joshua'!

Specific thematic connections with chapter 1 are made in the speech of the messenger. The charge brought against the Israelites is that they have disregarded Yahweh's prohibition against making any agreement with 'the people of this land' and his command to 'tear down their altars' (v. 2).[86] We have been prepared for the use of יושבי הארץ (the inhabitants of the land) in 2a by its two occurrences in the Joseph section of chapter 1 (32a, 33b). There it was used in connection with the co-existence at close quarters of Israelites and remaining Canaanites and the emergence of forced labour as a solution to the problems which this co-existence posed for Israel. The messenger's speech makes it clear that this 'solution' is totally unacceptable to Yahweh. The whole process of 'coming to terms' with these Canaanites is denounced as the making of a ברית (covenant) with 'the inhabitants of the land'[87]—a ברית which is ideologically incompatible with Yahweh's ברית with Israel (cf. 1f with 2a). Particularly offensive to Yahweh is the fact that Canaanite altars have been left standing, presumably in those Canaanite enclaves with whose inhabitants the Israelites have come to terms, but also, as will appear later (see 6.25-32), in areas which the Israelites themselves have occupied.[88]

Yahweh's ברית, which he has vowed never to break (1f) is the oath he swore to the fathers (1d) to give the land to their descendants.[89] The driving out of the Canaanites 'before' Israel (3b) is viewed in the speech as an activity of Yahweh; the reasons why he chose to do it gradually rather than all-at-once are taken up in 2.21-3.4. The Israelites are not charged in 2.2 with failing to expel all the Canaanites but with coming to terms with them.[90] The implication of the speech is that the process of dispossession and occupation would have been completed in due course if the Israelites had fulfilled their obligations to Yahweh, but that now their disobedience has put the completion of the conquest in jeopardy, for Yahweh 'also said . . .' (3ab). The language of the speech here is indeterminate:

> And I also said,
>> I will not drive them out before you;
>> but they will become [thorns] in your sides

Yahweh simply reminds his audience of what he *said* he would do in the kind of situation which has now materialized. The first consequence of Israel's disobedience is that they *may* have to share the land indefinitely with Canaanites who will become thorns in their sides (3c).[91] Yahweh's decision to *implement* this threat is not narrated until 2.21. The speech of the messenger in 2.1-5 anticipates the divine speech of 2.20-22. Between these two speeches lies Israel's lapse into apostasy (2.11-19); it is this lapse which is foreshadowed in the final words of Yahweh's messenger: 'their gods will become a snare to you' (3d). As if to repudiate the very suggestion, the Israelites weep and offer sacrifice to Yahweh (vv. 4-5). They may have failed in their obligations to Yahweh, but they have not yet forsaken him for other gods.

The speech of 2.1-5 portrays Yahweh as impaled on the horns of a dilemma—a dilemma which arises out of two things he has said:[92]

1e	I said,
1f	I will never break my covenant with you ...
3a	And I also said,
3b	I will not drive them out before you ...

How can Yahweh keep his oath to give the land to the Israelites and at the same time fulfil his threat not to give it to them (or at least not all of it)? A solution seems to present itself in vv. 4-5: repentant Israel will henceforth obey Yahweh; the threat need not be implemented. But what follows in 2.6-19 shows that this solution is illusory: the 'repentance' evaporates and the Israelites sink into an apostasy from which Yahweh himself seems powerless to retrieve them. This of course intensifies his dilemma, which is further dramatized in the soliloquy of 2.20-22 and the confrontations between Yahweh and Israel in 6.7-10 and 10.10-16.

1.18 *Excursus*

Bochim, by virtue of what happens there, becomes a sanctuary, a בית אל, 'house of God' (cf. Gen. 28.17-19, and my comments above at section 1.14a).[93] The burden of the divine messenger's speech is that Israel has come to terms with the Canaanites, a process which began at Bethel (בית-אל) according to 1.22-26. Because of this the new sanctuary becomes a place of weeping rather than of celebration. In 20.26-27 the ark is said to be located at Bethel and thither the Israelites go to weep again, and to sacrifice to Yahweh. The implied identification of Bochim with Bethel is made explicit in the LXX.[94] Compare the 'oak of weeping' at Bethel in Gen. 35.8.

1.19

2.6 (+ 7-10)

a	When Joshua dismissed the people,
b	The people of Israel went each to his inheritance to take possession of the land.

This verse raises the question of the text's coherence in an acute form. Formally (i.e. syntactically) the text flows on from v. 5 without

disturbance; ... וילכו ... וישלח ... ויזבחו ... ויקראו (and they called ...
and they sacrificed ... and he dismissed ... and they went ...); the
assembled Israelites are dismissed. But a moment's reflection on the
content of v. 6 makes it clear that a major temporal disjunction takes
place at this point; it is *Joshua* who dismisses the people! The content
demands that we read this as a flashback to an earlier assembly (see
further below) even though the formal indicators of a flashback are
absent (cf. 3.7).[95] It could simply be a case of defective syntax, for
which various kinds of diachronic explanation are possible.[96] On the
other hand (and this is generally overlooked)[97] there is a continuity
between 2.1-5 and 2.6 and following which is not *simply* formal. The
apostasy which is the principal subject matter of 2.6-3.6 as a whole
both follows and is derived from the gradual coming to terms with
the Canaanites described in 1.1-2.5, as anticipated in 2.3d: 'their
gods will become a snare to you'. While the particular content of v. 6
makes it clear that a major temporal break has taken place, the
syntax reflects a more fundamental continuity of thought.[98]

But then why the flashback at all? Why not proceed directly from
2.1-5 to the announcement of 2.11? The period between Joshua and
the assembly at Bochim has already been surveyed in chapter 1.
What narrative function(s) does 2.6-10 perform?

The survey of chapter 1 concerned itself primarily with the
military and political aspects of the period and only secondly with the
religious dimension; with Israel's relationships with the Canaanites
rather than their relationship with Yahweh. Yahweh's accusation
that they have 'made an agreement with the people of the land'
comes as no surprise after 1.22-36, but the focus is shifted by the
speech from the strategic to the religious implications of this. The
charge relating to the Canaanite altars further sharpens this new
religious focus, but is quite unexpected after chapter 1 since there has
been no mention at all there of these shrines. In chapter 1 we see the
period unfolding from the psychological perspective of the Israelites;
in 2.1-5 we see it for the first time from Yahweh's perspective. In
2.6-9 the whole period is reviewed from this new perspective. The
religious question (Israel's relationship with Yahweh) is now the
focus of attention, and it is the military and political aspects of the
period which are now passed over in silence. A three-phase analysis
is presented:

1. The days of Joshua the 'Servant of Yahweh'	Yahweh did a 'great work' for Israel	The Israelites served Yahweh

| 2. | The days of the elders who outlived Joshua (e.g. Caleb?) | They had seen the 'great work' which Yahweh had done for Israel | They served Yawheh |
| 3. | The time when another generation arose | They did not know 'the work' which he had done for Israel | They did not know Yahweh |

The first intimations of the 'arising' of this 'other generation' are to be found, upon reflection, in the second half of chapter 1, but its full manifestation does not come until the outright apostasy of 2.11sq. 2.6-10 as a whole serves as a preface to the announcement which is made there: 'the Israelites . . . abandoned Yahweh . . .' It offers an explanation of how this came about: the Israelites of this generation, unlike their forebears, did not have first hand experience of the 'great work' which Yahweh did for Israel under Joshua. At the same time it fully recognizes, in fact underlines, the evil character of the thing itself by setting it against the background of what Yahweh had done for Israel and contrasting it with the faithfulness of Joshua and his generation. A similar contrast is implicit in the startling transition made in v. 6 from the assembly addressed by Yahweh's messenger to the earlier assembly[99] presided over by Joshua.

Certain of the leading motifs and concepts of 2.6-10 recur as the larger unit, 2.6-3.6, draws to a close. The death of Joshua is adverted to once more in the divine speech of 2.22, and the contrast drawn again between the faithfulness of Joshua and his generation and the faithlessness of the Israelites of the judges era. Further, the connection made in 2.10 between 'knowing' Yahweh and 'knowing' the great work he had done for Israel is recycled in 3.1-2 in a new form: it is the Israelites who have 'not known' war (v. 2), and in particular 'the wars of Canaan' (v. 1) who fail the test of loyalty to Yahweh. Here the verb ידע (to know) acquires fresh dimensions of meaning through its assimilation to the new 'test' motif and becomes a key word (see further below). 2.6-10 serves as a preface, not just to vv. 11-19, but to 2.6-3.6 as a whole.

1.20

In the interests of clarity and readability I here anticipate my conclusions regarding 2.6-3.6 as a whole by offering the following outline of its compositional structure:

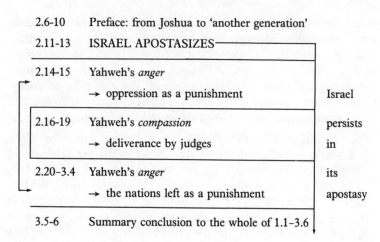

2.6-10   Preface: from Joshua to 'another generation'

2.11-13   ISRAEL APOSTASIZES

2.14-15   Yahweh's *anger*
           → oppression as a punishment   Israel

2.16-19   Yahweh's *compassion*
           → deliverance by judges   persists
                                                            in

2.20–3.4   Yahweh's *anger*
           → the nations left as a punishment   its
                                                            apostasy

3.5-6   Summary conclusion to the whole of 1.1–3.6

1.21

2.11-13

Here the gods whose altars were referred to in the speech of 2.1-5 come directly into view, and the prophecy of 3d is fulfilled. The unit is composed as follows:

A   The Israelites did הרע in the eyes of Yahweh.   v. 11

B₁   they served the *Baalim*   v. 11
           and they forsook *Yahweh*   v. 12

C   the god of their fathers   v. 12
               who brought them out ... of Egypt

           and went after

D   other gods   v. 12
               the gods of the people around them   v. 12
           and bowed down to them

E   they provoked Yahweh to anger   v. 12

B₂   they forsook Yahweh   v. 13
           and they served Baal and Ashtaroth   v. 13

B_1 and B_2 frame (as beginning and ending) a detailed exposition of A. הרע (that which is evil) is defined, first positively, 'served the Baalim', and then negatively, 'forsook Yahweh' (thus B_1; the order is reversed in B_2). C and D describe, respectively, the god the Israelites have forsaken and the gods they have embraced. Two expressions are used in each case. The description of Yahweh in C draws upon the two most fundamental elements of Israel's historico-religious credal confession: he is the god of patriarchal promise and of exodus deliverance. The two-fold description of the Baalim in D draws attention to their foreignness: they are 'other gods' worshipped by 'the people round about'. The two expressions which frame element D, 'went after' and 'bowed down to', express Israel's devotion to these gods and give more specific content to the עבד (served) of B_1 and B_2. The succession of verbs, 'served, forsook, went after, bowed down to, forsook, served', emphasizes the radical nature of the apostasy. Element E does not properly belong to this exposition but anticipates the subject-matter of vv. 14-15 and so helps to unify the larger composition.

1.22

2.14-15

Israel's apostasy kindles Yahweh's anger (14a). The balance of this unit describes the way in which this anger was expressed and the consequences which it had for Israel.

A   He gave them into the hand of plunderers
B   and they plundered them
A' and he sold them into the hand of their enemies round about
B' and they could no longer stand before their enemies

Within the parallel structure there is cumulative meaning.[100] In AB the focus is on the kind of depredation to which the Israelites were subjected (cf. 6.1-6); in A'B' it shifts to their powerlessness to resist it. It is this latter thought which is elaborated upon in the following verse:

15   Whenever they marched out,
b   the hand of Yahweh was against them for evil (לרעה),
c   as Yahweh had warned,
d   and as Yahweh had sworn to them;
e   and they were in dire straits.

Considerable pains are taken here to depict Yahweh's angry response as controlled and fully justified. לרעה of line b plays nicely upon הרע of 11a: the punishment fits the crime! With less subtlety the parallel in lines c and d doubly stresses that the punishment was entirely in accord with warnings previously given. (The language indicates clearly that it is such warnings as those of Deut. 31.29 and 28.25 which are presupposed.) Line e draws the unit to a close by neatly summarizing the consequences of the anger: Israel was in dire straits! (Cf. 10.9. ויצר in the last line of the unit echoes ויצאו in the first line).[101]

1.23

2.16-19

The subject matter of vv. 14-15 was Yahweh's anger expressed in his punishing Israel at the hands of 'plunderers' and 'enemies' (v. 14). The subject of this unit is Yahweh's compassion expressed in his saving them *from* 'plunderers' and 'enemies' (vv. 16 and 18 respectively). As in 14-15 repetition with elaboration is employed in the composition of the unit. It is composed of two sections, the second being subordinated to the first by the temporal clause at the beginning of 18a:

16-17   Yahweh raised up judges . . .
18-19   and whenever Yahweh raised up judges . . .

The unit as a whole reads as follows:

16   Then Yahweh raised up judges,
 b   Who saved them out of the power of those who plundered them.
17   And yet they did not listen to their judges;
 b   for they played the harlot after other gods
 c   and bowed down to them;
 d   they quickly turned aside from the way in which their fathers had walked,
 e   who had obeyed the commandments of Yahweh,
 f   and they did not do so.
18   Whenever Yahweh raised up judges for them,
 b   Yahweh was with the judge,
 c   and he saved them from the hand of their enemies all the days of the judge;
 d   for Yahweh was moved to pity by their groaning because of those who afflicted and oppressed them.

19 But whenever the judge died,
b   they turned back and behaved worse than their fathers,
c   going after other gods,
d   serving them and bowing down to them;
e   they did not drop any of their practices or their stubborn
    ways.

The statement that Yahweh raised up judges (16a) follows directly upon the statement that Israel was in dire straits (15e). The implication is that the 'raising up' of judges was an emergency measure taken by Yahweh from time to time in order to save Israel in dire circumstances. The implied motivation in 16a is his compassion, and this is made explicit in 18d: 'for Yahweh was moved to pity (בחם) by their groaning (מנאקתם) because of those who afflicted and oppressed them'. The formula, 'the Israelites cried (צעק/זעק) to Yahweh' does not occur here, a striking omission in view of its conspicuous occurrence in similar circumstances in 3.7–16.31 (3.9; 3.15; 4.3; 6.6; 10.10).[102] I shall return to this in my treatment of the central section of the book.

The closest possible connection is made in both parts of the unit between Yahweh's 'raising up' of the judge and the judge's role as a 'saviour' (16ab, 18a-c). In this role the judges were successful, liberating Israel from foreign oppression 'all the days of the judge' (18c). However, a different role, in which the judges were less successful, is implied in v. 17: the Israelites 'did not give heed to' (לא שמעו אל) their judges. The way of the fathers had been 'to give heed' (לשמע) to the commands of Yahweh (17de). This the Israelites of the judges era did not do (17f). By implication the judges, in addition to being 'saviours', were proclaimers of the מצות (commandments) of Yahweh,[103] but they were unable to stem the tide of Israel's apostasy.

In vv. 16-17 the Israelites of the judges era as a whole are contrasted with 'their fathers (אבותם)', that is, faithful Israelites of the past (cf. 2.6-10). In 18-19 a different perspective is introduced and אבותם undergoes a shift in meaning: each generation within the judges era is compared with the generation ('their fathers', 19c) which immediately preceded it. Both parts of the unit imply that there were periods of recovery, but neither draws attention to these. Rather they emphasize the persistent and worsening nature of the apostasy which characterized the era. In 17d, 'they quickly turned' (סרו מהר) from the way of the fathers. Although the language is not entirely perspicuous, vv. 16-17 seem to envisage apostasy already reasserting itself within the lifetime of the judge.[104] Verses 18-19, in keeping with their focus on succeeding generations, locate the time of decisive 'turning back (שוב)' *after* the death of each judge (19ab).[105] But here the turning back of each generation is to a *worse* state of apostasy than that which characterized the one before it: 'they turned back and behaved worse than their fathers' (19b). Israel is depicted as spiralling downwards into worse and worse apostasy. The closing line of the unit (19d) provides the final summary comment on the subject: 'they did not drop any of their practices or their stubborn ways'. (Contrast the 'way' of the fathers in 17d.)

1.24

2.20–3.6

The precise repetition in 20a of the words which introduced vv. 14-15 marks the beginning of a new unit in the composition and initiates a fresh narrative development. Verses 16-19 have shown Yahweh alternately punishing and rescuing Israel—to no effect: Israel has not desisted from its 'stubborn way'. Now his patience has been exhausted; his anger flares up again. His anger as expressed in this unit is his response to all that has gone before, that is, to Israel's behaviour throughout the judges period as a whole. We have reached a climactic point in the narrative. What will Yahweh do? The disclosure takes place in a divine speech (2.20-22); the balance of the unit (2.23–3.6) underlines the climactic nature of this speech by reviewing the background to it and the justification for the judgment which is announced in it.[106]

2.20-22 (+ 2.23–3.6)

20   So the anger of Yahweh was kindled against Israel;
b   and he said,
c   Because this people have transgressed my covenant
             which I commanded their fathers,
d   and have not obeyed my voice,
21   I also will not henceforth drive out before them
b   any of the nations that Joshua left when he died
22   in order to test Israel by them,
b   whether they would observe the way of Yahweh
c   by walking in it as their fathers did, or not.
23   So Yahweh left these nations . . .

There is nothing here of the indeterminacy and inconclusiveness which we noted in the speech of the messenger in 2.1-3. This speech consists of an 'announcement of judgment'[107] in two parts:

the reason (accusation)	20cd
the announcement	21-22

Yahweh no longer speaks *to* the Israelites (as in 2.1-3) but *about* them. By referring to them as 'this nation' (הגוי הזה) (20c) he implicitly associates them with 'the nations' (הגוים) (21c), whose gods they have embraced. He is angry, but tight-lipped. A firm rein is kept on his responses by the legal form of the speech. (There is nothing comparable here to the exclamation of 2d, 'What is this you have done!') although Israel itself is not addressed, the form of the speech (an announcement) implies an audience of some kind. Perhaps it is meant for the ears of the heavenly court where Yahweh presides as judge (cf. 11.27). Certainly Yahweh has distanced himself from Israel and adopted the measured tones appropriate to the handing down of a considered judgment.

It is in the context of 'Yahweh's covenant' *considered as a treaty* that this judgment is handed down. The wording of 20c, 'my covenant (בריתי) which I *commanded* their fathers' (my emphasis) implies that the obligations of the weaker party are determined and imposed by the stronger party as in a suzerainty treaty. Yahweh is judge because he is suzerain. In the speech of his messenger too, in 2.1-3, Yahweh referred to his covenant (בריתי, v. 1). There he struggled with the dilemma posed by the tension between his covenant considered as a promise which he had sworn never to break, and as a treaty or contract which required a certain response from Israel. Now he confronts that dilemma head-on by invoking the covenant purely as a treaty. The logical structure of the speech is indicated by the יען אשר (because) at the beginning of v. 20 and the וגם אני (I also) at the beginning of v. 21:

> *because this nation* has transgressed my covenant
> *I also* will not continue to drive out . . . the nations

Yahweh puts the promise aspect of the covenant into abeyance[108] in view of Israel's refusal to meet its obligation. By the 'I also' of 21a Yahweh tacitly acknowledges that in doing this he *technically* transgresses his own covenant (Yahweh himself is compromised);[109] his justification is Israel's prior transgression. The judges period ends with the relationship between Yahweh and Israel in a state of deadlock: no solution to the problem of Israel's apostasy is in sight.

A further, implicit, justification for the judgment is given in the closing words of the speech in which Yahweh identifies 'the nations' to which he has referred as those that were left by Joshua when he died 'to test Israel by them, [to see] whether they would observe the way of Yahweh by walking in it as their fathers did, or not'.[110] This provides the connection with the second part of the unit (2.23–3.6) in which the notion of the remaining nations as a test is elaborated upon in some detail, as follows:

A	*Recapitulation*: How it came about that there were nations left when Joshua died. They were left by Yahweh.[111] He did not drive them out quickly by giving them into the hand of Joshua.	2.23
B	*Who the remaining nations were*. 'These are the nations which Yahweh left to test Israel. . .'	3.1a
C	*Parenthesis on the test.*	

a	The *subjects* of the test: those Israelites who had not known (ידע) the wars of Canaan.	1b
x	The *object* of the test: so that they might know (ידע)—to teach them war.	2a
a'	The *subjects* of the test: those who had not known (ידע) them previously.	2b

B'	*Who the remaining nations were* (The list anticipated in B is now given).	
A'	*Recapitulation*: These nations were left to test Israel, so that Yahweh would know (ידע) whether they would keep his commands.	4
D	*Conclusion*: the result of the test. The Israelites lived among the Canaanites, intermarried with them, and served their gods. (That is, Israel failed the test, as implied by the closing words of Yahweh's speech).	5–6

The concentric structure of 2.23–3.4 gives surface unity to a passage which is highly repetitious and, on a first reading at least, not very coherent. It also alerts us to the fact that the parenthesis (C) in fact contains the central subject matter of the piece as a whole, which is about the *test* rather than the remaining nations as such. The repetition of the key word, ידע (know), further helps to unify the passage and to establish links between apparently disparate elements. Thus, for example, the 'war' which the Israelites were to 'know' by being taught it (Cx) was the war which earlier generations had known' (Ca), that is, the 'wars of Canaan', or holy war. Further, the two objects of the test in Cx and A′ are complementary: Yahweh would 'know' whether they would keep his commands by giving them the opportunity to 'know' holy war. The conclusion (D) confirms what is implied by the closing words of Yahweh's speech: Israel failed the test. The nations which were originally left as a test are now to be left as a punishment.

Element D, however, has a more independent status within the sub-unit 2.23-3.6 than the other elements do. (See my diagrammatic outline at 1.20 above.) It stands outside the concentric structure of 2.23-3.4 and does not contain any of the key words נסות (to test), ידע (to know), or גוים (nations). It does contain a list of Canaanite peoples (v. 5) but in a much more standardized form than that of v. 3. In fact vv. 5-6 serve a double function. As well as drawing out the implication of 2.23-3.4 and relating this back to Yahweh's speech in 2.20-22, they provide a summary conclusion to the whole introduction to the book. This introduction is composed, as we have seen, of two major segments: 1.1-2.5, which deals with the way in which conquest gave way to co-existence as Israel 'came to terms' with the Canaanites, and 2.6-3.6, which deals with the apostasy which followed upon and was the consequence of this accommodation. The final two verses of the introduction now summarize these two developments as follows:

v. 5   the Israelites lived among the Canaanites . . .   (cf. 1.1-2.5)
(v. 6a) (and intermarried with them)
v. 6b   and served their gods   (cf. 2.6-3.6)

Intermarriage (mentioned in 6a) is entirely understandable as a middle term, or as an aspect of the 'living among the Canaanites' of v. 5. But its specific mention here is unexpected since there has been no reference to intermarriage as such in 1.1-3.6. What *has* been featured, however, is the marriage of Othniel, whose career as the first judge is about to be reported (3.7-11). The mention at this point, therefore, of intermarriage with Canaanites, sharpens up the background against which we are to view Othniel.

1.25 *Summary remarks on the coherence of 1.1–3.6*

As chapter 1 progresses it gradually becomes apparent that the expectations created in the opening verses will not be fulfilled. Conquest gives way to co-existence as the Israelites begin to come to terms with entrenched Canaanites. The full significance of this does not become clear until the Israelites are confronted by Yahweh's messenger in 2.1-5 where the issue of 'making an agreement with the inhabitants of the land' is taken up directly. It is in this confrontation that the first climax of the narrative is reached. The story then breaks off and a second major movement begins from a different starting point. There is an overlap in the periods covered by the two movements but the second movement continues far beyond the point at which the first ended, including in its scope developments over the entire judges period. From the outset of the second movement the focus lies on the specifically religious question of Israel's relationship to Yahweh, and apostasy quickly emerges as the central issue; but again a process of deterioration is traced, climaxing in the divine speech of 2.20-22. This is the second climax of the narrative and the point at which the two movements ultimately converge, since it is here that the judgment that was threatened in 2.1-3 is put into effect. The speech at 2.20-22 is therefore climactic with respect to the whole of 1.1–3.6 and not just with respect to the second movement. The *issue* which is at stake here (will Yahweh do what he threatened to do at 2.1-3?) is the issue with which the composition as a whole is ultimately concerned. The issue of 'coming to terms with the Canaanites' (central to 1.1–2.5) and the issue of Israel's persistent and worsening apostasy (central to 2.6–3.6) are both directly relevant to it. The composition as a whole is ultimately concerned with the question of why the Canaanites were not wholly expelled from Canaan; why Israel did not come into possession of the whole land according to the promise which Yahweh had sworn to their fathers. The answer given is that Yahweh withdrew the promise (whether permanently or temporarily is not clear)[112] in view of what happened in the judges period. The whole of 1.1–3.6 is an elaborate justification for his decision to do so. This issue with which 1.1–3.6 as a whole is ultimately concerned is what I shall call its theme.

'To tell and to follow a story is already to *reflect upon* events in order to encompass them in successive wholes.'[113] This process is clearly at work in 1.1–3.6. A configuration is elicited from scattered events extending over a lengthy period (from before Joshua's death to the end of the judges period) by grasping them together into successive wholes. The text realizes its theme principally through its narrative shape, or plot. This plot is a teleological structure which draws us forward through the succession of events to the climax which is reached at 2.20-22. The plot structure (two movements featuring two divine speeches) is similar to that of the Jephthah story (five movements, or episodes, featuring five dialogues) and performs a similar function in relation to the theme.

Within this overall shaping of the material at the level of plot, considerable formal patterning of a more detailed kind occurs. Summaries of the observations I have made on the composition of particular parts of the text are to be found in the body of the present chapter as follows:

1.1–2.5	(§ 2.17)
1.2-19	(§ 2.11)
1.3	(§ 2.03)
1.3-17 (+ 18-21)//1.22-35 (+ 36)	(§ 2.13)
1.22-34	(§ 2.15)
2.6–3.6	(§ 2.20)
2.11-13	(§ 2.21)
2.23–3.6	(§ 2.24)

The details need not be repeated here, but this compositional patterning is quite extensive and includes symmetrical arrangement of corresponding blocks of material, closure, chiasm, repetition (with variation or elaboration) and the use of key words. This patterning of the material is aesthetically pleasing and greatly enhances the coherence and intelligibility of the text. Two examples must suffice:

(i)   The key word עלה (to go up) in 1.1-2.5. By its frequency and distribution it serves to unify this extended segment of text and to demarcate the several units of which it is composed (see §1.17 above). Cf. ידע (to know) in 3.1-4 (§1.24 above).

(ii)   The compositional parallel between the Judah and Joseph sections within chapter 1 throws the treatment of the Canaanite informer in the Bethel campaign (first item in the Joseph section) into sharp relief against the treatment of the Canaanite lord of Bezeq in the Bezeq campaign (first item in the Judah section). (See §1.13 above). This comparison helps us to perceive more clearly the basic shift that has already begun to take place at this point in the relationship between

Israelites and Canaanites in spite of the fact that the second
section, like the first, begins with a notable victory.

Finally, I note here once again (cf. §1.19 above) the temporal-causal
connection which is made at 2.3 ('their gods will become a snare to
you') between the coming to terms with the Canaanites which takes
place in 1.1–2.5 and the apostasy which is described in 2.6–3.6. In
terms of subject-matter the two major components of 1.1–3.6 are
complementary. There is a fundamental continuity of thought which
links them as parts of a conceptual whole.

2.00 *1.1–3.6 as an introduction to the book*

2.01
                          1.1–2.5

The account of the wars waged against the Canaanites by the various
tribes (ch. 1) begins with the exploits of Judah and ends with the
problems encountered by Dan. The central section of the book (3.7–
16.31) begins with the career of a Judahite judge, Othniel, and ends
with that of the Danite, Samson. In general the south-north sequence
of the tribes in chapter 1 corresponds to the south-north sequence of
the judges in 3.7–16.31. The sequel to the difficulties encountered by
the Danites at the end of chapter 1 is to be found in their northward
migration which is narrated in the closing section of the book (ch.
18).

Certain elements of chapter 1 assume greater significance as the
book proceeds. The question which is asked at 1.1 will be echoed by
the question which the captains of Gilead ask, in different circumstances, in the middle of the book (10.17, see my comments in
§4.00 of Chapter 2 above). It will appear again in almost the same
form as in 1.1, and receive the same reply, in the final section of the
book (at 20.18). There it is asked in the context of a civil war. Its
occurrence in all three major sections of the book has a unifying
effect upon the whole and helps to alert the reader to the
deterioration in Israel's circumstances which takes place in the
course of the period covered by the book. The vignette of 1.11–15 in
which Othniel is featured as a hero-figure anticipates his reappearance
as the first judge in 3.7–11. The note about the Kenites prepares us
for the ambivalent role they play when they reappear at 4.11, 17sqq.

(see p. 89, above). The failure of the Israelites to dislodge the Canaanites of the Plain of Jezreel, especially those of Taanach and Megiddo (1.27) is the background to the fierce battle which is fought there in chapter 4 and recalled in chapter 5 (see especially 5.19).

The mini-narratives which punctuate the summary reporting of chapter 1 contain motifs which will recur at significant points in the rest of the book:

1.4-7	the lord of Bezeq	Negative portrayal of (Canaanite) kingship	Cushanrishathaim, Eglon, Jabin, (Gideon, Abimelech)
		Retribution	Abimelech (9.56,57)
1.11-15	Achsah	The woman with initiative who exercises power over men	Deborah, Jael, the 'certain woman' who kills Abimelech, (Jephthah's daughter),[114] Delilah.
1.22-26	Conquest of Bethel	Conquest by devious means	Ehud, Jael, (Gideon), Delilah, (Samson), the conquest of Gibeah.

The full significance of these recurring motifs will become apparent only in retrospect, but it is apparent even at this stage that they form a network of interconnections which is part of the texture of the larger composition.[115]

As I have noted above (§1.17) the confrontation between Yahweh and Israel which takes place in 2.1-5 is the first of a series of such confrontations which extend from this point into the very centre of the book (2.1-5 → 6.7-10 → 10.10-16). They dramatize Yahweh's increasing frustration and anger at Israel's persistent apostasy despite all his interventions on its behalf. The climax which is reached at 2.20-22 belongs temporally at the end of this series but is disclosed in advance.

2.02

2.6–3.6

1.1-2.5 is full of the names of particular tribes, persons, events, and places. Even where similar kinds of events are reported (as in 1.27-33) each particular event is reported separately with the detail appropriate to it.

A different mode of narration comes into play in 2.6-3.6.

Particular tribes, persons, events, and places are now lost to view (after 2.6-9) and replaced by generalizations: Israelites, plunderers, enemies, judges, generations. Events of the same kind are grouped together: 'Yahweh raised up judges . . .', 'whenever Israel went out to fight . . .', 'when the judge died . . .', and so on. Particular 'nations' are named (3.3, 5) but only in lists, unconnected to specific events.

This difference in the mode of narration reflects a difference in the way 1.1-2.5 and 2.6-3.6 respectively function in relation to what follows. The events narrated in 1.1-2.5 all take place prior to the onset of apostasy and the advent of the first judge. The relevant details are contained within 1.1-2.5 itself, which serves as a narrative prelude to what follows. The developments described in 2.6-3.6, on the other hand, coincide (temporally) with those narrated in the bulk of the book. The details are contained, not in 2.6-3.6 itself, but in what follows. 2.6-3.6 is a narrative abstract, an outline of the plot. It reduces suspense (we already 'know' the story), but it does not necessarily hinder our ability to appreciate the detailed presentation of character, situation, and theme in the fully presented narrative which follows. Indeed, it may enhance it, as when one is given a summary of the plot of a complex drama before it is presented on the stage. In any case suspense is not eliminated from individual episodes, where it may play a very significant role.

But clearly 2.6-3.6 is *more* than an outline of what follows. It contains one crucial element, 2.20-22, which is not paralleled at all in the rest of the book. Further, it is not presented with the authorial detachment of a mere plot-summary. Here we touch upon other ways in which the narrative mode of 2.6-3.6 differs from that of 1.1-2.5.

In 1.1-2.5 the narrator does not comment directly on the rightness or wrongness of the actions of any of the characters. The only evaluation of behaviour is to be found in the reported speech of Yahweh's messenger (2.1-3) in which he, as one character in the story, passes judgment on the behaviour of other characters. It is otherwise in 2.6-3.6. The only human individual who is named is Joshua. He is an ideal figure (*the* servant of Yahweh, 2.8), a foil for the Israelites of the judges era, who are characterized *en masse* as religiously incontinent (זנו, 2.17), corrupt (השחיתו, 2.19), and stubborn (קשה, 2.19). These are the narrator's own evaluative terms; they reveal his ideological perspective directly.

Again, in 1.1-2.5 all the characters, including Yahweh, are

portrayed entirely from without. Our only access to their state of mind is through their reported behaviour, including, in some cases, their reported speech. In 2.6–3.6, by contrast, Yahweh's state of mind (and only his) is described directly: he becomes angry with the Israelites (v. 14), he is moved to pity by their groanings (v. 17), he becomes angry again (v. 20). This description of the ebb and flow of Yahweh's emotions draws our attention (admittedly in an unsubtle manner) to the depth of his personal attachment to Israel and to the reluctance with which he finally takes the decision announced in 2.20-22. It has the effect of making that decision more understandable, and therefore acceptable, to the reader. The narrator's explicit condemnation of the Israelites serves the same end. The same concern to justify Yahweh's action is expressed in another way, as we have seen, in 2.23–3.6.

In short 2.6–3.6 is much more directly manipulative of the reader's responses than 1.1–2.5. It provides orientation to what follows, not just at the level of plot, but also at the level of theme. (See note 116 for comparison with 10.6-16 of the Jephthah narrative.)

2.03 *Prospectus: 1.1–3.6 and the theme of the book*
I have argued that 1.1–3.6 is a coherent literary unit which serves as an introduction to the rest of the book by orienting us to it in various ways.

It contains an exposition of the initial complication (Israel comes to terms with the Canaanites, 1.1–2.5) out of which the basic conflicts of the ensuing narrative emerge, as outlined in 2.6–3.6. Israel is ensnared by the gods of the remaining Canaanites. This brings Israel into conflict with Yahweh and, via his intervention, into conflict with surrounding peoples. As a result Yahweh is torn between his pity for Israel and his anger at its apostasy. According to 2.6–3.6 all these conflicts grow more intense as the judges era runs its course and at the end no solution to them is in sight. In particular, Israel (more addicted to other gods than ever) continues to eke out a precarious existence in a land which it has never fully possessed and in which it is subjected to constant harassment by surrounding peoples. Here the ideological perspective of 2.6–3.6 comes to the fore and provides us with at least a provisional understanding of the conception (in a thematic sense) of the work as a whole. This state of affairs is interpreted as Yahweh's reluctant but just judgment on Israel (2.20-22). Israel has not come into secure possession of the land sworn to the fathers because of its persistent apostasy despite all Yahweh's interventions. The non-fulfilment of the promise is acknowledged but Yahweh is vindicated.[117]

In the following chapters I will argue that the thematic developments which take place in the rest of the book are in keeping with this conception of the judges period which is presented in the introduction.

Chapter 4

VARIATIONS, 3.7–16.31

1.00 *Compositional distinctives*

1.01

A detailed exposition of the formula, 'the Israelites did הרע (that which was evil) in the eyes of Yahweh', has been given in the introduction to the book at 2.11-13 (see §1.21 of Chapter 3). Within 3.7–16.31 it introduces the career of Othniel as the first saviour-judge at 3.7, and that of Gideon at 6.1. In a slightly modified form, 'the Israelites *continued* to do הרע' ... (my emphasis),[1] it introduces the careers of Ehud, Barak, Jephthah, and Samson at 3.12, 4.1, 10.6 and 13.1 respectively. The Abimelech narrative of chapter 9 is not introduced by this formula although the circumstances appropriate to its use are clearly indicated (8.33-34). Instead a lengthy transitional piece (8.29–9.5) firmly splices the stories of Gideon (father) and Abimelech (son) together: the latter does not simply follow the former but is a continuation of it. The formula does not occur at all in chapters 17–21. It divides 3.7–16.31 into six major narrative episodes (here I differ from Gooding)[2] featuring Othniel, Ehud, Barak, Gideon and Abimelech, Jephthah, and Samson respectively.

1.02

A number of other figures who, like those just mentioned, are said to have saved and/or judged Israel, are referred to in brief summary notices, introduced as follows:

3.31	And after him was Shamgar ...
10.1	And there arose after Abimelech ... Tola
10.3	And there arose after him, Jair

12.8	And there judged after him ... Ibzan
12.11	And there judged after him ... Elon
12.13	And there judged after him ... Abdon

There is more variation here than in the formula which introduces the major episodes. These short notices are distributed over three separate locations in 3.7–16.31, with a variation in the introductory formula at each new location (see above). (Incidentally their frequency follows an arithmetic progression: first one of them, than two, then three.) What all the opening lines have in common is אחריו, 'after him', a proper name standing instead of the pronoun suffix in one case only (that of Abimelech). This consistent use of אחריו, together with the extreme brevity of the notices, and the fact that they all stand at the end of a major narrative episode, marks them (from a compositional point of view) as subordinate units, attached as supplements to the narratives which they follow.[3] (Compare the supplementary notes to the Judah and Joseph sections in Chapter 1.)

1.03

Taking these two formulae as markers of where units and sub-units begin, we may represent the compositional design of 3.7–16.31 as follows:

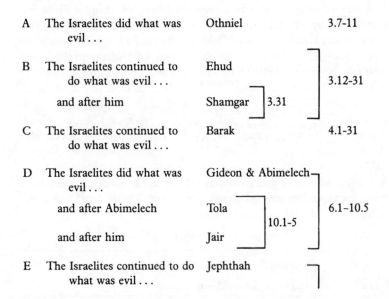

A	The Israelites did what was evil ...	Othniel	3.7-11
B	The Israelites continued to do what was evil ...	Ehud	3.12-31
	and after him	Shamgar 3.31	
C	The Israelites continued to do what was evil ...	Barak	4.1-31
D	The Israelites did what was evil ...	Gideon & Abimelech	6.1-10.5
	and after Abimelech	Tola 10.1-5	
	and after him	Jair	
E	The Israelites continued to do what was evil ...	Jephthah	

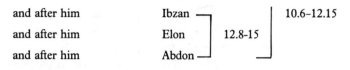

and after him	Ibzan		10.6–12.15
and after him	Elon	12.8-15	
and after him	Abdon		

F   The Israelites continued to do   Samson   13.1–16.31
     what was evil . . .

The 'eight years' of 3.8 introduces a chronological scheme which is
continued through to the 'twenty years' of 16.31, but not into
chapters 17–21.[4] In addition, the two introductory formulae also
contain temporal indicators, namely, 'continued to do . . .', and 'after
him'. That is, 3.7–16.31 is not simply an anthology of judge stories
and summary notices but a long and complex narrative movement. It
has an episodic structure with an underlying linear ground-plan (cf.
the Jephthah story).

2.00 *Method*

2.01
The preliminary observations about composition made above have
certain implications for the way the following analysis of 3.7–16.31
will proceed:

(i)   The Abimelech narrative will be read as a continuation of the
        Gideon narrative.
(ii)   The significance of the short notices will be sought, in the first
        instance, in their function within the compositional unit to
        which they belong.
(iii)   Each of the six major units will be read as an episode within a
        larger narrative composition extending from 3.7–16.31. Inter-
        pretation of particular episodes will take account both of the
        distinctive features of that episode and of the function(s) of the
        episode in its literary context.
(iv)   The whole of 3.7–16.31 will be read in the light of the
        orientation which has been provided in 1.1–3.6, but with an
        openness to the possibility that new issues, not anticipated
        there, may emerge as thematically significant.

2.02
An analysis of the Jephthah story has already been given in Chapter
2. At the appropriate point this will be expanded to include the

summary notices which are appended to that narrative, as well as some additional comment on the significance of the Jephthah episode in the context of 3.7–16.31. In order to keep this study within reasonable limits the analysis of other episodes will, regrettably, have to be presented in less detail. The analysis in each case has involved the same kind of close study of the text as was used for the Jepthhah narrative (and for 1.1–3.6), but the 'workings' will be presented in less detail and the conclusions approached more directly. Some of the excellent literary studies which have been made of certain of the episodes will be drawn upon and acknowledged where appropriate. A section at the close of the chapter will summarize my conclusions about 3.7–16.31 as a whole.

3.00 *Othniel*

3.01

3.7-11

7   And the people of Israel did what was evil in the sight of Yahweh,

b   forgetting Yahweh their God,

c   and serving the Baals and the Ashtoreth.

8   Therefore the anger of Yahweh was kindled against Israel,

b   and he sold them into the hand of Cushan-rishathaim King of Aram-naharaim eight years.

9   But when the people of Israel cried to Yahweh,

b   Yahweh raised up a saviour for the people of Israel,

c   who saved them,

d   Othniel the son of Kenaz, Caleb's younger brother.

10   The Spirit of Yahweh came upon him,

b   and he judged Israel;

c   he went out to war,

d   and Yahweh gave Cushan-rishathaim King of Aram into his hand;

e   and his hand prevailed over Cushan-rishathaim.

11   So the land had rest forty years.

b   Then Othniel the son of Kenaz died.

3.02

After the sweeping survey of the entire judges period in 2.6–3.6 we are returned in 3.7 to the same time and circumstance referred to in

2.11 of the introduction. As in 2.6 there is no formal (syntactical) indication of the time-shift; the content alone is sufficient to confirm that it has taken place: 3.7 recapitulates 2.11-13, and 3.8a repeats the opening words of 2.14 exactly. But now for the first time we have a particular judge and a particular enemy (although his identity remains an enigma)[5] and some chronological data. But narrative detail is minimal. A victory is reported, but not one concrete detail of the struggle is given. There is no dialogue, no reported speech of any kind, no dramatization of events, no scenic presentation.

This account of Othniel's career as the first saviour-judge is firmly anchored in its literary context by the extensive re-employment of terminology and formulas introduced in 2.11-19. This is the first clue to its significance. Othniel is the embodiment of an institution; all the key words applied to judgeship in chapter 2 are applied to Othniel here, and his career conforms to the paradigm given there. He is 'raised up' by Yahweh; he 'saves' Israel by 'judging' and going out to war.[6] It is Yahweh who gives him victory over the enemy, a victory which ushers in an era of peace which lasts until after his death.[7] But there are also new elements. The Israelites 'cry' (זעק) to Yahweh, and Yahweh's spirit comes upon Othniel (cf. the more general statement, 'Yahweh was with the judge . . ' in 2.18). Both of these new elements will recur in subsequent episodes (the cry: 3.15; 4.3; 6.6-7; 10.10; cf. 15.18; 16.28; the spirit: 6.34; 8.3; 11.29; 13.25; 14.6, 19; 15.14; cf. 9.23). But in 3.7-11 there are no complicating details. The cry meets with an immediate response. Yahweh, his anger apparently assuaged, becomes assiduously active on Israel's behalf, 'raising up' (9b), empowering (10a), and 'giving' (10d)—all of which is summarized in the emphatic repetition of (ישׁע) in 9bc: 'Yahweh raised up a *saviour* . . . who *saved* them'.[8] Here, it seems, is an institution which holds the key to Israel's survival. Subsequent episodes will show how open to abuse it was.

3.03

A further connection with the literary context is made in 9d, which identifies Othniel in precisely the same terms as 1.13.[9] We are left in no doubt that Othniel the saviour-judge is the same person as the Othniel who displayed his prowess and won Achsah as his prize in 1.12-15.[10] There his feats were his own; here he is supernaturally empowered—a charismatic leader. But what we know of him from chapter 1 makes his eleter by contrast. His wife is a true Israelite if ever there was one; a daughter of the illustrious Caleb, no less! Further there is a certain appropriateness, in view of 1.1-2 and the creditable performance of Judah in chapter 1 that the first judge should be one whose Judahite connections have been so firmly established. Altogether we feel that we *know* why Yahweh acted as he did in choosing Othniel. But we are in for a surprise. The confidence that we feel at this point (even the workings of the divine mind are within our grasp) is going to be subtly subverted in subsequent episodes. Things will turn out to be not quite as straightforward as the introduction and the Othniel episode have led us to believe.

3.04

Those who choose to serve (עבד) foreign gods (7d) are made to serve (עבד) a foreign tyrant (8c)—the punishment fits the crime (cf. 1.7). The Masoretic pointing of the tyrant's name makes explicit what is probably an intentional corruption of a received name into 'Cushan-of-double-wickedness' or the like, a reading of the name which is encouraged by the way it is echoed by 'Aram-naharaim', 'Aram of the two rivers', in 8b where it first appears. The name encapsulates a certain perception of the tyrant; in it we see him through the eyes of his victims. But the name also serves a compositional function with wider thematic implications. It is twice used in quick succession in 8bc, and then twice again in 10de, forming a frame around the intervening account of Othniel's exploits.[12] In both halves of this frame the tyrant is called a מלך ('King', cf. the portrayal of Canaanite kingship in 1.7). Like Othniel he is the embodiment of an institution. The clash between Othniel and Cushan-rishathaim is a clash between two institutions, but both alike are seen as expressions of Yahweh's rule over Israel; kingship in punishment, and judgeship in deliverance. The relationship between the rule of Yahweh and these two institutions will be explored further in subsequent episodes.[13]

4.00 *Ehud (plus Shamgar)*

4.01

The same basic sequence of events unfolds in this episode as in the previous one: apostasy, subjugation, appeal, the raising up of a saviour, defeat of the oppressor, peace. But instead of the shadowy Cushan-rishathaim we have now the very corporeal presence of the fat Eglon, and instead of the 'knight' Othniel we have the devious

left-handed assassin, Ehud. The 'service' עבד of the tyrant (v. 14, cf.
v. 8) now takes the specific form of the conveying of tribute to him,
and this provides the opportunity for Ehud to take a daring personal
initiative which effectively decides the issue *before* he rallies the
Israelites and engages the Moabites on the field of battle. Within the
predictable framework emerges a highly entertaining, satirical
narrative which moves through two climaxes to the resolution which
is reached in v. 30.

4.02
The kind of detailed stylistic analysis of the story which is the
necessary precursor to a treatment of its thematics has already been
done by Alonso Schökel.[14] I will not duplicate his work, with which I
am largely in agreement, by offering a detailed stylistic analysis of
my own, but proceed directly to a consideration of the thematics of
the story in its literary context.

4.03
The most striking feature of the style of the story is its satirical
quality. The principal target of the satire is, of course, the tyrant
Eglon. He is four times given his full title, עגלון מלך מואב (Eglon king
of Moab, vv. 12, 14, 15, 17) and then, climactically, Ehud addresses
him as המלך (O king) in v. 19.[15] The details of his subjugation of
Israel, given in vv. 13-14, give no hint of the satire which is to follow:
he gathers allies, goes and smites Israel, occupies the city of Palms,[16]
and maintains his hold over Israel for eighteen years. He is
apparently no mean hand in military matters. Certainly the Israelites
have no answer to him; that is why they cry out to Yahweh. But from
the moment the one-to-one Ehud-Eglon relationship is established
(protagonist-antagonist) Eglon is held up to ridicule. His obesity is
presented in the most grotesque terms (his fat belly swallows up
Ehud's sword, hilt and all, v. 22). By fattening himself on the tribute
he has extorted from Israel (מנחה is probably tribute in the form of
agricultural produce)[17] Eglon has turned himself into a large, slow-
moving target. His obesity symbolizes both his greed and his
vulnerability to Ehud's swift blade (v. 21). But much is made also of
his gullibility. He is easily deceived by the crafty Ehud, so much so
that he seals his doom by dismissing his own bodyguard (v. 19) and
by rising from his throne to receive the דבר אלהים (word of God)
which Ehud offers him, totally deceived as to its real nature (v. 20).

The narrator has developed dramatic irony at Eglon's expense; *we* know what Eglon does not. Ehud's words, 'double-edged like his sword', have a totally different meaning for us and for Ehud than they have for Eglon.[18]

The satirical handling of the subject-matter is continued beyond the murder scene to the comic scene which follows (vv. 24-25), in which Eglon's servants belatedly discover their master's corpse:

> The courtiers' erroneous assumption that their bulky monarch is taking his leisurely time over the chamber pot is a touch of scatalogical humor at the expense of both king and followers, while it implicates them in the satiric portrayal of the king's credulity.[19]

Eglon's courtiers are as gullible as their master and equally helpless against Ehud's deadly cunning. His troops fare no better. In full flight, trying desperately to make their escape across the Jordan, they are cut off there by the Israelites who have rallied behind Ehud. Not one of them escapes. The unusual use of שמן in v. 29[20] contains one final satirical touch. They were 'all of them stout (שמן) and all of them warriors (men of substance איש חיל)'. שמן, like איש חיל can be read in more than one sense. Like בריא which is applied to Eglon in v. 17 ('Now Eglon was a very *fat* man') it is used elsewhere in the Old Testament as an antonymn of רנה, 'lean'[21] and in this context is capable of the same kind of *double entendre* as the word 'stout' in English.[22] These stout warriors are 'laid low . . . under the hand of Israel' (v. 30) as their portly master has already been laid low under the swift hand of Ehud:[23]

> Ehud's assassination of Eglon . . . is not only connected causally with the subsequent Moabite defeat, but it is also a kind of emblematic prefiguration of it.[24]

The point is not that Eglon, his courtiers, and his troops were all blundering incompetents (witness the past eighteen years!) but that they were no match for a saviour raised up by Yahweh. Eglon has served his purpose (v. 12); now he is removed with such ease that it is laughable. Inasmuch as our attention is specifically drawn to his office, the satirical portrayal of the man, Eglon, involves an implicit critique of kingship (cf. 1.4-7 and 3.7-11, and see the table in section 2.01 of ch. 3).

4.04

Equally as striking as the satirical tone of the story is the absolutely central role that deception plays in it.[25] There is something deceptive about the very physical constitution of the protagonist. He has a physical abnormality[26] which appears to fit him for one role (conveyor of tribute),[27] but actually, at the same time, fits him for a quite different role (assassin). Ehud destroys Eglon by means of a weapon purpose-made by Ehud himself (v. 16).[28] The contrast between the final line of v. 15 ('the Israelites sent tribute by his hand') and the opening line of v. 16 ('but Ehud made for himself a sword') implies that the weapon is crafted in secret. Only when he blows the trumpet in the hill-country of Ephraim (v. 27) will the Israelites recognize Ehud as their מושיע ('saviour', v. 15). After its manufacture the murder weapon is doubly concealed. First it is concealed physically on Ehud's person (v. 16); then it is concealed verbally by the deliberately misleading expressions דבר סתר (secret thing/word), and דבר אלהים (word of God) in vv. 19 and 20 respectively. Ehud has accompanied the porters as far as certain פסילים (sculptured stones) near Gilgal and returned alone from there, a manoeuvre which may have been intended to give added plausibility to his claim that the 'secret thing' is in fact an 'oracle' (דבר אלהים).[29] Deception is crucial to the success of the murder. But so is it to the escape. The locked doors (v. 23) deceive the courtiers into the crucial confusion and delay which allow Ehud to make good his flight (v. 26). The only straightforward piece of action in the story is the successful military action in vv. 27-29, but this is possible only because of the whole series of skilfully executed deceptions which have gone before.

The grotesquely comic character of the story makes moral judgments irrelevant. We are clearly meant to identify with the protagonist and to enjoy the sheer virtuosity of his performance. It is a classic example of the underdog coming out on top, a scenario with universal comic appeal.

But the entertainment is given an ideological twist by the statement that Ehud was raised up by Yahweh, and by Ehud's rousing summons in v. 28: 'Follow me, because Yahweh has given your enemies (Moab) into your hand!' The perfect tense here, 'has given', is nuanced by its narrative context. It is not simply an instance of the customary use of the past tense to assure the troops that the victory is as good as won, but a reference to the very tangible grounds for such assurance in this particular case: the Moabite tyrant has already been given into the hand of Ehud[30] and lies dead in his chamber. Ehud now stands unveiled as Yahweh's chosen 'saviour'.[31] He has been 'raised up'; his deceptions have been providentially directed and guaranteed, although even Ehud himself may not have been aware of it at the time. We, the readers, have been initiated into the divine secret by the omniscient author quite early in the narrative, but even so we cannot explain the choice of 'Ehud the Benjaminite'[32] with quite the same assurance that we could the choice of Othniel. Why not another knight? Why a devious assassin? And why a Benjaminite, in view of what has been said about them in 1.21? Only on the purely formal plane, Benjamin after Judah, as in chapter 1, is there any perceivable appropriateness in the choice.

In short, while the same broad parameters apply (Yahweh punishes the Israelites for apostasy but saves them when they appeal to him) Yahweh's activity in this episode assumes a new aspect. It is secretive, deceptive, less accessible to human perception and explanation than it was in the Othniel episode.

4.05 *Shamgar*

3.31

a   After him was Shamgar ben Anath,
b   who killed six hundred of the Philistines with an oxgoad;
c   and he too saved Israel.

This brief account of the career of Shamgar is marked by the same grotesque, satirical quality as the Ehud story to which it is attached. Again the enemy is not only defeated, but made to look utterly ridiculous by the single-handed virtuoso performance of a saviour who is a most unlikely hero. Again our attention is specifically drawn to the weapon used.[33] This time it is makeshift rather than purpose-made, and it marks its bearer even more clearly as a non-professional, a makeshift warrior. As for Ehud, a man who is apparently fitted for one role (in this case, farmer) fulfils a quite different one (warrior). But as his weapon is much less subtle than Ehud's, so is his method. He overcomes the six hundred professional warriors[34] ranged against him by a feat of superhuman strength and dexterity, goading them to death like so many oxen that have incurred his displeasure (cf. Samson in 15.15).

The note is connected to the preceding Ehud story not only by the ואחריו (and after him) of line a, but also by the עם הוא (he too) of line c: 'And after him [Ehud], was Shamgar ben Anath[35] . . . and *he too* saved Israel'. The implication is that Shamgar was another saviour like Ehud, that is, an agent of Yahweh. If confirmation of this is needed it is supplied later at 10.11: 'Didn't I [Yahweh] save you from the Philistines?'[36] Yet Shamgar's tribal and geographical connections are not given as Ehud's were (contrast also the details regularly given in the short notices of 10.1-5 and 12.8-15), and his name only adds to the mystery surrounding his person, leaving open the possibility that he was not even Israelite.[37] Thus, by means of a more extreme example, this note adds to the impression created in the Ehud narrative itself, that while it is a small thing with Yahweh to save Israel from its enemies, his chosen means of doing so may not be easy to predict or explain. This issue will be taken up again in the Barak episode which immediately follows, and in which 'the days of Shamgar ben Anat' are explicitly recalled (5.6).[38]

5.00 *Barak*

5.01

The oppressor is again a foreign king, 'Jabin, King of Canaan, who ruled in Hazor',[39] but the prologue (4.1-3) already prepares us for the fact that Jabin will remain a shadowy background figure by directing our attention immediately to his army commander, Sisera.[40] Both pieces of information which we are given about Sisera—that he is based in Harosheth-haggoyim, and that he has nine hundred chariots at his disposal—will be alluded to again in the body of the narrative, where they are directly relevant to the unfolding action (vv. 13, 16). Although Jabin falls into the background we are reminded of his existence twice in the course of the narrative (vv. 7, 17) and then he is brought pointedly into view again with the threefold repetition of his name and title in the closing lines:

> So God subdued on that day *Jabin king of Canaan* before the
>   Israelites,
> And the hand of the Israelites bore continually harder upon *Jabin
>   king of Canaan*,
> Until they had destroyed *Jabin king of Canaan*.[41]

What seems to be envisaged here is that with the destruction of his army at the Kishon and the death of his commander, Jabin is isolated in Hazor and eventually overcome by the Israelites who thus finally establish their supremacy over the Canaanites in the north.[42]

5.02

The body of the narrative, telling how the Israelites were liberated, opens in vv. 4-5 with what D.F. Murray has aptly described as a 'tableau',[43] in which Deborah sits under her palm-tree in the hill-country of Ephraim, judging Israel (cf. Moses in Exod. 18.13-16). This scene serves to introduce the character who will set the plot in motion in v. 6 by sending for Barak, and to provide certain relevant information about her, in particular that she is a prophetess and hence the vehicle by which Yahweh's word enters the story to summon Barak to fulfil the role of 'saviour' (the term does not occur in the text but this is certainly Barak's role). Hence for the first time 'judging' and 'saving' are clearly distinguished from one another.

'The hill country of Ephraim in v. 5 is the topographical link by means of which we pass from the southern setting of the Othniel and Ehud episodes to the northern setting of this and subsequent ones.[44] It was in this region that Ehud sounded his trumpet and from which he led his volunteers south to engage the enemy at the fords of the Jordan (3.27). From this same locality Deborah now sends northwards to summon Barak to a battle to be fought at the Kishon. In terms of the schema of chapter 1 this is the first major episode which, with regard to both its setting and the Israelite tribes principally involved, falls within the sphere of the 'house of Joseph' (note the reference to Bethel in v. 5, cf. 1.22). It is the failure of the northern tribes to dislodge the Canaanites from key fortified cities, as described in 1.27-33 which provides the demographic/political background to the conflict which comes to a head here (the catalyst probably being an influx of Sea Peoples, as suggested by the name Sisera).

The initial focus upon a woman is quite surprising in view of the complete absence of women from the Othniel and Ehud episodes. The fact that she holds a position of authority and takes the initiative in relation to the prospective male hero is the first intimation of a thematic development that will give this particular episode its unique character.

5.03

Deborah charges Barak solemnly in the name of Yahweh (vv. 6-7). Barak responds by imposing a condition:

> If you go with me I will go
> but if you do not go with me I will not go.

Deborah is clearly taken aback, as her rejoinder in v. 9 shows. Saving Israel by force of arms is men's work. Barak has already received his orders and has been assured of victory. She will go with him if he insists, but he will have a price to pay:

> there will be no honour for you on the path you travel, for Yahweh will sell Sisera into the hand of a woman.

On the face of it, this need mean no more than that the victory will redound to Deborah's credit rather than Barak's. But a complication arises when Sisera escapes from the scene of battle (v. 17). The story cannot reach its dénouement until Sisera is accounted for. That dénouement is reached with the ironic juxtaposition of victor and vanquished in the tent of Jael, the woman who has in effect conquered them both: Sisera, by depriving him of his life, and Barak, by depriving him of the honour that should have been his as the chosen deliverer. Murray,[45] following Alonso Schökel,[46] has drawn attention to the compact irony of Sisera's last words (spoken to Jael):

> Stand at the entrance to the tent,
> and if anyone (אִישׁ) should come and ask you
> 'Is there anyone (אִישׁ) here?'
> You will say, 'No (אַיִן).'

The אִישׁ (lit. 'man') who comes to the door of the tent is, of course Barak, and the אִישׁ within is Sisera, dead by the time Barak arrives. To quote Murray,

> the confrontation is not now of two leaders at the head of vast armies, but of two men in the presence of a woman; and one word put with dreadful irony into the mouth of Sisera who has so cravenly abandoned his position of leadership, adumbrates the impending fate of them both: אַיִן [lit. 'nothing, no-one'].

This ultimate convergence in the destinies of the two men has been foreshadowed obliquely in the course of the narrative by a whole series of word-plays and syntactical parallels which have been identified by Murray; I will not repeat the details here. The final tableau in the tent of Jael balances the initial focus on the woman Deborah.

5.04
I have already drawn attention to the links with the preceding Ehud

narrative and its Shamgar supplement which are provided by
הר אפרים (the hill-country of Ephraim) in 4.5 and by the reference to
'the days of Shamgar ben Anat' in 5.6. Further connections of a more
substantial kind may now be observed.

Both narratives feature a murder scene followed by a discovery
scene, as follows:

	Ehud narrative	*Barak narrative*
Murder scene	Ehud murders Eglon	Jael murders Sisera
Discovery scene	The courtiers discover	Barak discovers the
	the dead Eglon	dead Sisera.

In the Ehud narrative the murder takes place before the battle, in the
Barak story it follows it, but in both it, rather than the battle, is the
high point of dramatic interest. Jael's murder of Sisera is narrated in
the same vivid style as Ehud's murder of Eglon; each separate
movement is described precisely (cf. 4.21 with 3.20-22). The verb תקע
occurs at the height of the action in both scenes: Ehud thrusts (תקע)
his dagger into Eglon's belly; Jael drives (תקע) her tent-peg into
Sisera's temple. (Compare the way in which, within the Ehud
episode, this same word links Ehud's private initiative with its
national consequences: Ehud thrusts [תקע] his dagger, and then
blows [תקע] his trumpet in the hill-country of Ephraim.)[47] Barak's
discovery of the dead Sisera is likewise narrated in the same style as
the courtiers' discovery of the dead Eglon. Alonso Schökel has
summarized the matching stylistic elements in the two scenes as
follows:[48]

	[Ehud narrative]		[Barak narrative]	
Entdeckung	hinne		hinne	
	hinne		hinne	
	hinne			
beinahe wörtlich:				
	adonêhem nopel 'arṣa		met	
	sîs⁰ra' nopel		met	

The similarity of style and situation in adjacent narrative units
invites us to read the second in the light of the first and to compare
the roles played by the characters in the corresponding scenes.

5.05

Deborah's charge to Barak in vv. 5-6 indicates that he is destined for a role comparable to that played by Othniel in 3.7-11. He does win a notable victory, but his insistence that Deborah accompany him already detracts from his heroic stature. Subsequently he is reduced to playing a role analagous to that of Eglon's courtiers, who were held up to such ridicule in 3.24-25. He arrives too late, to find that the man he is seeking is dead. Paradoxically that death is a defeat for himself; the honour that should have been his has been taken away and given to a woman (cf. v. 9). He can only stand and stare. It is his punishment for trying to manipulate Deborah, Yahweh's prophet (v. 8).[49] It is also a foretaste of the far greater evil that Jephthah will bring upon himself by trying to manipulate Yahweh directly. (Just as the vow and its fulfilment is the axis along which tension is developed and resolved in the Jephthah story, so the bargain struck in vv. 8-9 [Deborah will go with Barak, but Yahweh will sell Sisera into the hand of a woman] is the axis along which tension is developed and resolved here.)

It is Jael who finally emerges as the real hero of the narrative. But she is not an orthodox hero on the Othniel model, as Barak was destined to be; she partakes rather of the unorthodox qualities of Ehud and of Shamgar. Like Ehud, Jael is a lone assassin, who accomplishes her ends by deception. Like him she despatches her victim when the two of them are alone in a private chamber (hers, in this case, rather than her victim's). Like Shamgar she is a makeshift fighter who uses an improvised weapon. And if Shamgar was *probably* not an Israelite, Jael is *certainly* not; she is a member of a Kenite splinter group which is at peace with Jabin, Israel's arch-enemy (4.11, 17)! Her action is morally ambiguous, but her courage and the sheer virtuosity of her performance are sufficient to silence criticism on that score (5.24).[50] The crowning aspect of her unorthodoxy as a hero is her sex: Yahweh sells Sisera into the hand of a woman.

5.06

In the Barak narrative Yahweh's providential activity assumes an even more mystifying character than it did in the Ehud story, and this time mystification is of the very essence of the story's narrative art. In the Ehud story we were initiated into Yahweh's secret designs quite early in the piece, so that when Eglon failed to perceive the true

nature of the 'secret thing', the 'oracle (דבר אלהים)' which Ehud
brought to him, the irony was entirely at *his* expense. In the Barak
story we find out belatedly that we ourselves have been misled as to
the true significance of an oracle. Our discovery of the true identity
of the 'woman' is delayed as long as possible so that the irony is
nicely turned against the reader.[51] The effect of this use of the
technique of literary estrangement is to enhance the impact, when it
comes, of the revelation that Yahweh's choice has fallen not merely
on a woman, nor even on an Israelite prophetess (as we were led to
expect), but upon 'Jael, the wife of Heber the Kenite'.

5.07

To summarize: as in the Ehud narrative the basic subject-matter
(how Israel was freed from oppression—in this case that of Jabin and
Sisera) has been given a forceful thematic shape, in which the
principal dramatic interest lies in how Yahweh, in the course of
rescuing Israel, took the honour of the victory away from a man who
showed himself unworthy of it and gave it to a woman. At the same
time the Barak story is firmly anchored in its present literary context
and participates in larger thematic developments which are taking
place there. It complements the preceding Ehud narrative by
depicting Yahweh as realizing his providential designs by means
which completely overturn human expectations. By showing how
Barak was disciplined for manipulating Deborah it raises in a
preliminary way an issue which will assume increasing importance
in the confrontations between Yahweh and Israel in 6.7-10 and 10.10-
16 and will become the central theme of the Jephthah narrative, as
we have seen. In common with the Othniel and Ehud narratives it
depicts kingship as an oppressive foreign institution which Yahweh
uses at his discretion to discipline Israel, but this thematic element,
like Jabin himself, is marginal to the present narrative, in contrast to
the more integral role it plays in preceding units. (See, however, the
conspicuous mention of 'kings' at 5.19.)

5.08 *The song (5.1-31)*

5.081

In the finished form of the book the song of chapter 5 appears as part
of the Barak narrative. The ביום ההוא (on that day) of 5.1 picks up the
ביום ההוא of 4.23, locating the performance of the song in the

immediate aftermath of the victory which it celebrates (cf. Exod. 15.1), and the prose narrative is not formally concluded until the song is completed (see 5.31b and cf. 3.11, 30). Further, the song assumes the reader's familiarity with the events which have just been narrated. The well-known facts are alluded to obliquely rather than being re-presented in detail: Deborah is cryptically referred to as 'a mother in Israel' (cf. 4.4-6), Sisera first appears, without explanation, in 5.20 (cf. 4.2-3), and so on. At other points, however, the song takes up elements from the story and elaborates upon them, giving them a dramatic force they lack in the body of the narrative. Thus Deborah's brief rhetorical question in 4.14, 'Hasn't Yahweh gone forth (יצא) before you?', finds its counterpart in the majestic picture of Yahweh going forth (יצא) from Seir as the divine warrior in 5.4-5,[52] and the summary treatment of the battle in 4.15 finds its counterpart in the dramatic scene of 5.19-22: kings—stars—the river—pounding horsehooves. One scene, Sisera's mother waiting in vain, has no countepart in the narrative proper but greatly enhances the effectiveness of the song, as we shall see.

5.082
Many attempts have been made to find a clear metrical and/or strophic pattern in the song,[53] but the task has proven to be an extremely difficult one. The difficulty arises partly because the composition is of mixed genre (part ballad, part hymn),[54] partly because the text is obscure at many points (perhaps due, in part at least, to disturbance suffered in transmission), and partly because the mode of composition of such early Hebrew verse is still not sufficiently well understood.

In what is arguably the most thorough stylistic and structural analysis of the song in its finished form so far produced, M.D. Coogan[55] has discerned five stanzas in the song, the first and last being divided into two strophes each, as follows:

I	⎡A	vv. 2-5
	⎣B	vv. 6-8
II		vv. 9-13
III		vv. 14-18
IV		vv. 19-23

$$
V \begin{cases} A & \text{vv. 24-27} \\ B & \text{vv. 28-30} \end{cases}
$$

This analysis does not quite cover the song in its finished form since Coogan follows J.M. Myers, W. Richter and others in eliminating v. 31a from consideration on the grounds that it is 'a liturgical gloss and hence not part of the original song'.[56] Criteria used to identify the limits of the stanzas include shifts in subject and, in some cases, of metre as well, boundary-marking inclusions, and extended compositional patterns which are repeated. I will not repeat the details here.

In most cases the shifts of scene or subject-matter between strophes or stanzas is clear. This is especially so in the second half of the song where III deals with the varying responses of the tribes, IV with the battle, VA with the murder of Sisera by Jael, and VB with Sisera's mother waiting in vain for her son's return. In the first stanza the second strophe (vv. 2-5) is more heterogeneous in content than Coogan appears to recognize. It consists of a prelude to the song in two parts (vv. 2 and 3 respectively) and a section dealing with the coming of Yahweh as divine warrior (vv. 4-5). Stanza II is the part of the song with the most semantic and textual uncertainties and (the evidence adduced by Coogan notwithstanding)[57] would scarcely be identifiable as a stanza were it nor for the fact that it is of similar length to stanzas already identified and is preceded and followed by units which are clearly distinct from it. Its content is perhaps best summed up as a call to participate in the battle.[58] The response of the tribes follows in stanza III as I have noted.

The following table correlates my own content-analysis of the song with Coogan's formal (stanzaic) analysis:

Content		Stanzas
A. Prelude to the Song		
(i) Preliminary ascriptions of praise to Yahweh for what is about to be recounted	v. 2	
(ii) A call to hear the song	v. 3	IA
B. The coming of Yahweh as divine warrior	vv. 4-5	
C. Conditions prevailing before the battle	vv. 6-8	IB
A call to participate in the battle	vv. 9-13	II

E.	The response of the tribes	vv. 14-18	III
F.	The battle itself	vv. 19-23	IV
G.	The death of Sisera	vv. 24-27	VA
H.	His mother waits in vain	vv. 28-30	VB
I.	Concluding invocation of Yahweh	v. 31a	

Apart from the obvious difference in genre, it is clear that the same basic subject-matter (how Israel was freed from the predicament described in 4.1-3) has been handled quite differently in the song from the way it was handled in the preceding narrative. After the preliminaries of vv. 2-3 the focus falls, not on Deborah, but on Yahweh, who comes upon the scene from the south with terrible majesty as Israel's champion. The preliminaries have in fact prepared the way for his advent in this capacity by drawing attention very pointedly to the special bond existing between 'Israel' and 'Yahweh'. These key words occur as follows in vv. 2-3:

v. 2   Israel—Yahweh

v. 3a   Yahweh

v. 3b   Yahweh—Israel

Both A (vv. 2-3) and B (vv. 4-5) end with the same words: 'Yahweh, God of Israel'.[59] In the prose narrative Yahweh's 'going forth' to fight for Israel occurs on the day of battle (4.14); here, in the song, it is given special prominence by the fact that it occurs, out of chronological sequence, at the very outset of the composition. The time-shift which follows in 6a takes us back to a situation before the advent of Deborah, and from there developments are traced up to the battle itself which occurs in its proper chronological position at vv. 19-23. But the theophany of vv. 4-5 already focuses our attention upon Yahweh, whose victories (צדקות)[60] are to be the chief burden of the song (v. 11), and the storm imagery used in the theophany already anticipates the participation of cosmic elements in the battle.[61]

The advent of Yahweh is paralleled, in the second strophe of this first stanza, by the advent of Deborah, and thus an implicit equation is drawn between the two: the power of Yahweh, mythically described in the theophany, is historically revealed in the arising of

Deborah as 'a mother in Israel'.[62] Here are the seeds of a potentially fruitful thematic development, but strangely, in view of the preceding narrative, this parallel between the action of Yahweh and the activity of a woman remains a muted note in the song. Little is said about Deborah, as I have already observed. There is no mention of her summons to Barak or of his dialogue with her, nor any reference to the prediction, so central to the prose narrative, that Yahweh will sell Sisera into the hand of a woman. In the next stanza[63] Deborah reappears in company with Barak (Deborah sings while Barak leads the troops into battle, v. 11), but the dramatic interest remains centred in the forthcoming battle itself, not in the role that a woman will play in it. The third stanza, with its listing of the tribes which did and did not take part builds up expectancy that there is to be a truly great battle, such as the theophany of vv. 4-5 foreshadowed.[64] At the same time it reveals a lack of unity among the tribes—an issue that will assume growing importance in the remainder of the book (see 8.1-3; 12.1-6; 15.9-13 and the Samson episode in general, and, climactically the civil war of ch. 20). Verse 18, dealing with Zebulun and Naphtali ('they hazarded their lives to death on the heights of the field') provides the transition to the battle, and incidentally confirms that these were the tribes most directly concerned, as in the prose narrative.[65]

The description of the battle in the fourth stanza fully realizes the expectations built up in the preceding sections of the song.[66] The opening two lines, with their climactic parallelism (kings . . . kings of Canaan)[67] impress upon us the scale of the conflict (as did the list of participants in vv. 14-18). The fighting itself takes on cosmic dimensions: the stars fight from the heavens, and on earth the Wadi Kishon responds by becoming a torrent and overwhelming the enemy.[68] The description ends with the pounding (*daharot, daharot*) of the horsehooves of the defeated chariotry trying to escape.[69] The style is impressionistic and allusive. We are left to conclude that the stars have acted under Yahweh's orders and that their action took the form of a colossal storm;[70] but we have been prepared for this by the storm imagery of vv. 4-5 as I noted earlier. The human element in the victory is so completely eclipsed by the intervention of heavenly powers that Barak and his forces are not even mentioned in the description of the battle! But there is one heroic deed on the human plane which, even in this context, cannot be overlooked. The cursing of Meroz in v. 23 serves as a foil to what immediately follows (the first strophe of the last stanza) in which Jael, by contrast, is blessed (v. 24).[71]

The killing of Sisera is dwelt upon with savage delight, as in the prose narrative, and the vividness of the style if anything surpasses that of the previous account. But this time Barak makes no appearance. Unlike the corresponding scene in chapter 4 this one is not concerned with how the honour was taken away from Barak and given to a woman, but solely with the fate that Sisera suffered. Nothing is allowed to distract our attention from the spectacle with which the scene concludes: Sisera lying shattered (שׁדוּד) at the feet of Jael (v. 27). To die thus at the hand of a woman is the ultimate humiliation; Abimelech will later commit suicide rather than be exposed to the shame of it (9.54)! Jael is 'most blessed among women' for her part in bringing Sisera to such an end. This strophe completes the action which was begun in the battle, but since there is no oracle carrying us forward to it and no mystery, to be solved, it does not have the same quality of dénouement that the corresponding scene in the prose narrative had.

In the second strophe of this last stanza the scene changes from Jael's tent to Sisera's stately home where his mother watches anxiously from the window. The inaction (waiting) of this scene is the complement of the action (murder) in the previous one. The tone is subdued. The waiting mother's two questions 'convey with wonderful psychological insight her state of nervousness and impatience',[72] and the answers given by her maids without any real conviction only thinly veil an unspoken dread. *We* know that Sisera will never return. The scene evokes strong and conflicting emotions. The bereaved mother-figure, the psychological realism, and the heavy irony in combination are powerful generators of pathos.[73] But it is clear that the author finds the scene deeply satisfying and that this is meant to be our response to it also, as the final invocation of v. 31a confirms:

> So let all your enemies perish, Yahweh!

The second strophe, like the first, shows how completely Yahweh's enemies have been undone. At the same time it serves as an artistic closure to the whole song by providing, in the mother of Sisera, a counterbalance to Deborah, the mother in Israel.

5.084

To summarize: the song is not concerned, as the narrative of chapter 4 was, with how Yahweh took the honour of victory from Barak and gave it to a woman. It pays tribute to those individuals and tribes which 'came to the help of Yahweh' and rebukes those that did not (thus alerting us to a lack of unity among the tribes—a harbinger of things to come). But its chief burden is the 'victorious deeds' of Yahweh himself, who went forth as Israel's champion and over-whelmed the enemy by unleashing the powers of heaven against them. The battle itself is the climax of the song; the two strophes in the final stanza show how completely his enemies were undone.[74] And so the Barak episode concludes with a victory hymn in praise of Yahweh and his loyal supporters—but especially of Yahweh. The Gideon episode which immediately follows will end very differently (a striking example of the progressive decline outlined program-matically in 2.19). At the beginning of that episode Yahweh will have to despatch a prophet to remind the Israelites, so soon apostate again, of his earlier interventions on their behalf (6.8-9).

6.00 *Gideon (plus Abimelech, Tola, Jair)*

6.01

'The Israelites did what was evil in Yahweh's sight' (6.1a). The familiar words mark the beginning of another major episode. But here they stand in abrupt contrast to the high praises of Yahweh that have been sung in the previous chapter and confront us in a particularly striking way with the fickleness of the Israelites, who cannot for long resist the allurements of other gods no matter how much Yahweh exerts himself on their behalf. As we shall see, the problem of apostasy is explored much more fully in this episode than in previous ones.

This time the Israelites are punished by being subjected to the depredations of hordes of Midianites and other 'easterners' (6.3).[75] As in the Barak episode the struggle between the two sides centres on the plain of Jezreel (6.33), making this episode the natural and logical sequel to what has gone before. Barak's victory over the Canaanite chariot forces has opened the broad fertile plain to Israelite settlement and the cultivation of crops (6.3a), but now a different kind of enemy appears in the same region and a new struggle for control of it ensues.[76]

The plight of the Israelites is described here much more fully than in previous episodes. The pitiful decline in their lifestyle is conveyed by piling detail upon detail: they live in dens and caves like animals; their produce is destroyed, and their sheep, oxen and donkeys are carried off by the enemy (v. 4b).[77] The entire land is laid waste[78] and with it their means of sustenance. The enemy is as numerous and destructive as a plague of locusts (v. 5a) and has a huge tactical advantage in its possession of 'camels, without number' (v. 5c). The sequence of iterative verb-forms in vv. 3-5 captures stylistically the wave after wave of pillage and destruction. The whole is summarized in v. 6a, 'Israel became utterly destitute because of Midian'.[79] In their desperation the Israelites appeal, as usual, to Yahweh, and this becomes the point of transition to the next major unit in the narrative, vv. 7-10. (Note how v. 7 repeats, in reverse order, the substance of v. 6.)

6.02

Yahweh immediately sends a prophet (איש נביא, 6.8a), who appears at precisely the same point in the plot as Deborah the prophetess (אשה נביאה, 4.4) had appeared in the Barak narrative.[80] But his function contrasts sharply with hers: not to set in motion the process of deliverance, but to indict the Israelites and tell them that they have forfeited all right to deliverance (6.10b). Calling (צעק/זעק) upon Yahweh is an activity with ancient precedent in Israelite tradition: their fathers had cried to Yahweh in their desperate circumstances in Egypt and had been sent a saviour in the form of Moses (Exod. 2.23–3.12. זעק is used in Exod. 2.23 as in Judg. 6.6). The appeal to Yahweh is part of the pattern established in the preceding episodes, but the response which it receives here breaks the pattern and is wholly unexpected. Yahweh's frustration begins to show for the first time. The effect of the prophet's speech is to caution us against drawing any simple equation between calling upon Yahweh and repentance (this is developed further in 10.10-16 as we have seen) and to make it clear that the appeal is not a device by which Israel can automatically secure its future. To call upon Yahweh is to invoke a relationship, but this relationship (acknowledged in the speech) is one which lays certain obligations upon Israel, obligations which she has not fulfilled (v. 10). The speech ends on this note of indictment and it is not clear what the divine decision concerning Israel's future has been. For that we must look to the ensuing narrative.

6.03

With the advent of Yahweh's angel in 6.11 it is at once apparent that Yahweh has resolved to rescue Israel yet again. But we are aware that the problem of Israel's apostasy remains unresolved (the exchange in 6.6-10 has had more the character of confrontation than of rapprochement) and that this issue is of fundamental concern to the narrator. The body of the narrative, dealing with how Israel was freed from Midianite domination, extends from 6.11 to 8.28 where it is formally concluded, as in previous episodes, by the statement that the enemy was subdued before the Israelites and the land had rest for forty years (cf. 3.10b, 11; 3.30; 4.23; 5.31). This long section consists of two distinct narrative movements, as I will now show.

After the enlistment of Gideon in 6.11-24 there follows a series of incidents which build the sense of mounting tension by simultaneously anticipating the inevitable clash between Gideon and the enemy and delaying its arrival. The climax is reached at the end of chapter 7 with the successful surprise attack on the Midianite camp, the rout of the enemy, and the slaughter of their two commanders (7.19-25). A brief epilogue follows (8.1-3) in which Gideon successfully averts the threat of civil war by quelling intertribal jealousies which have been aroused in the course of the campaign. Thus, with the external threat removed and internal harmony restored, we appear to be set for the customary conclusion, namely, that 'the land had rest for X years'.

But then, quite unexpectedly, the story is resumed in 8.4 from the point at which Gideon and his men crossed the Jordan, and a whole new narrative development begins to emerge.[81] Once again a series of incidents builds the suspense; again it is Gideon and his three hundred who take the encamped enemy by surprise; again the enemy is panicked, routed and pursued, and again two Midianite leaders are captured and executed; it seems that the climax of this second movement has been reached. But this time the two leaders are kings (מלכים, 8.5, 12) rather than commanders (שרים, 7.25), and are captured and slain by Gideon himself. Gideon's personal success so elevates him in the estimation of his fellow Israelites that they offer him dynastic rule (8.22). With this, Gideon has reached the peak of his power and influence, and this, rather than his victory over the kings becomes the true climax of the second movement and, retrospectively, of the story as a whole, as implied by the terms in which the offer is made, 'Rule over us . . . for you have saved us out of the hand of Midian'. As in the first movement, a brief epilogue follows the climax and brings the movement to a close. This relates how, ironically, Gideon proceeds to make an ephod which becomes a 'snare' not only to himself and his family but to 'all Israel' leading to the establishment of an all-Israel idolatrous cult in Ophrah, the very place where Gideon had begun his career by tearing down the idolatrous Baal-altar (6.25-32). Nevertheless, 'the land had rest for forty years' (8.28), and with this formula the story of Gideon's career is effectively at an end. The next four verses (8.29-32) relate the birth and naming of Abimelech and the death and burial of Gideon. They serve as a bridge to the account of Abimelech's career which follows.

To summarize, then, the body of the narrative begins and ends at Ophrah and consists of two distinct movements, the second of which begins from the point at which Gideon and his men cross the Jordan. We may represent this as follows:

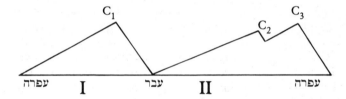

Certain events which occur in the second movement are strikingly reminiscent of events which have occurred in the first. These observations about how the narrative is constructed are taken as the basis for the following thematic analysis.

6.04
As noted earlier, appealing to Yahweh for deliverance from intolerable oppression has as its precedent not only the appeals of the preceding episodes but that which finds classical expression in Exod. 2.23-24.[82] This long-range precedent is implicitly acknowledged in the opening words of the prophet in 6.8b:

> Thus says Yahweh,
> I brought you up from Egypt,
> and brought you forth out of the house of bondage.

Indictment follows. Gideon, in 6.13, rather cheekily picks up these words and turns them into a challenge:

> Didn't Yahweh bring us up from Egypt?
> But now Yahweh has forsaken us . . .

His challenge is answered, ironically, in his own call and commissioning which follows the classical paradigm for the call and commissioning of a deliverer, namely, the call and commissioning of Moses in Exodus 3.[83] Gideon receives his commission in similar circumstances to Moses: in hiding from the enemy, working for his father Joash who is clan head and priest of a pagan shrine (cf. Jethro, Moses' father-in-law, whose flocks Moses is tending when Yahweh's angel appears to him, Exod. 3.1). He receives the same word of authorization, שלחתיך, 'I have sent you' (Judg. 6.14; Exod. 3.12). Like Moses, he protests that he is inadequate for the task (Judg. 6.16; Exod. 3.11) and receives the same assurance of divine aid, כי אהיה עמך, 'Surely I will be with you' (Judg. 6.16; Exod. 3.12)[84] and, again like Moses, is given a sign (אות) to reassure him (Judg. 6.17; Exod. 3.12). In both cases the commissioning is accompanied by a fire theophany which induces fear in the one who is called (v. 22, cf. Exod. 3.6). In Exodus 3 this proof of the divine presence is given unsolicited at the outset; in Judges 6 it is withheld until the end, so that the recognition of the messenger becomes the climax of the scene:

> Ahh! my lord, Yahweh!
> I have seen Yahweh's angel face to face! (v. 22)

But Gideon is told not to fear; it is not Yahweh's intention to slay him (v. 23). Gideon has been commissioned, not by the prophet (contrast Barak), nor by any human agency, but by Yahweh in person,[85] and Yahweh and Gideon will be in almost constant dialogue with one another in the sequence of events leading up to the battle (6.25, 36, 39; 7.2, 4, 7, 9). Again we are reminded of Moses who received his commission direct from Yahweh and whom Yahweh knew 'face to face' (Deut. 34.10).

This comparatively long account of Gideon's recruitment is without parallel in the preceding episodes and serves to establish a distinct perspective on the protagonist at the outset of the narrative. I shall return to this in due course. The miraculous fire of 6.21 introduces a formal motif (fire) which will punctuate the Gideon-Abimelech story (6.26; 7.16, 20; 9.15, 20, 49). The aetiological note in v. 24 about Gideon building an altar to 'Yahweh-Shalom' in 'Ophrah of the Abiezrites' serves a double function. With v. 11 ('Ophrah which belonged to Joash the Abiezrite) it forms an inclusio around the account of Gideon's call. At the same time it effects the transition to the next scene, vv. 25-32, by anticipating the issue to be resolved there, namely, the rivalry between Yahweh and Baal as symbolized by the juxtaposition of their two altars.

Gideon's encounter with Yahweh has isolated him within his family and clan. Yahweh, to whom Gideon has pledged his allegiance, will not tolerate their easy syncretism; Gideon must convert them to pure Yahwism or perish. Fearful of the consequences he carries out Yahweh's orders under cover of darkness with the help of ten of his servants. The men of the town are outraged at the sacrilege, with the result that Joash is forced to decide between Baal and his son (v. 30). He decides on a ploy to save Gideon and save face at the same time by referring the case to higher authority: if Baal is god let him take up his own cause against the desecrator (v. 31). Nothing happens, the townsmen are impressed, and Gideon emerges as a hero. He is, as it were, reborn, and his father gives him a new name which marks him as living proof of Baal's impotence (v. 32). Gideon has begun his career by driving Baal from the field, and the stage is now set for him to rally the Israelite militia to fight a holy war under Yahweh against the external, human foe, the Midianites (vv. 33-35). We note that in its broad patterning the narrative follows the same order as the Moses narrative of Exodus: first the call, then the exposure of foreign deities, then holy war. Here however the exposure is for the sake of Gideon's own clansmen, not for the enemy.[86]

Gideon, it seems, is not altogether without resourcefulness when it comes to uniting the scattered Israelites in a common cause and commanding them in the field. With the fighting men of his own clan first firmly consolidated as his power base (v. 34) he engages in diplomacy, in the form of messengers, to call for wider support, first from Manasseh as a whole (35a) and then from neighboring northern tribes who have common cause with his own against the invaders (35b). The (as it turns out) successful strategy to induce panic in the enemy is reminiscent of Joshua's strategy against Jericho, but unlike Joshua, Gideon does not receive the strategy ready-made from a heavenly visitor; it is apparently his own idea. His calling up of reserves in 7.23 and his deployment of the Ephraimite militia along the Jordan to cut off the enemy's escape in 7.24-25 likewise show a considerable competence in military strategy. Finally he shows himself a master of diplomacy when it comes to settling internal disputes (8.1-3). Clearly his self-deprecatory words in 6.15 are not to be taken at face-value. He is, after all, addressed by Yahweh's angel at the outset as a גבור חיל ('mighty man' 6.12), not necessarily a professional soldier, but certainly not either a man devoid of resources (witness his ten servants in 6.27).[87] There is an intimation of Gideon's natural potential for leadership in his first defiant retort in 6.13, and in the rather surprising response of the divine visitor:

> Go in this your strength[88]
> and save Israel . . . (6.14)

Gideon is not without either resources or resourcefulness. This is clearly implied in the text, but it is not stressed. What is thrust upon our attention repeatedly in the first movement is Gideon's fearfulness and sense of inadequacy for the task, and hence his constant need for reassurance and moral support. This perspective on Gideon is strongly developed in the three scenes which intervene between the call-up of the militia in 6.34-35 and the attack on the Midianite camp at the end of chapter 7.

The scene involving the fleece (6.36-40) highlights Gideon's diffidence in a particularly striking way. Even after it is clear that he has popular support and that he has a considerable fighting force at his disposal, he hesitates. He needs to be doubly assured that God is with him and will give the promised victory. In 7.1-8 his fighting force is reduced to three hundred[89] (the rest are made reservists) in order to secure the victory against misinterpretation: 'Lest Israel vaunt themselves . . . saying, My own hand has delivered me' (7.2). (In the absence of information to the contrary we may assume that Yahweh's predilection for unlikely heroes in earlier episodes was similarly motivated.) But along with this drastic reduction in his forces comes a further word of reassurance:

> By the three hundred men that lapped I will save you
> and deliver the Midianites into your hand (7.7).

In the final scene before the attack Yahweh, anticipating that Gideon will be too fearful to reconnoitre the enemy camp alone, even under cover of darkness, gives him permission in advance to take his servant Purah for moral support (7.10; cf. Exod. 4.14-16, where Moses is permitted to take Aaron for the same reason). This neatly recapitulates 6.27, another night scene. They are shown that the feared Midianites are in fact in a state of near panic—Yahweh has already unsettled them with ominous dreams[90]—and only then does

Gideon settle on his plan to stampede them. But there is no real fight; they are already 'given' into his hand before the battle begins (7.14-15).

In this first major movement then, Gideon is a reluctant conscript, who distrusts his own competence and relies wholly upon Yahweh. In short, he is a model of Mosaic piety. He is commissioned by Yahweh and invested with Yahweh's spirit (6.34). The war in which he engages is holy war in which the victory is not his personal achievement but the gift of Yahweh.

6.05

A rather different Gideon appears in the second movement, beginning in 8.4. His declared purpose is to capture 'Zebah and Zalmunna, the kings of Midian' (8.5), and he presses towards this goal with frenzied determination despite the hunger and weariness of his men and the refusal of the leaders of Succoth and Penuel to give him support. He expects these two kings to be given into his hand as surely as Oreb and Zeeb were (8.7), but in fact there is no indication of any involvement by Yahweh, and the holy war motifs which were so prominent in the first movement are entirely lacking here (contrast 8.11-12 with 7.21-22). Gideon's diffidence has completely disappeared. He now throws diplomacy to the wind, demanding support from towns on his route with threats of retribution to those who fail to comply. Gideon's personal resourcefulness which, in the first movement, had been subordinated to the holy war perspective is now given full play and it is clear that what he now achieves is by his own strength of character and tactical skill. His actions against Succoth and Penuel anticipate the similar but more brutal actions of his son Abimelech against Shechem and Thebez (cf. in particular Gideon's action against the tower of Penuel, 8.17, with Abimelech's action against the tower of Shechem, 9.46-49). At length Gideon's motivation is revealed in the dialogue in 8.18-19: Zebah and Zalmunna had been responsible for the death of his brothers.[91] It is a personal vendetta which Gideon has been prosecuting with such ruthless determination in Transjordan. Jether, Gideon's firstborn, who is unexpectedly introduced at this point (v. 20) serves as a foil for his father and points up the contrast between Gideon as he was and Gideon as he now is. The father's earlier diffidence is now mirrored in the son, who hesitates when he is told to kill the prisoners, 'because he was afraid' (20b). Gideon, by way of contrast is now a man of 'strength' (גבורה) (v. 21), and has 'the appearance of a king's son' (כתאר בני המלך) (v. 18).

The offer of dynastic rule follows immediately on Gideon's slaughter of the two kings (8.21-22). The slayer of kings has *ipso facto* achieved a kingly status in the eyes of his followers, who now attribute their escape from the Midianite yoke directly to Gideon and make this the basis of their offer:

> Rule over us, you and your son and your son's son, *For you have saved us* (הושעתנו) out of the hand of Midian. (My emphasis).

The key word, ישע (to save), has occurred six times previously in the narrative, all in the first movement (6.14, 15, 36, 37; 7.2, 7). In every case the same point is made either directly or implicitly: it is Yahweh, not Gideon or the Israelites themselves, who saves Israel. The point is made particularly forcefully in 7.2 as we have seen. Here Yahweh says to Gideon,

> The people with you are too many for me to give the Midianites into their hand, *lest Israel vaunt themselves against me saying, My own hand has saved me.*

The danger is that the Israelites will fail to give Yahweh the credit for the deliverance. This is now precisely what happens in the offer made to Gideon. Gideon recoils from the impiety and gives the theologically correct response:

> I will not rule over you
> neither will my son rule over you
> Yahweh shall rule over you.

If the rationale of the offer is that he who saves is entitled to rule, that entitlement belongs to Yahweh, not Gideon. The irony of the situation is that the impiety from which Gideon recoils is of his own making. From the moment he crossed the Jordan he has acted more and more like a king, especially in his dispensing of summary punishments on those who resist his authority. In crossing the Jordan he had already exceeded his commission and begun to move towards the kind of rule which is now formally offered to him.

Gideon's request for materials to make an ephod is a logical sequel to his assertion that Yahweh shall rule Israel. If Yahweh is to rule he must be inquired of, and it is apparently with the intention of facilitating such inquiry that Gideon makes an ephod and puts it in Ophrah where Yahweh had appeared to him and an altar to Yahweh now stood.[92] But it is an act of piety that goes wrong, for the ephod becomes an object of worship rather than inquiry, and Gideon is implicated in the impiety, both by his manufacture of the ephod and by his involvement in the irregular worship which came to be associated with it: 'it became a snare to Gideon and his house' (27b).

Exodus motifs are less conspicuous in this second movement but are present nonetheless and serve to accentuate the changed perspective in which Gideon is viewed. Gideon and his followers are in the 'wilderness' (8.16) and are 'faint' (8.4-5; cf. Deut. 25.18). But no heavenly provisions sustain them. The self-assertive and vindictive Gideon of this movement contrasts nicely with the meek Moses of the exodus traditions. But this does not necessarily mean that he ceases to be a Moses figure. The Moses of the exodus traditions, too, overreached his authority in the wilderness, and there is even a tradition which surfaces in 2 Kgs 18.14 to the effect that the bronze serpent which he made, like Gideon's ephod, became an idolatrous cult object to which the Israelites burnt incense.

The way in which we are pointedly returned, at length to Gideon's 'own city, Ophrah' in 8.27 is a classic example of ring composition which invites us to read the end of the story in the light of its beginning. Ophrah at the beginning of the story was the centre of a clan cult, a family affair. At the end it has become a centre where, according to 8.27, '*all Israel* played the harlot' after the ephod, presumably under Gideon's superintendence. So here, at Ophrah, the final irony of the story is enacted: Gideon, champion of Yahweh against Baal, presides over the national apostasy. Only after his death, however, is the impiety carried to its logical conclusion: the Israelites reject Yahweh outright and make Baal-berith their god (8.33). So Gideon's challenge to Baal has been answered in full and Gideon himself has contributed significantly to the answer. The name Jerubaal has acquired an ironic twist; Baal has indeed taken up his own cause (6.31-32). One aspect of the initial crisis (Israel vs. Midian) has, we are told, been decisively resolved: 'so Midian was subdued before Israel and lifted up their heads no more' (8.28), but the other and more fundamental aspect of the crisis (Israel vs. Yahweh) has become more acute. The conclusion of the Gideon episode contrasts sharply with the conclusion of the preceding Barak episode as I noted earlier.

6.06 *Transition (8.29-32)*

'Jerubaal son of Joash went and lived in his own house' (v. 29), that is, retired into private life in keeping with his protestation that Yahweh, not he, was to rule Israel. This retirement presumably took place soon after he had installed the ephod in Ophrah. But the details of Gideon's family life are of interest principally with reference to what follows (the career of Abimelech) and so are held over until the events of primary interest for Gideon's own career have been narrated. Now, with a pun on בית (house), v. 29 picks up the reference to Gideon's 'house', that is, household, that was made at the end of v. 27.

Paradoxically Gideon's household as described in vv. 30-31 looks far more like that of a ruler than of a private citizen. He had 'many wives' (cf. Deut. 17.17) by whom he sired 'seventy sons' (cf. Abdon, 12.14; and Ahab, 2 Kgs 10.1). He also had a concubine in Shechem who bore him a son whom he named Abimelech. Here in the pointed distinction between the seventy and the one is the seed from which the fratricide of chapter 9 will grow, and it is of Gideon's own making. The name Abimelech (My-father-is-king) is an ironic comment on the contradiction between Gideon's public pronouncements and private practice. It is also a portent; for, as the ensuing narrative clearly indicates, Gideon did become a dynast, in fact if not in name, and the succession was decided in the bloody intrigues which attended Abimelech's rise to power, a son who had far fewer scruples about the acquisition and exercise of power than his father had had.

6.07 *Abimelech*

In this sequel to the Gideon story two explicit statements of theme are provided by the narrator himself. They occur at 9.23-24, at a crucial point in the development of the plot, and at 9.56-57 after the climax has been reached with the death of Abimelech. These two statements complement one another and point to retribution as the thematic key to the story: God causes the evil which Abimelech and the men of Shechem did to rebound upon their own heads.

The details of the narrative show this process being worked out with almost mathematical precision from the point at which God sends an evil spirit between Abimelech and the men of Shechem (9.23). Abimelech's going to Shechem to incite its leaders to conspire with him against the sons of Jerubbaal (9.1-2) is answered by Gaal's

arrival in Shechem to incite its leaders to conspire with *him* against
Abimelech (9.26-29).⁹³ The ambush (ויארבו) set by the men of
Shechem in 9.25 is answered by the ambush (ויארבו) set by Abimelech
in 9.34 on the advice of Zebul. Finally Abimelech, who, as we are
told twice, killed the sons of Jerubbaal 'on one stone' (9.5, 18) is
himself slain beside a stone which has been dropped on his head by a
woman of Thebez (9.54).⁹⁴ So in the outworking of the plot act
answers to act, and evil to evil. The evil spirit (רוח רעה) sent by God
to set the whole process of retribution in motion (9.23), itself answers
to the evil (רעה) committed by Abimelech and the men of Shechem
(9.56, 57). This evil spirit is not exorcized until the chief instigator of
the evil is struck down, whereupon his followers, as if waking from a
bad dream, down weapons and go home without completing their
assault on Thebez (9.55).

Jotham appears on the scene in 9.7 to confront the men of
Shechem with the evil they have done. He calls on the men of
Shechem to listen, and on God to witness their response to his words
(v. 7). He adapts a fable to his purpose, but the main thrust of the
speech lies not in the fable itself (vv. 8-15) but in his application of it
to the present situation (vv. 16-21).⁹⁵ The central charge he brings
against his hearers is that they have not dealt 'truly and sincerely'
(באמת ובתמים) with Jerubaal as they were obliged to do in view of the
benefits he had conferred upon them.⁹⁶ He rehearses Jerubaal's past
good deeds on their behalf and the benefits they had enjoyed (v. 17),
charges the men of Shechem with disloyalty (v. 18), and sets before
them the alternatives of blessing (v. 19) or curse (v. 20). The blessing
is of course delivered with heavy irony; it has ceased to be a real
alternative because the crime is irrevocable. The detailing of the
curse in v. 20 is in effect a pronouncement of judgment. The narrator
shows how the words of Jotham were fulfilled in the action of God
which followed (v. 23), and the concluding words of the narrative
describe the retribution which was visited upon the evildoers as 'the
curse (קללה) of Jotham, son of Jerubbaal' (9.57).

There is a very close functional parallel, then, between the speech
of Jotham and the speech of the prophet in the Gideon narrative
itself. The prophet brings a lawsuit against the Israelites in the name
of Yahweh; Jotham brings a lawsuit against the men of Shechem in
the name of Jerubbaal. The covenant language is part of the
rhetorical form of the speech, just as the fable form of vv. 8-15 is.⁹⁷ It
does not necessarily presuppose the existence of a literal treaty

between Jerubbaal and the citizens of Shechem. It is, however, the ideal form for a speech whose central thrust is that benefits conferred entail an obligation to show loyalty to the one who conferred them. It is also an ideal rhetorical form for a speech delivered in a city which, ironically, boasted a temple to 'Covenant God' (אל בריה) (9.46; cf. 8.33; 9.4).

Whatever Jotham's personal motives may have been, it is clear that he has been adopted by the narrator as his own *alter ego*, the character in the story who gives voice to the narrator's own interpretation of the situation. Jotham's interpretation of the evil which the men of Shechem have committed is fundamental to the thematic connection which the narrator makes in 8.34-35 between the Gideon narrative itself and its sequel:

v. 34	The Israelites did not remember Yahweh their god who had rescued them out of the hand of their enemies on every side	=	the theme of the Gideon narrative
v. 35	Neither did they deal faithfully (חסר) with the house of Jerubbaal/ Gideon in return for all the good he had done for them	=	related theme in its sequel, the story of Abimelech

Retribution remains the primary theme in the Abimelech narrative, by by interpreting the evil done by Abimelech and his followers as faithlessness, the narrator has established a firm thematic link with the Gideon narrative proper.[98] The statement in 9.22 that Abimelech ruled over *Israel* for three years involves, by implication, the whole of Israel in this evil, and not just the men of Shechem. Abimelech's followers are called 'men of Israel' in 9.55.

6.08 *Summary: Gideon and Abimelech*

a. The theme of the Gideon narrative is Israel's infidelity to Yahweh. This is explored much more fully here than in previous episodes. In the first movement Yahweh establishes his claim to Israel's loyalty by rescuing them, yet again, from their enemies. In the second movement Gideon raises a lone voice in defence of this claim (8.23), but the drift back into apostasy is already too strong. The Israelites credit Gideon with the victory, make an idol out of his ephod, and finally abandon Yahweh altogether (8.33). The way the narrative starts out from Ophrah and returns us there reinforces the theme. Even while Israel was appealing to Yahweh there was an altar to Baal at Ophrah. It is removed only to be replaced by a shrine where all-Israel plays the harlot after Gideon's ephod. The thesis advanced at the climax of the narrative (ironically, by the Israelites themselves) is that he who saves Israel should be acknowledged as its ruler. The conclusion of the narrative shows how the Israelites did exactly the opposite to what the thesis required. The narrator has succinctly summarized the theme in 8.34: 'the Israelites did not remember Yahweh their god who rescued them . . '.

In the sequel the theme of infidelity is transposed into a lower key. It now has to do with the חסד due to Gideon for 'all the good he had done for Israel' and the way that this was totally disregarded by those who made the murderer of Gideon's sons their king. The narrator makes the connection directly in 8.35, and, indirectly in Jotham's speech (esp. 9.16-20).

b. Three striking new developments in the Gideon narrative and its sequel serve as indicators to the way in which this major unit participates in larger narrative developments taking place progressively through the book.

The first is the fact that here for the first time Israel's appeal to Yahweh meets with a stern rebuke rather than immediate assistance. It is clear that the appeal is being abused and that Yahweh is beginning to lose patience with Israel. In the next major episode the appeal will meet with a much more heated response from Yahweh, as we have seen (10.10-14). In the Samson episode there will be no appeal at all.

The second new feature is the fact that the slide back into apostasy is already well advanced before Gideon dies[99] and that he himself contributes to this regression by his own actions. The narrator puts the best possible construction on Gideon's conduct (he is presented as a flawed hero rather than as a cynical double-dealer) but the evidence of his contribution to all that went wrong is not concealed.[100] The next major saviour-judge, Jephthah, is more obviously flawed than Gideon. His self-interest is evident from the start and his vow is as plainly manipulative as Israel's 'repentance', as we have seen.

Samson is virtually incontinent, wilful Israel personified and is scarcely recognizable as a saviour-judge.

The third new feature is the *internal* fighting which takes place under Gideon and Abimelech. Gideon is the first judge to turn the sword against his compatriots (8.16-17). Abimelech is like this Gideon of the second movement with all the constraints of Yahwistic piety removed. The civil war which erupts under him is a harbinger of worse things to come (12.1-6; 20.1-48). After 8.28 the formula, 'the land had rest . . ' does not occur again.

With the Gideon episode and its sequel the pattern of decline *within* the repeating pattern of the successive episodes begins to come sharply into focus. This theme of progressive decline was presented schematically in the introduction to the book (2.16-19).

c. The process of exact retribution in the Abimelech story is an aberration from the alternating pattern of punishment and rescue in the succession of stories about the saviour-judges. The separateness of these two modes of divine operation is accentuated by the fact that the divine name Yahweh is not used in connection with the retribution in the Abimelech narrative. After 8.34-35 in which the Israelites reject Yahweh and make Baal-berith their god only אלהים (Elohim) is used (9.7, 23, 56, 57). In the stories of the judges god, as יהוה (Yahweh), has operated on a different principle, namely, punishment tempered by compassion, with compassion (expressed as rescue) having the final say in each episode.[101] The significance of a story of such thorough and exact retribution appearing at this point in the book must be sought in the context of the serious and rapid deterioration in Israel's relationship with Yahweh to which the Gideon episode has drawn our attention, and of the connection made in 8.34-35 between the unfaithfulness of the Israelites towards Yahweh and their unfaithfulness towards Gideon's household.

Ironically the Israelites as a whole benefit from the retribution worked upon their bramble king:

> When the men of Israel saw that Abimelech was dead
> they departed every man to his home (9.55).

The process of retribution has had the precision of a surgical operation. Only those directly responsible have been destroyed. Retribution brings the evil to an end, and normal life can be resumed. But the story also has a chilling aspect. The 'evil spirit from Elohim' (9.23), agent of retribution, is the dark counterpart of 'the spirit of Yahweh' (6.34), agent of deliverance. It is a reminder that God has a different principle of operation he can invoke at his discretion, and if it can be invoked against Abimelech and the men of Shechem, why not against Israel in general, and if against unfaithfulness in the one sphere, why not against unfaithfulness in the other? This story of retribution sounds an ominous note in the deteriorating situation to which the Gideon episode has drawn our attention.

d. The issue of kingship figures much more prominently in the Gideon episode and its sequel than it has done in previous episodes. For the first time the institution of kingship is experimented with in an Israelite context and the result is disastrous. However, neither the Gideon nor Abimelech stories is about kingship as such, nor is it suggested in either of them that the institution as such is evil.

This is particularly clear in the Abimelech story. There the major theme is well established, namely, retribution. But nowhere is there any hint that Abimelech's crime was that he became a king. Nor is it suggested that the crime of the men of Shechem was that they made Abimelech a king. The crime is quite specifically the unfaithfulness shown to the house of Gideon by the rulers of Shechem who conspired with Abimelech to kill Gideon's sons. That kingship as such is not the issue is clear from Jotham's words in 9.16:

> If you then acted in good faith and honour
> > with Jerubbaal and his house today
> then rejoice in Abimelech, and let him also
> > rejoice in you;
> but if not . . .

The same is true of Gideon's refusal of the offer made to him. His refusal must be seen in relation to the specific terms in which the offer was made (8.22). Israel's future could not be secured by creating a new institution. Only a wholehearted return to Yahweh could do that, and that was what was conspicuously lacking in the offer made to Gideon. Gideon had to refuse, not because kingship is incompatible with Yahwism, but because Yahweh, not he, should have been given the credit for the victory. The story as a whole is about the religious problem implicit in the offer, not with the institution of kingship as such. As in previous episodes, kingship is seen in an unfavourable light but it is not rejected in principle.[102]

6.09 *Tola and Jair*

6.091

'Now after Abimelech there arose to save Israel, Tola . . .' (10.1). The explicit naming of Abimelech is a feature of this particular notice unparalleled in the notices about the other so-called minor judges. It brings the career of Abimelech into sharp focus as the backdrop to the career of Tola. These words clearly do not mean that Tola arose to save Israel as Abimelech had done. That would be patently absurd in view of what has just gone before and in any case would more naturally be expressed in other terms, as for example are used for Shamgar in 3.15:

> and after him [Ehud] was Shamgar
> and *he too* (גם הוא) saved Israel (my emphasis).

The opening words of 10.1, by contrast, simply indicate that after Abimelech Israel needed saving and that Tola arose to do this.

Despite the use of ישע (to save) no military activity is attributed to Tola, nor is there mention of any external threat during his period of office (contrast Shamgar). We are told that he 'sat' or 'presided' (ישב) at Shamir in Mt Ephraim and judged Israel for twenty-three years. This use of the verb ישב is another feature of the Tola notice which distinguishes it from the other short notices. The language is strongly reminiscent of that used of the early career of Deborah who sat/ presided under her palm tree in Mt Ephraim and judged Israel (4.4-5). She, too, is said to have 'arisen' when Israel was in disarray (5.7). Such details as *are* given of Tola's activity, together with the explicit reference to Abimelech's career which had immediately preceded strongly suggest that it was the disastrous effects of Abimelech's rule that Israel needed saving from, and that Tola did this by providing a period of stable administration.[103] Tola saved Israel from disintegration. The similarity to Deborah suggests that he, too, may have been a charismatic leader without being a military one.

6.092

The notice about 'Jair the Gileadite' in 10.3-5 prepares the way for the story of 'Jephthah the Gileadite' which immediately follows (cf. 10.3 with 11.1). Jair arises after the crisis which Tola faced has passed. The reference to his thirty sons riding upon thirty asses and enjoying possession of thirty towns bespeaks the peacefulness of the times and the prosperity and prestige enjoyed by the judge. It also shows the unpreparedness of the Gileadites for the disaster about to fall on them (10.7). Small use Jair's pampered sons will be when the Ammonites invade! Then the Gileadites will search desperately for a *fighter* (10.17-18). In order to win Jephthah over the elders of Gilead will offer to make him 'head of all the inhabitants of Gilead' (11.8). The portrait of Jair presented here gives some indication of what was on offer and why Jephthah found it so attractive. But the reality was very different for Jephthah from what it had been for Jair. Jephthah had to maintain his position by force (12.1-6) and he had no family to parade his greatness; he was rendered childless by his vow.

7.00 *Jephthah (plus Ibzan, Elon, Abdon)*

For Jephthah himself see Chapter 2.

7.01 *Ibzan, Elon, and Abdon (12.8-15)*

After the two Gileadites, Jair and Jephthah, the judgeship returns to the northern tribes west of Jordan. The Bethlehem associated with Ibzan in vv. 8-10 is taken by most scholars to refer to the northern Bethlehem of Josh. 19.15, on the Asher-Zebulun border.[104] The tragic story of Jephthah and his one daughter, an only child, is followed by this note about a judge who had *thirty* daughters and brought in a further thirty daughters from outside his clan as wives for his thirty sons! Of all the judges, daughters are mentioned only in connection with these two, Jephthah and Ibzan. After Jephthah's barrenness comes Ibzan's fulness; the contrast serves to underscore the tragic barrenness suffered by Jephthah in consequence of his vow. Nothing is reported about Elon the Zebulunite except the length of his judgeship and the place of his burial. Abdon's judgeship was centred on 'Pirathon in the land of Ephraim' according to v. 15. The note about his sons and grandsons riding upon seventy donkeys (v. 14) recalls the similar ostentation of Jair and his family (10.4).

In the light of the Gideon episode and its sequel there is a suggestion, in the mention of the numerous sons of certain judges, that from Gideon onwards judgeship was always on the verge of turning into kingship, in which sons would succeed their fathers to office.[105] But it is not until 1 Samuel that a father actually appoints his sons to succeed him. The corrupt behaviour of the sons precipitates the demand that he appoint someone else—a king (1 Sam. 8.1-5).

In general, however, the interest in numbers of sons and daughters, grandsons, donkeys and weddings in the notes about the minor judges presents a striking contrast to the preoccupation with apostasy, oppression, war and deliverance in the major episodes. To be sure, the brief note about Shamgar in 3.31 does not lose contact with these concerns, and the two notices in 10.1-5 are closely connected to what precedes and follows them as I have indicated; but in the three notices of 12.8-15 we have a longer interlude between major episodes in which contact with the major themes of the work is all but lost. It seems that the narrative is on the point of losing its way and that the story of Yahweh's struggle to reclaim Israel from apostasy and dissolution is going to peter out into a mere chronicle of the careers of judges who were so undistinguished that scarcely anything about them could be recalled—a chronicle of trivialities. It's as though both Israel and Yahweh have wearied of the struggle and the conflict between them has resolved itself into a kind of truce in which there is nothing of substance to report.

But there is an air of unreality about this situation. We know Israel and Yahweh too well by this point in the work to believe that it could last. In fact it lasts just long enough to enhance the impact, when it comes, of the Samson episode, as the climax of the series of major episodes which span the central section of the book. Here the major themes are taken up again and receive their definitive treatment before the epilogue of chapters 17–21.

8.00 *Samson*

8.01

The formula which has introduced all the major episodes now appears for the last time (13.1a). The problem of apostasy is still unsolved and Israel is made to feel Yahweh's displeasure once more. His use of the Philistines has already been anticipated in the introduction to the Jephthah story:

> So Yahweh's anger was kindled against Israel
> and he sold them into the hand of the Philistines
> and into the hand of the Ammonites.

The order is reversed in what follows. The Ammonite oppression provides the setting for the Jephthah narrative, the Philistine oppression for the Samson story.[106]

Conspicuously absent is the appeal to Yahweh which has preceded his intervention to save Israel in all previous episodes. In the Gideon and Jephthah narratives, as we have seen, the practice of appealing to Yahweh comes under close scrutiny and the apparent connection between Israel's call and Yahweh's saving intervention in the earlier episodes is broken. Israel neither deserves (6.7-10) nor influences (10.10-16) Yahweh's intervention to rescue it. In the Samson episode the Israelites show little sign of even *wanting* to be rescued. Manoah and his wife are intent only on avoiding contact with the Philistines as much as possible (14.3). Samson does not want to fight the Philistines; he wants to intermarry with them. He is propelled into conflict with them by Yahweh's Spirit (13.25; 14.6, 19; 15.14).[107] The Judahites (contrast their crusading spirit in chapter 1!) accept the Philistine dominance as unassailable and are intent only on maintaining the status quo (15.11). It is Yahweh, and Yahweh alone who seeks 'an occasion against the Philistines' (14.4).

This progressive phasing out of the appeal to Yahweh is anticipated in the programmatic introduction in 2.11-19 where there is no mention of the Israelites calling upon Yahweh, and his interventions to save them are attributed solely to his compassion at their plight (18b). But the Samson episode has a surprise in store for us. The motif of calling upon Yahweh reappears at two crucial points in the account of Samson's career, as we shall see.

8.02

The plot of the Samson story is set in motion by the unsolicited appearance of Yahweh's angel to a barren woman, the wife of Manoah the Danite (13.2-3). He makes two predictions: the barren woman will bear a son (3b), and this son will begin to deliver Israel out of the hand of the Philistines (5b). The first is fulfilled in 13.24, 'the woman bore a son and called his name Samson'; the second is fulfilled progressively in two major narrative movements spanning chapters 14 to 16. The first movement begins with Samson's going down to Timnath in 14.1 and climaxes in the slaughter of the Philistines at Ramath-lehi in 15.14-20. The second movement begins with his going to Gaza in 16.1 and climaxes in his slaughter of the Philistines and his own death in the temple at Gaza in 16.31. The references to Zorah and Eshtaol in 13.25 and 16.31 form an inclusion around these two movements, and the references to Manoah, Samson's father in 13.2 and 16.31 form a second inclusio around the entire narrative.[108]

This formal patterning of the narrative is very similar to that which we observed in the Gideon narrative. In Judges 6 the Yahweh angel commissions Gideon directly; in Judges 13 he commissions Samson indirectly through his mother, anticipating the significant role that women will play in his career. The two major movements of the Samson narrative exhibit a similar symmetry to those in the Gideon episode, but much more extensive. In both movements Samson sees a woman (the Timnite, the harlot of Gaza), becomes involved with a woman who betrays him by revealing a secret (the Timnite, Delilah), is bound and given into the hands of the Philistines (by the Judahites, by Delilah) and is then empowered by Yahweh to slaughter them in great numbers.[109] The Samson story begins and ends at Zorah (and Eshtaol) as the Gideon narrative began and ended at Ophrah.

There are some striking points of contact with the Gideon episode in content as well as style. The motifs common to the theophanies of chapters 6 and 13 are numerous and conspicuous and need not be detailed here.[110] The motif of fire common to the two theophanies is also common to the Gideon and Samson narratives proper. Compare in particular the torches (לפדים) used by Samson with his three hundred foxes (15.4) with the torches (לפדים) of Gideon and his three hundred men (7.16, 20). But here we are on the verge of discovering a wider network of motifs which extends far beyond these two episodes. For the word לפיד, torch, has also occurred in its abstract plural form לפידות as the name of Deborah's husband (4.4), and the Deborah/Barak episode, like that of Gideon, has some striking points of contact with the Samson story. Delilah's fastening (תקע) Samson's hair with a pin (יתר) (16.14), recalls Jael's striking (תקע) the tent-peg (יתר) into Sisera's temple (4.21). Both scenes take place in the woman's private quarters and the sleeping Samson of 16.19 recalls the sleeping Sisera of 4.21.[111] Further there is an echo of the name Deborah (דבורה), bee, in the colony of bees (עדת דברים) which Samson finds in the carcass of the lion (14.8),[112] and the prodigious feats of strength which mark the career of Samson (שמשון) give a new, ironic twist to the closing lines of the song of Deborah and Barak:

may those who love you be like the sun (שמש)
going forth in its strength! (5.31)[113]

But we are not finished yet, for Samson's singled handed slaughter of a thousand Philistines with a jawbone of an ass in 15.15 can hardly help but recall to our minds the remarkably similar feat of Shamgar which occurs as early as 3.31. And so we could go on. The frequency with which narrative elements from earlier episodes reappear in the Samson story is striking to say the least.[114] And when we press beyond motifs to themes we find further, more significant connections between the Samson episode and those which have gone before.

8.03

Since the Samson story reaches its climax in the great festival of Dagon in 16.23-30 it is here that we may expect to find some indication of the main issues with which the narrative as a whole is concerned. Here I quote, with permission, from an unpublished paper by David Gunn.[115] At the opening of this final scene

> the narrator reiterates the claim of the Philistines to the supremacy of their god (16.23-24):
>
>> Now the lords of the Philistines gathered to offer a great sacrifice to Dagon their god, and to rejoice; for they said, 'Our god has given Samson our enemy into our hand'. And when the people saw him, they praised their god, for they said, 'Our god has given our enemy into our hand, the ravager of our country, who has slain many of us'.
>
> They are, of course, wrong. They do not know that it was precisely Yahweh who gave Samson into their hands. (We are reminded of the theme of the exilic prophets—is this story, too, a sermon for the exile?) And by deserting Samson at the cutting of his hair, Yahweh deceives the Philistines into thinking that Samson's strength is merely a magical-mechanical thing, to be manipulated at will by humans. The ensuing scene of death and destruction is for Dagon a debacle of the greatest magnitude. The words of praise for their god must have died coldly on the lips of his devotees. Subtly, and without any crude fanfare of the explicit, the narrator underlines the power of Yahweh, the irrelevance of Dagon. The victory is unquestionably Yahweh's, even if it is only achieved through the suffering of his servant. Israel's deliverance from the Philistines 'begins' with the sine qua non of deliverance—the recognition that it is Yahweh who controls the destiny of his people. Yahweh gives

his people into the hand of their enemies (cf. 13.1). Yet Yahweh, if he chooses, can also turn such defeat into victory.

> So the dead whom Samson slew at his death were more than those whom he had slain during his life

- undoubtedly, since the dead include this time a god! To take into Sheol with him all those lords of the Philistines and the others may no doubt be seen as a blow against the occupiers of Israel, and hence, proleptically at least, the beginning of more telling battles in years to come. But to bring low the *god* of the Philistines is Samson's real contribution to Yahweh's purpose here. His achievement is, ironically not an (heroic) physical blow, but a theological one!

So briefly, but significantly, God is 'made known' by Samson.

8.04

But it is not only in his death that God is made known by Samson. Samson's life-to-be assumes a distinctive shape from its very inception, and there are many intimations in the birth account of chapter 13 of what is to come. The climax of the narrative casts a very long shadow before it. Consider, in particular, the words of Samson's mother as she tells Manoah of the message she has received from her mysterious visitor: 'the child shall be a Nazirite of God from the womb *to the day of his death*'. The underlined words were not part of the original message as reported in vv. 3-5; they are her own. Does she have a premonition? Certainly she speaks better than she knows. The announcement of Samson's birth is accompanied by a theophany, a disclosure of God which anticipates the climactic disclosure of God which is achieved by his death.[116] For Samson is the gift of God to a barren woman. His birth is a miracle. As the theophany approaches its climax Manoah asks the messenger, 'What is your name?', and is told that it is 'wonderful' (פלאי) (v. 18). He then prepares a sacrifice and offers it upon a rock 'to Yahweh, the one who works wonders' (ליהוה ומפלא לעשות) (v. 19). The syntax is anomalous,[117] but the terminology echoes the classic ascription of praise to Yahweh in Exod. 15.11:

> Who is like you, Yahweh, among the gods?
> Who is like you,
>   majestic in holiness,
>   fearful in praises,
> doing wonders (עשה פלא)?

As the flames rise up from the altar the messenger goes up in them, and Manoah and his wife go down—face down, on the ground (v. 20). They know that they have seen God, and the experience leaves Manoah in a state of mortal fear:

We shall surely die, because we have seen God.

Not so, says his wife:

If Yahweh had intended to kill us, he would not have received a burnt offering... at our hands, or shown us all these things... (v. 23).

Then, at last, the miracle itself is reported:

The woman bore a son
and called his name Samson
and Yahweh blessed him (v. 24).

What is disclosed by this account of Samson's miraculous birth is that the issues of barrenness and fertility, life and death, are in the hands of Yahweh. Twice Samson will call upon Yahweh in the course of the narrative, and both times his call will be answered; in the first case he will be granted life (15.18-19), and in the second case death (16.31). In dying he will bring down Dagon and demonstrate the supremacy of Yahweh.

8.05

All the major episodes from Othniel to Jephthah have involved a competition between Yahweh and other gods for the allegiance of Israel. This is implicit in each of them but is a particularly prominent motif in the Gideon episode which has strong stylistic affinities with the Samson story as we have seen. Gideon *begins* his career by tearing down Baal's altar at Ophrah and erecting an altar to Yahweh in its place, thus earning for himself the name Jerubbaal, 'Let Baal strive [against him]' (6.32). But the end of the story is a defeat for Yahweh and a victory for Baal (8.33). Samson tears down not just a local shrine, but the very temple of Dagon, and this is the *climax* towards which the whole narrative moves. The affinities between the Gideon and Samson episodes are not just stylistic; they are thematic as well. And here we must reflect again on the introduction to the *Jephthah* episode where we noticed that the mention of the Philistines in 10.7 anticipates the Samson story. For there, in 10.6, is a list of the 'other gods' to whom the Israelites gave their allegiance in the period of the judges—a list which culminates, significantly, in 'the gods of the Philistines'. In this way the narrator has prepared us to see the larger significance of the defeat of Dagon. He is representative of all those 'other gods' who hold such fascination for the Israelites (cf. 2.11-12). In the theological point which it makes, Samson's action in the temple of Dagon is comparable to Elijah's demonstration on Mt Carmel.

8.06

The transition from the Samson-Delilah scene of 16.4-21 to the climactic scene of the narrative is made in 16.22 with what James Crenshaw has aptly described as 'one of those pregnant sentences that is the mark of genius':[118] 'But the hair of his head began to grow again after it had been shaved'. After the apparently final humiliation of Samson in v. 21 these words raise our expectations high again. Perhaps Yahweh who forsook Samson when his hair was cut will return to him again? Perhaps there may yet be 'some great service'[119] to crown Samson's career and restore his dignity? The sentence is so pregnant because of the associations which Samson's hair has acquired in the course of the narrative.

In the announcement made by the angel in 13.4-5 Samson's long hair is the sign *par excellence* of his separation to God for the work of beginning to deliver Israel from the Philistines. The three marks of his separation are curiously split between the mother and the son she is to bear, with only the prohibition against the cutting of the hair being specifically applied to Samson himself.[120] Further, in contrast to the order in Numbers 6 (no strong drink, no cutting of the hair, no contact with a dead body) the prescription concerning the hair comes last in Judges 13, anticipating its association with the climax of the narrative.[121] If Samson's behaviour makes us wonder whether he is aware that he has been designated 'separate' his own words finally remove any doubt:

> A razor has never come upon my head
> for I have been a Nazirite of God from my mother's womb.
> If I were to be shaved, my strength would leave me
> and I would become as weak as any other man (16.17).

The narrator tells us that in saying this to Delilah Samson 'told her all his heart', that is, told her (at last) what he really believed the secret of his strength to be. Samson associates his strength directly with his separation to God as symbolized particularly in his hair. If he renounces his separation to God by allowing his hair to be cut his strength will leave him. But whence, then, his confidence in v. 20? For here again the omniscient author comments directly upon Samson's state of mind:

he said
'I will go out as at other times . . . '
But he did not know that Yahweh had left him.

Samson is portrayed as acting irrationally in the grip of strong emotions. His supernatural strength is the one aspect of his separation to God that he has genuinely relished, but alone with Delilah he sees his strength as the source of all his troubles.[122] He wants to be done with fighting the Philistines and settle down with the woman he loves.[123] His words indicate obliquely what his action (laying his head in Delilah's lap) indicates directly: he *wants* to be 'like any other man'. He delays so long because he knows he is tempting fate, but his delaying tactics are at the same time a form of love-play. But with the Philistines upon him his mind works quite differently. Yahweh has apparently been willing to overlook his flagrant disregard of his Nazirite status in the past and come to his aid when he needed help (14.6; 15.14). Surely he will not *really* forsake him now when he needs him most? But he is wrong. Yahweh withdraws; Samson is captured, blinded, and brought down—what grim irony—to gateless Gaza.[124] This 'bringing down' of Samson is the climax of all his 'goings down' in the course of the narrative (14.1, 5, 7, 19; 15.8).[125]

From the moment when Yahweh's Spirit begins to move Samson (13.25) up to the point when his hair is cut Yahweh seems as unconcerned with the ritual aspects of Samson's Naziriteship as Samson himself. Samson's eating of the carcass-polluted honey is his own chosen action, but his initial tearing of the lion *with his bare hands* (14.6) is prompted by Yahweh. Yahweh's Spirit also contributes to Samson's seeking a wife among the uncircumcised (ritually impure) Philistines (14.3-4), and his slaughter of a thousand Philistines—'heaps upon heaps' of corpses—with a jawbone pilfered from the 'fresh' (polluted) carcass of an ass (15.14-16). Why then does he forsake Samson when his hair is cut? Not, I would suggest, because of outrage at Samson's disregard for the ritual requirements of his status as a Nazirite, but to preserve his separateness at a much more fundamental level. Yahweh will not let Samson be 'as other men'. By temporarily withdrawing he deceives the Philistines into engineering their own downfall by transferring Samson to Gaza and eventually to the temple of Dagon itself where he will fulfil the purpose for which he was separated to God even before his birth.[126]

In the Nazirite legislation of Numbers 6 the shaving of the hair signifies that the period of separation has come to an end, either because the terms of the vow—voluntarily taken—have been fulfilled (in which case the hair is offered to Yahweh on the altar, v. 18) or because the terms of the vow have been broken (in which case the hair is not offered to Yahweh ; it is shaved off so that a fresh start may be made, vv. 9-12). In Samson's case the separation is not voluntarily assumed, nor is it temporary. He remains *nazir* (separate) 'to the day of his death'. He may wish to be as other men but Yahweh will not let him be so. His hair is shaved off only to grow again, and at the climax of the narrative it is not his hair only that is offered in sacrifice, but Samson himself.[127] Yahweh's apparent disregard for ritual prescriptions which he himself has enjoined on Samson through his mother is highly paradoxical, but it is a paradox which takes us right to the heart of the relationship between divine freedom and religious institutions. We are told that Samson will be a 'Nazirite of God' and we think we know what this means, but as the narrative unfolds our initial expectations are overturned and replaced by a more profound understanding. To quote Gunn again, 'it is as though the shell of the ritual institution has been broken open to reveal its vital essence'.[128]

8.07

As Naziriteship is treated in the Samson episode, so judgeship is treated in the whole narrative complex extending from chapter 2 to the end of chapter 16. After the programmatic introduction in 2.11-19, and the example of Othniel in 3.7-11, we think we know what a judge is. But almost at once that initial understanding is challenged: Ehud is a devious assassin rather than a warrior, Shamgar is probably not an Israelite, Deborah is a woman, and so on, until finally we are presented with Samson, who is the polar opposite of Othniel:[129] Othniel's marriage is exemplary, Samson's liasons with foreign women are the reverse;[130] Othniel leads Israel in holy war, Samson is a loner who doesn't even *want* to fight the Philistines; Othniel saves Israel and ushers in an era of peace, Samson leaves the

Israelites under the Philistine yoke. And yet the narrator insists that Samson was a judge, and the point is made with particular emphasis. The body of the Samson narrative consists, as we have seen, of two parallel movements, climaxing respectively in the slaughter of the Philistines at Ramath-lehi and the overthrow of Dagon and his assembled devotees at Gaza. Each of these two major movements ends with a note about Samson's judgeship (15.20; 16.31). As far as their location in the narrative is concerned the two notices are symmetrical,[131] but they are not identical. The first begins with the verb in the conjunctive (converted imperfect) formation, 'and he judged Israel in the days of the Philistines for twenty years'; the second begins, disjunctively, with the personal pronoun followed by the verb in the perfect, 'and he *had* judged Israel for twenty years'. That is, Samson's judgeship began effectively at Ramath-lehi and concluded with his death at Gaza.[132] To be a judge, then, is to be the person in whom Yahweh's administration of Israel is realized at a particular time. Retrospectively we see that what we initially thought were the defining characteristics of the institution were its outer husks; the Samson episode discloses the 'vital essence' of *this* institution also.

8.08

'Calling upon Yahweh' is perhaps best regarded as a *de facto* rather than formal institution. As a narrative motif it has figured prominently in the major episodes from Othniel to Jephthah as we have seen. It now recurs at the climax of both the major narrative movements of the Samson episode, and as Cheryl Exum has pointed out, in both cases the importance of the motif is emphasized by a play on the word קרא (to call):

> In ch. 15 Samson's calling on Yhwh provides the background for the presentation of the etymology of En-haqqore, the spring of the caller. In ch. 16, the narrator gives the motif of calling an ironic twist, using it first to refer to the summoning of Samson; and then to Samson's invocation of Yhwh. The people call (קרא) Samson to make sport (two times in v. 25); but while they watch Samson making sport, Samson calls (קרא) on Yhwh! The result stands in sharp ironic contrast to their expectation.[133]

In his first appeal to Yahweh, at Ramath-lehi (15.18) Samson acknowledges that the 'great deliverance' he has just experienced has been the gift of Yahweh and not his own achievement. He acknowledges that he is Yahweh's 'servant'.[134] On the point of death he asks for life and is granted it. In the temple of Dagon Samson no longer desires life, but in his blindness he knows that Yahweh is his god still,[135] and turns to him with one last appeal. And if he has an intensely personal stake in what he asks for ('let me be avenged on the Philistines for one of my two eyes')[136] at least he at last desires what Yahweh also desires.[137] Samson is allowed to die with dignity and in so doing to fulfil the purpose for which he was born. The preceding episodes indicated that 'calling on Yahweh' was a practice much used and abused in the days of the judges. The Samson episode, again, lays bare its essence: to call on Yahweh is to know that Yahweh alone is your god and to place yourself in his hands, for life or for death.

8.09

In the previous episodes it was Israel that called on Yahweh; in this final episode it is Samson himself. This is only one aspect of a more general pattern of identification which emerges in the narrative. Samson's awareness of his separation to God, and yet his disregard for it, his fatal attraction to foreign women, his wilfulness and his presumption all hold the mirror up to the behaviour of Israel itself. So too does his fate. 'O mirror of our fickle state', the chorus exclaims as it contemplates the blind, fallen Samson in Milton's recreation of the story.[138] It is because of this implicit identification of Samson with Israel[139] that the conclusion of the episode captures so powerfully the twin qualities of hope and grim foreshadowing.[140] Samson, the angel had said, would begin to deliver Israel from the Philistines. The key words turns out to be 'begin'. It occurs in 13.25 where the plot is set in motion ('the spirit of Yahweh began to move him . . .'). It occurs again twice as the narrative nears its climax, in 16.19, after the shaving ('she began to torment him and his strength left him'), and then finally in 16.22 ('but his hair began to grow again after it had been shaved'). The climax combines, paradoxically, achievement and failure, blindness and recognition, resentment and acceptance. Samson dies, Israel does not, but neither is it delivered (the situation envisaged in the judgment speech of 2.20-21 is beginning to materialize), and Samson's tragic fate makes us wonder to what straits Yahweh will have to reduce Israel before it, too, is reconciled to its separateness.

8.10

Finally, a few observations on the role that the motif of knowing and not knowing plays in the Samson story. It occurs explicitly—by the use of the verb ידע (to know)—six times in the narrative, twice in each of the three major units of which it is composed.[141] In the account of Samson's birth in chapter 13 Manoah does not know the identity of the divine visitor (v. 16), and then he does, but only, ironically, when the visitor is no longer present (v. 21). In the first major movement of the narrative (chs. 14–15) Samson's parents do not know that Samson's determination to marry a Philistine is from Yahweh (14.4), and the men of Judah challenge Samson with the question, 'Don't you know that the Philistines rule over us?' (15.11). Of course Samson knows this, but what neither he nor his questioners know is that Yahweh is seeking an occasion against the Philistines through Samson. In the second major movement (ch. 16) the secret of Samson's strength is not known (v. 9) and then, when it is, Samson does not know that Yahweh has left him (v. 20).

To these must be added the many oblique references to the same theme. When Manoah finally knows the identity of the messenger he also knows something else, 'We will surely die because we have seen God' (13.22). But he is wrong. His mortal fear stems from his knowledge of the rules of holiness,[142] but it is misplaced, for what might confidently be predicted on the basis of the rules does not happen in this case. Nor does knowledge of the ritual requirements of Naziriteship enable Manoah and his wife to understand how God is at work in the bizarre behaviour of their son, and we would be no more enlightened than they if the omniscient narrator did not come to our aid. Samson attempts to exercise power over his wedding guests by proposing a riddle which he knows they will not be able to solve. But he, too, is wrong. The Philistines resort to intimidation to get the knowledge which will enable them to turn the tables on Samson (14.15). In the second movement the stakes are higher. The Philistines need to know the secret of Samson's strength so that they can bind him, and having acquired this knowledge (this time by bribery, 16.5) they seem to have the power they desired. But they do not know that it is Yahweh who has given Samson into their hands in order to destroy them.

Knowledge is elusive in the Samson story,[143] and not least the knowledge of God, for God acts in this story with a freedom which sets very definite limits to the kinds of knowledge which mortals can have of him. He may be known in the sense that he is recognized by Manoah's wife, and is at hand to respond to Manoah's and Samson's prayers. And he may be known as the true author of Dagon's discomfiture.[144] But what none of the characters in the story is allowed to have is the kind of knowledge which would enable them to use God, to pin him to predictability, to manipulate him by religious rituals, even those of his own making. We are reminded of Jephthah with his vow, and Israel with its calling upon Yahweh and its 'repentance'. The Samson story with its striking use of the literary technique of 'contrary-to-expectation' underlines a theological concern which we have seen surfacing in one way or another in most of the preceding episodes.

Manoah, with his insistent demand for answers and explanations serves as a foil for his wife, to whom our attention is continually directed in the annunciation scene which opens the narrative.[145] Gunn has nicely pointed out the contrast between the two:

> There is Manoah who must be sure, must map out the future, must fit his experience to the rules of religious life. There is Manoah's wife who is blessed in her barrenness, knows God when she meets him, trusts him, and is satisfied to ask (or presume) no more. [See especially vv. 6 and 23 of chapter 13.][146]

The dignity which Samson acquires at the end of the narrative derives in part from the fact that he, too, does not demand explanations, but evinces something of that same calm acceptance of his place in the divine scheme of things that his mother evinced at the beginning. Samson, we feel, knows God in his death better than he knew him in his life.

9.00 *Summary Remarks on 3.7–16.31 as an integrated narrative sequence*

9.01 *Distinctive content*
In terms of content 3.7–16.31 is distinguished from what precedes and follows in that it consists of accounts of the careers of individual judge-figures. The only exception to this is chapter 9 which narrates, in the form of an appendix to the Gideon episode, a temporary aberration from the norm. The various narrative episodes and summary notices of which 3.7–16.31 are composed are set within a chronological scheme which begins with the 'eight years' of 3.8 and is

continued through to the 'twenty years' of 16.31, but not into chapters 17-21.[147] This scheme is part of a more general chronological ordering of the material which makes 3.7-16.31 a complex narrative movement rather than a mere anthology. (See sections 1.01-1.03 of this chapter.)

9.02 *Redactional unity*
The Othniel, Ehud, Barak, Gideon, Jephthah, and Samson episodes are superficially related to one another by a repeating redactional framework consisting of six elements:

1. Israel does what is evil in Yahweh's sight
2. Yahweh gives/sells them into the hand of oppressors
3. Israel cries to Yahweh
4. He raises up a deliverer
5. The oppressor is subdued (reversal of element 2)
6. The land has rest

Minor variations occur in particular elements, variations which either do not affect meaning at all or affect it only minimally, as for example, the variation between זעק and צעק in element 3 or that between 'gives' and 'sells' in element 2.[148] Variations in the pattern itself occur through the omission of one or more of its elements, such omissions being related to the content of particular episodes. Elements are omitted in certain cases because the content of a particular episode makes them redundant. Thus element 4 fades out as an explicit statement after the first two episodes because the Barak, Gideon, and Samson narratives themselves focus in some detail on the activity of Yahweh in enlisting the destined deliverer. Jephthah at first appears to be a purely human appointee, but Yahweh's involvement is indicated in the text, first in a passive role (11.11), then in an active one (11.29).[149] Elements of the framework pattern are omitted also when the content of a particular episode suggests that their inclusion would be inappropriate. Thus element 6 does not occur again after the end of the Gideon episode because the land does not regain its rest under Jephthah[150] or Samson, and elements 3 and 5 as well as 6 are dropped from the Samson episode because there Israel does not actively seek deliverance and the oppressor is not subdued.

In short the editorial framework of these episodes is not a fixed grid into which the narrative material is forced regardless of its content. The framework pattern is varied in such a way as to reflect the changing state of Israel as seen in the succession of episodes. The change is one of progressive deterioration in Israel's condition, in relation to Yahweh, in relation to its enemies, and in relation to its own internal stability. (Compare, in the introduction to the book, the schematic overview of the period in 2.16-19.)

The short notices of 10.1-5 and 12.8-15 are constructed according to a pattern which is quite distinct from that which frames the major episodes. Its four elements are

1.   There arose/judged after him . . .
2.   he judged Israel for (term of office)
3.   he died
4.   he was buried in (place of burial)

The first element is the only one which shows any variation;[151] all four elements occur in each of the five notices. The perspective of this pattern appears to be purely antiquarian and secular. The theological concerns which are so prominent in the framework pattern of the major episodes are entirely lacking here. This raises the question of how these two contrasting patterns are integrated into the larger composition.

None of these short notices refers to any external threat or to any military activity on the part of the judge. Argument from silence is admittedly precarious, but two additional observations are relevant here. First, it is not paucity of information alone which is the distinguishing feature of the short notices; Othniel, about whom very little specific information is given, is nevertheless accorded the full formulaic treatment of a military deliverer.[152] Second, such details as *are* given in these notices suggest conditions of peace and prosperity. I suggest that Boling is in accord with the textual evidence when he argues that these notices represent generally peaceful interludes.[153] Their inclusion effectively excludes the notion that any form of cyclic determinism governed Israel's fortunes in the judges era.

There is of course one other short notice which I have not mentioned here, namely, that of Shamgar in 3.31. Its brevity and the way it is introduced (with the characteristic 'after him') associate it with the other short notices, making six in all distributed in a 1:2:3 progression as we have seen. But its content links it with the major episodes. Elements of both the characteristic framework patterns are combined in the Jephthah episode as has long been recognized.[154] The burial of the judge in a specified place, which receives only formulaic treatment in the short notices is part of the narrative proper in the Gideon and Samson episodes (8.22; 16.31a), and the two notes concerning Samson's term of office (15.20; 16.31b) are similar in form to those used in the short notices. So then, the two patterns are not simply juxtaposed but alternate and overlap in the larger composition.

Each of the six major episodes and the six short notices features one individual who is either explicitly said to have judged Israel or is clearly identifiable as a judge on other grounds. Deborah delegates responsibility for saving Israel (in a military sense) to Barak, but Barak remains subordinate to her and it is she alone who is said to have judged Israel (4.4). Neither Ehud nor Gideon are explicitly said to have judged Israel but must clearly be considered judges in view of the description of judgeship given in 2.16-19. Shamgar is another deliverer *of the same kind* as Ehud as we have seen: 'he too saved Israel' (3.31). It follows therefore that twelve judge-figures are featured in 3.7-16.31. They are not distributed one to each tribe in accordance with any of the traditional lists (e.g. Gen. 49; Num. 26; Deut. 33) but they are presented in a schematic arrangement corresponding broadly to that of the tribes in chapter 1, beginning with Judah and Benjamin (Othniel, Ehud) and concluding with Dan (Samson). The pan-Israelite perspective of the stereotyped formulae in both the major episodes and the short notices finds a subtle reinforcement here. It is to be noted in this connection that a concern for the completeness of Israel, as expressed in its 'twelveness', is to be found in the closing chapter of the book; it is imperative that wives be provided for Benjamin so that the full complement of the tribes can be maintained (21.3, 6, 15, 17).

9.03 *Unifying motifs*
My analysis in this chapter has attempted to demonstrate coherence not only at the level of overall structure, but also at the level of narrative texture. A dense network of interlocking motifs has been uncovered which unifies the material of 3.7-16.31 at a deeper level than that of the repeating surface patterns. In particular, motifs have been found which serve as links between adjacent episodes, for example:

1.   The verb תקע (to thrust/stike) which occurs at the high point of the action of both the Ehud and Deborah/Barak episodes (3.21; 4.21), drawing attention to other striking similarities between the actions of Ehud and Jael.

2. The twin expressions, אשה נביאה (a woman, a prophetess)
    and איש נביא (a man, a prophet)—unique in the Old
    Testament—used, respectively, of Deborah in the Deborah/
    Barak episode and of the prophet in the Gideon episode
    which follows (4.4; 6.8). These two figures are introduced
    at the same juncture in the respective narratives but there
    is a significant contrast in their roles.[155]

3. The worthless fellows (אנשים ריקים) which follow
    Abimelech (9.4) are matched by the worthless fellows
    (אנשים ריקים) which follow Jephthah in the following
    episode (11.4), drawing attention to a number of striking
    similarities and contrasts between Abimelech and Jephthah
    themselves.

By means of such motifs successive episodes are hinged together like
the panels of a triptych, or to be more precise, a polytych,[156] and the
reader is invited to read each episode in the light of what has gone
before. They are an important part of the linguistic design of the
book.

Similar linking motifs are to be found between the short notices
and what precedes and/or follows them in the larger composition.
Thus Shamgar's improvised weapon (ox-goad) anticipates Jael's
improvised weapon (tent-peg) in the Deborah/Barak episode which
immediately follows. The note about Jair 'the Gileadite' (10.3) is
followed by the story of Jephthah 'the Gileadite' (11.1), and this story
about the judge who sacrificed his only child, a daughter, is linked to
the note about Ibzan which follows by the pointed reference to
Ibzan's many daughters (12.9).

Longer range connections are made by such recurring motifs as
'seizure of the fords of the Jordan' (Ehud, Gideon, Jephthah),
'contention with the Ephraimites' (Gideon, Jephthah), 'the apparently
weak woman who overcomes a male hero' (Jael, the 'certain woman'
of Thebez, Jephthah's daughter, Delilah), 'flaming torches' associated
with the number '300' (Samson, Gideon), or 'slaughter of large
numbers of Philistines with an improvised weapon' (Samson,
Shamgar). The annunciation scene in chapter 13 recapitulates many
motifs found in 6.11-24, and the Samson story in general contains an
unusually high concentration of motifs which have occurred in
earlier episodes.

9.04 *The Samson episode as the climactic realization of major themes*

My analysis has been concerned ultimately with the thematics of 3.7–16.31 considered as one complex narrative movement. Taking my cue from the climax towards which the Samson episode moves I have argued that this final episode is principally concerned with issues which also figure centrally in 3.7–16.31 as a whole. They are as follows:

1. Israel's special status as a nation separated to Yahweh

2. Israel's going after other gods in wilful violation of this special status

3. The implied contest between Yahweh and these other gods

4. The freedom of Yahweh's activity over against Israel's presumption that it knows him and can use him, as required, to secure its own future

These themes are brought to a unique focus in the story of Samson whose personal history recapitulates that of Israel as a whole in the judges era, especially in his *nazir* (separate) status, his going after foreign women,[157] and his calling upon Yahweh.

Chapter 5

CODA, 17.1–21.25

1.00 *Distinctiveness*
Chapters 17–21 contain two major narrative complexes, 17–18 and
19–21 respectively, which are clearly different in kind from those
which appear in 3.7–16.31. They are formally distinct in that they
stand outside the redactional framework which unifies 3.7–16.31,
and they are distinct in content in that neither of them features the
career of a judge. They are set in the period when 'there was no king
in Israel', but are not linked to what precedes by more precise
temporal indicators.

2.00 *Unity*

2.01
The transition from the first major narrative complex to the second
is effected by 19.1a:

> Now it came to pass in those days when there was no king in Israel
> that . . .

This alludes to the similar transitional comments which occur *within*
the first complex at 17.6 and 18.1, and anticipates the closure which
is effected at 21.25 where the same expression occurs as a
summarizing comment not only on chapters 19–21, but also on
chapters 17–21 as a whole. The comment occurs in an expanded
form in 17.6 and 21.25 and an abbreviated form in 18.1 and 19.1
giving the following inverted pattern:

A   (17.6)   In those days there was no king . . .
                         every man did what was right in his own eyes

B   (18.1)   In those days there was no king . . .

B′   (19.1)   In those days when there was no king . . .

A′   (21.25)   In those days there was no king . . .
                   every man did what was right in his own eyes

2.02
The two narratives which are brought together into a *redactional*
unity by this structure have so much in common that their
conjunction is a very natural one. They both feature a Levite who, in
each case, has connections with 'Bethlehem Judah' on the one hand
and 'Mt Ephraim' on the other (17.7-8; 19.1). The Levite of the first
story is resident in Bethlehem Judah, but journeys from there to Mt
Ephraim; the Levite in the second story is resident in Mt Ephraim
but travels to Bethlehem-Judah. (This inversion of corresponding
narrative elements mirrors the inverted pattern of redactional
elements noted above.)[1] In both cases the personal fortunes of the
Levite become the mainspring for larger action. In the first story it is
the presence of the Levite in Micah's house which attracts the
attention of the Danites (18.3) who transfer both the Levite and
Micah's image to Dan. In the second story it is the presence of the
Levite and his concubine in Gibeah which triggers off the outrage
committed there and the war which follows (19.22). The first
narrative concludes with a reference to the sanctuary at Shiloh
(18.31); the second concludes with the abduction of 'the daughters of
Shiloh' (21.19-23).

3.00 *Cultic chaos: Micah and the Danites, 17.1–18.31*

3.01
In this first major narrative the redactional comments at 17.6 and
18.1 occur at nodal points in the development of the plot. These are
points of discontinuity at which one stage of the narrative reaches a
point of rest and a further development is then initiated from a
different direction.[2] The resulting three-part structure of the plot is
as follows:

17.1-5   Micah acquires a molten image and installs it, along with
            an ephod and teraphim, in his private shrine in Mt
            Ephraim.

17.7-13   A Levite from Bethlehem-Judah travels to Mt Ephraim, meets Micah, and is installed by him as a priest in his shrine.

18.1b-31   The Danites, in the course of migrating northwards, come to Micah's shrine. They take both his image and his priest and install them in their own newly established shrine at Dan.

3.02

17.1-5

Micah enters the narrative as a self-confessed thief. The money he stole had been the subject of a vow sworn by his mother in Micah's hearing. Apparently conscience-stricken, he tells his mother what he has done and returns the money to her.[3] She is so glad to have it back that she utters not one word of reproach, but blesses her son in the name of Yahweh. She then discloses the purpose for which she had dedicated the money:

> I had wholly consecrated the money to Yahweh
> > from my own hand, my son—
> To make a molten image![4]

The incongruity of the statement[5] is typical of the way the scene as a whole is handled. The whole 'eleven hundred of silver'[6] is dedicated, but only 'two hundred' of it is given to the smith to be made into an image. What did Micah's mother do with the rest? And the man who becomes the proud owner of the image and installs it in his shrine along with his ephod and his teraphim (v. 6) has a name, מיכיהו, which means 'Who is like Yahweh?'.[7] This long form of the name Micah occurs only twice in the narrative, as an inclusio around this particular scene:

v. 1   There was a man of Mt Ephraim and his name was מיכיהו
v. 4   There it was [the image] in the house of מיכיהו!

And so the narrative opens with a scene full of heavy irony bordering on farce. The irony arises from the fact the characters are apparently unaware of the incongruity of their own words and actions. Micah's mother has made her brief appearance and will take no further part in the action. Her function has been to put Micah in possession of his image and to provide us with some insight into how it was that Micah came to be the kind of man he is.

17.7-13

Money again changes hands in this second scene. As soon as Micah discovers that his visitor is a Levite he offers him 'ten of silver' per year, as well as lodgings, clothing and food, if he will stay and become his priest (v. 10). The Levite is well pleased with these terms and is duly installed. The scene ends with Micah confident that his future is now well secured:

> Now I know that Yahweh will prosper me because I have a Levite for a priest (v. 13).

He is mistaken of course, and we have come to a major turning point in the development of the plot. Micah's personal fortunes, which have risen steadily throughout the first two scenes are about to undergo a sudden reversal. From now on nothing will go right for him.

18.1-31

This final segment of the narrative consists of several scenes (featuring dialogue) with connecting narration,[8] reflecting the movement of the Danites to and fro and their encounters with various persons en route.

There are two scenes involving the Levite, the first being in vv. 3-7a where he is consulted by the spies. Passing close to Micah's house the spies recognize the voice of the young Levite[9] and turn aside to investigate. And so the Levite that Micah thought would guarantee his good fortune inadvertently triggers off the events leading to his downfall. The Danites want to know what he is doing there. The Levite explains:

> This is what Micah did for me,
> He hired (שׂכר) me
> and I have become his priest (v. 4).

The narrator himself in the previous chapter has expressed it differently: literally,

> Micah filled the hand of the Levite
> and the young man became his priest (17.12).

The phrase 'to fill the hand' is quite unexceptional in itself (cf. for example, Exod. 28.41; 29.9, 29, 33, 35; Lev. 8.33), and probably refers to the ceremonial filling of the appointee's hands with some token of his office. But the Levite's use of שכר (hired) suggests that it is the filling of the hand in quite another sense which occupies *his* mind! The hint is not lost on the Danites. On their next visit in vv. 15-20, the other scene involving the Levite, they outbid Micah for the Levite's services and find him more than willing to abandon Micah and go with them:

> And the priest was pleased;
> and he took the ephod, teraphim, and molten image
> and went with the people (v. 20).

In the scene which immediately follows (vv. 21-26), Micah makes his last appearance in the narrative, now a pathetic figure, half protesting, half pleading, blurting out his words in short, disjointed sentences:[10]

> My god which I made—you have taken!
> And the priest!
> And you have gone away!
> What do I have left?
> How can you say to me, 'What is the matter with you?' (v. 24).

But it's no use. The Danites are too strong for him. He turns, and makes his way home.

Micah's undoing takes place in the context of the migration of the Danites and their campaign against Laish. It is this which provides the basic storyline for this final segment of the narrative. An analogy with the traditional account of *national* migration, conquest, and settlement is suggested by the comparison between Dan and Shiloh which is drawn in 18.31:

> So they [the Danites] set up Micah's image which he made
> all the time the house of God was at Shiloh.

It was at Shiloh, according to Josh. 18.1, that the Israelites had first set up the tent of meeting after they were established in Canaan. The Danites, like the Israelites, acquire a priesthood and cult objects en route and conclude their campaign by setting these up in their newly acquired territory (vv. 17-30). The mission of the spies in Judges 18 is strikingly reminiscent of that in Numbers 13-14 and Deut. 1, and the 'six hundred fighting men' of Judg. 18.11, 16, 17[11] recalls the 'six hundred contingents' of Exod. 12.37 and Num. 11.21. The Danite conquest of Laish follows the same basic pattern as the Israelite conquest of Canaan, but on a smaller scale.[12]

But the difference is not simply one of scale. Certain key elements of the pattern appear in an inverted form in Judges 18, giving the account of the Danite campaign a distinctly satirical thrust. For all their show of strength the Danites are actually in retreat! They are not advancing into the heart of the land to claim their inheritance as Israel was, but withdrawing in the face of Canaanite pressure to a substitute holding on the perimeter (18.1; cf. 1.34). They are having to make do in a situation where Yahweh no longer drives out the Canaanites from before Israel, as anticipated in the judgment speech of 2.20-21.[13] Encouraged by the made-to-order oracle given them by Micah's Levite (v. 6)—we know how mercenary he is!—the spies of Judges 18 travel on until they discover a town in the remote north which is isolated, unsuspecting, and unfortified (v. 7), the very antithesis of the cities 'great and fortified up to heaven' referred to in Deut. 1.28 (cf. Num. 13.28). Unlike the spies in Numbers 13–14 they return a unanimous recommendation that a campaign be mounted at once (vv. 8-10), but we sense that their confidence lies less in an indomitable faith in Yahweh than in the knowledge that they have found easy prey. It is impossible to take their pious exhortation as seriously as we can the brave words of Joshua and Caleb (Num. 13.31; 14.6-9). When the Danites are about to fall on Laish the narrator dwells again on the peaceful, defenceless existence of its citizens in a way which suggests that his sympathies lie more with the conquered than with the conquerors:

> The Danites came to Laish
> to a people quiet and unsuspecting
> and smote them with the edge of the sword
> and burnt the city with fire.
> And there was no deliverer
> because it was far from Sidon
> and they had no dealings with anyone[14] (vv. 27-28).

In Dan, Micah's shrine is re-opened, as it were, on a new site and under new management (vv. 30-31). A cryptic note, 'until the captivity of the land...',[15] implies that it eventually suffered the same fate there as it had suffered in Mt Ephraim. The account closes, as I noted above, with a statement which contrasts the outcome of the Danite campaign with that of the classic Israelite one: Dan versus Shiloh.

3.03

Implicit in the story as a whole are a number of particular criticisms of the Danite sanctuary: its cult was syncretistic, its priesthood mercenary, and its (indirect) founder a thief. Interestingly it does allow that it was served by levitical priests whose ancestry could be traced to Moses himself (18.30).[16] If this mutes slightly its polemic against the sanctuary[17] it gives, at the same time, a sharper edge to its implied criticisms of the levitical priesthood as an institution. But the theme of the story cannot be stated adequately in terms of particularist polemics of this kind. A far more fundamental issue emerges in Micah's confident assertion:

> Now I know that Yahweh will prosper me
> because I have a Levite for a priest.

This is a major turning point in the development of the plot, as we have seen, and is of quite pivotal significance in the development of the story's central theme.[18] It is, above all, a story about the false confidence men have that they know God in such a way that they can manipulate him by cultic and institutional means, and so secure their own futures. The Danites make essentially the same error as Micah, and their shrine eventually suffers the same fate. The treatment is satirical throughout.

4.00 *Moral chaos: The outrage at Gibeah and its consequences, 19.1–21.25*

4.01

This time the redactional comments about there being no king and every man doing what was right in his own eyes do not occur in the body of the narrative as they did in chapters 17–18, but at its two extremes (19.1; 21.25). The difference is in keeping with the fact that the plot of this second narrative does not have points of discontinuity comparable to those at 17.6 and 18.1 in the first narrative, but is unilinear, each development emerging directly out of the one which precedes it.[19] There are four episodes, as follows:

I	19.1-28	The outrage at Gibeah
II	219.29–20.11	Preparations for war: the Levite's call and Israel's response

III   20.12-48   The war itself

IV   21.1-24   Post-war reconstruction: wives for the Benjamite
                  survivors

The principal action takes place in the third episode. The first two
episodes trace developments leading up to it and the last deals with
the consequences that flowed from it.

4.02

Episode I, 19.1-28

This first episode gives the narrator's perspective[20] on the outrage
committed at Gibeah and on the characters who were involved in it.

At the beginning of the episode the concubine 'plays the harlot'
(זנה);[21] at the end she becomes the common property of the men of
Gibeah (19.2, 25). The grim irony suggests that from the narrator's
point of view there was an element of justice in the concubine's fate.
We are reminded of Samson who did what was right in his own eyes
and ended up by having his eyes put out (14.3; 16.21), or of
Abimelech who killed his brothers on a stone and was killed himself
by having a stone dropped on his head (9.5, 53). Such censure of the
concubine does not of course imply moral approval of those
responsible for her fate. And the censure itself is muted somewhat by
the narrative details. Damning though it is, it seems that זנה is used
metaphorically rather than literally in 19.2. The concubine 'plays the
harlot' by walking out on her husband,[22] but far from giving her
favours to other men she goes straight home to her father and stays
there, and the Levite's attempt to win her back by 'speaking kindly to
her' (19.3) suggests that she had not left without provocation on his
part.

The night scene at Gibea in which the concubine is raped is the
climax of a series of scenes in which hospitality is featured in one way
or another. The exaggerated hospitality shown by the concubine's
father creates a situation in which the Levite, in exasperation at his
host's continued importunity, finally draws the line and takes his
leave at about mid-afternoon on the fifth day. He would have done
better to have asserted himself earlier in the day or to have yielded to
his host's urgings to stay yet another night. As it is, he and his
companions are forced to make an overnight stop on their way home.
Late in the day the travellers arrive opposite Jebus. The servant

wants them to stop and seek lodgings there, but the Levite is reluctant to entrust himself to the hospitality of foreigners:

> We won't turn aside to a city of foreigners who are not Israelites.
> We'll go on to Gibeah (v. 12).

It is a fateful decision, but only subsequently does the full irony of it emerge. In Gibeah they are at first offered no hospitality at all, despite the fact that their two laden asses give assurance that no great liability would be incurred. This downright boorishness of the citizens of Gibeah is an ominous harbinger of the far worse abuse of the travellers which is to follow. At length a temporary resident in Gibeah—not a Benjaminite—takes them in and soon shows himself to be a model host, foddering their asses, washing their feet, and plying them with food and drink (v. 21). The atmosphere quickly lightens as host and guests settle down to a convivial evening together. But then the worst elements of the local population gather outside and begin to beat on the door, demanding that the host bring his principal guest out to them so that they can rape him! Now at last the full irony of the Levite's decision to travel on to Gibeah becomes apparent. Having eschewed the hospitality of foreigners and entrusted himself to Israelites he finds himself in a virtual Sodom![23] The host is faced with a crisis, and being a model host his response is governed entirely by his understanding of the rules of hospitality:

> No, my brothers! Do not act so wickedly
> for this man has come into my house.
> Don't commit this folly!
> Look, my virgin daughter and his concubine—
> Let me bring them out now.
> Rape them. Do with them as you please.
> But to this man do not do this foolish thing! (vv. 23-24).

So the model host turns out to be the one who conceives the idea of throwing the concubine to the dogs. It is a comedy of correctness; he is a conscientious host to the last! That he should volunteer the Levite's concubine as well as his own daughter is surprising to be sure.[24] Perhaps the rules of correct behaviour in such circumstances, as he understands them, apply to male guests only, or more likely, he is simply doing the best he can: two women instead of one man; at least he will have saved his principal guest. At any rate, there is no protest from the Levite who is the person chiefly at risk. He seizes his concubine and turns her out to the mob himself.[25] We are spared the harrowing details of what she suffered at their hands. Three graphic verbs in quick succession tell it all: they knew her, they abused her, they discarded her (v. 25). They are 'sons of Belial' (v. 22); their appetites and motives are uncomplicated and brutal. They are the chief culprits, but they are not the principal characters in this closing scene of the episode. What they do takes place off stage and is left largely to our imagination. Interest is centred on the host and the Levite, and especially the latter. As dawn approaches the discarded concubine falls at the door of the house, too weak to knock or cry out, perhaps already dead. Inside, at daybreak, the Levite 'gets up'. The expression is chilling in what it implies by its sheer ordinariness. After thrusting out the concubine and seeing that he himself is no longer personally threatened, the Levite has retired to bed. He rises without any apparent remorse for what he has done or concern for the concubine. In fact he appears to give no thought to her at all until he is preparing to leave and finds her on the doorstep and tells her with almost unbelievable callousness to get up because he is ready to go. There is no answer. He picks her up, puts her on his ass, and completes his journey home. And so ends this first episode.

Episode II, 19.29–20.11

Israelite hospitality received satirical treatment in the first episode; in this one the assembly (עדה)[26] receives similar treatment. Its convenor is the Levite; the matter of national importance is the outrage committed in Gibeah. Dramatic irony is generated by the fact that we, the readers, know more about both the convenor and the matter in hand than the members of the assembly do. To us the Levite's systematic dismemberment of the concubine—all very businesslike—is an extension of the cool callousness he displayed towards her at Gibeah; to those who receive the pieces and the accompanying summons it is an act of holy zeal.[27] They are galvanized into action and come out 'as one man, from Dan to Beersheba, including the land of Gilead!' (20.1). That is, the call of this Levite elicits a response which far surpasses anything achieved by the saviour-judges raised up by Yahweh.[28]

In his speech to the assembly he chooses his words carefully. The facts are not grossly distorted, but quite a different impression is created from that which the narrator has given in the previous episode. In the narrator's account the rapists are 'the men of the city,

worthless fellows [lit. sons of Belial]' (19.22); the Levite speaks of
'the nobility (בעלי) of Gibeah' rising against him (20.5). To the
members of the assembly, who do not know the facts as we do, this
would presumably be taken at face value as an assertion that the
crime was committed by the leading men of the city (cf. 9.2). In the
narrator's account the offenders demand that the host bring the
Levite out so that they can 'know' him (19.22). The Levite says, 'Me
they intended to kill' (20.5). Considering what happened to the
concubine it is perhaps a reasonable inference that they intended
more than a mere sex orgy. But the Levite's choice of words lays
particular stress on the threat to himself, thereby diminishing his
own responsibility by implication. In the absence of further
information, what he says could conjure up a totally different
scenario from the actual one, namely: his life was threatened; he
escaped, but his concubine was caught and raped; he later recovered
her body, and so on. Finally, the narrator's account is suggestively
vague about whether the concubine died solely as a result of the rape
or as a result of the combined effects of the rape and the Levite's
subsequent treatment of her. Was she unconscious or dead on the
doorstep? Did she die while the Levite was taking his rest, or during
his preparations to leave, or on the journey home? The narrator's
account even allows us to entertain the suspicion that having turned
her out to the mob the Levite considered her as good as dead,[29] but
then, having conceived the possibility of using her corpse to avenge
himself on the men of Gibeah, deliberately contributed to her death
or even caused it directly with his knife when they got home.[30] This
would explain the extraordinary callousness he displays. In the light
of these possibilities there is an eerie ambiguity about the כזאת, 'such
a thing as this', of the message which accompanies the pieces:

> Has such a thing as this happened or been seen from the time the
> Israelites came up from Egypt until today? (19.30).

The Levite's account to the assembly, by way of contrast, is
deceptively simple:

> my concubine they ravished, and she died (20.5).

He implies, without explicitly stating it, that she died solely as a
result of the rape. His speech arouses none of the suspicions that the
narrator's account does. This is the second time in the narrative that
we have had the opportunity to compare the Levite's retelling of
events with the narrator's own account of them. His speech to the old

man at Gibeah in 19.18-19 does not have the sinister overtones of the present speech but displays the same ability to choose words with care in order to produce a desired effect on the hearer.[32]

The members of the assembly are as impressed by the Levite's speech as they were by his grisly summons. They arise 'as one man' and resolve at once on united punitive action against Gibeah (20.8-11; cf. v. 1). The action they take may well be justified in principle; by the pointed irony of 19.12 the narrator has implied that the outrage at Gibeah is an act which challenges the very concept of 'Israel' as a distinctive people. But what will become of Israel when its assembly can be convened and used by a person of such dubious morals as this Levite? That is the serious issue raised by the satirical portrayal of the assembly in this episode.

Episode III, 20.12-48

The outcome of the assembly's decision is a holy war, an institution especially associated with Israel's heroic age in the biblical traditions. The present narrative incorporates virtually all its formal features, distributed over Episodes II-IV as follows: the summons, the assembly of the people of God, the vow of concerted action—Episode II; inquiry for divine guidance, offerings in the face of reverses, divine assurance of victory, panic among the enemy, the execution of the ban—this episode; dispersal of the assembly—Episode IV.[33] The peculiar horror of the present account is that it is one of the tribes of Israel which is the enemy and that the war is prosecuted with a determination and a thoroughness surpassing anything evidenced in Israel's wars with the Canaanites elsewhere in Judges. The action in Episode III alternates between engagement with the enemy and inquiry of Yahweh, giving the following compositional pattern:

> Attempt at negotiation
> > Inquiry of Yahweh
> Defeat
> > Inquiry of Yahweh
> Defeat
> > Inquiry of Yahweh
> Victory

The failure of the attempt at negotiation (20.11-14) is a narrative development for which there has been careful preparation in the preceding episodes. In Episode I the citizens of Gibeah in general abuse the Levite and his companions passively (by refusing them hospitality) before the rapists abuse them actively (19.15, 22). In Episode II the Benjaminites as a whole hear of the assembly but do not attend it. Now they openly declare their solidarity with the rapists by refusing to extradite them. The evil committed at Gibeah has now led to an open breach between one whole tribe and the rest of the confederation. The very fabric of Israel is threatened. The focus of the narrative is now no longer on the Levite's involvement in the outrage, but on the seriousness of it in its own right. The Levite simply disappears without trace. The tone of the narrative changes too. We miss in this episode the satirical element we found in the previous two. The subject-matter is now handled in an entirely serious vein.

Most of the space in vv. 18-48 is devoted to a description of the fighting, with the fluctuating fortunes of the opposing sides. But the three inquiries and the three responses which punctuate the account open an important window onto the psychological plane of the narrative. They enable us to see what is happening besides the fighting itself; that is, what is happening in the minds of the Israelites and between them and Yahweh as the war proceeds through its various phases. The contents of the respective inquiries and responses may be summarized as follows:

	Inquiry	Response
v. 18	Who will go first?	Judah.
v. 23	Shall we go again against our brothers?	Yes.
v. 28	Shall we go again against our brothers or shall we desist?	Go again; I will give them into your hand.

The three inquiries exhibit a pattern of incremental repetition which expresses the growing anxiety of the inquirers. Their first inquiry reflects their confidence regarding the rightness and eventual outcome of their cause. They are already committed to the war and Yahweh's approval is assumed. They therefore raise a purely procedural matter; how is the campaign to be conducted? Yahweh puts Judah in the van, appropriately so, since the ravished concubine was a Judahite.[34] But there is no promise of victory and none materializes; quite the reverse. The second inquiry shows the drastic loss of confidence the inquirers have suffered as a result of their disastrous defeat. They are now doubtful about the wisdom, and perhaps also the rightness, of continuing the war. A conciliatory note is struck by the reference to the Benjaminites as 'our brothers' (also in the third inquiry). But Yahweh sends them into battle again, to another severe mauling at the hands of the Benjaminites. After their first setback they wept before Yahweh; now they weep and fast and offer sacrifices. In their third inquiry they explicitly ask whether they should desist, a possibility which now looms very large in their minds. But Yahweh sends them into battle again, this time with an assurance of victory. In the ensuing battle the fortunes of the two sides are suddenly reversed when Yahweh intervenes on the side of 'Israel' (20.34, 35).

To summarize then, in this episode in which Israelites wage holy war on Israelites, Yahweh takes his place at the head of the assembly and distributes victory and defeat in such a way that the punishment of Benjamin by the other tribes is made the occasion for the whole of Israel to be chastised by Yahweh.

Episode IV, 21.1-24

Just as the narrative seems set to move swiftly and smoothly to its conclusion a fresh complication appears in the plot with the revelation that the Israelites had sworn an oath at Mizpah not to give their daughters in marriage to Benjaminites (21.1; cf. 20.1). To this ill-considered oath they have now added excessive slaughter. In the heat of the battle the passion for revenge seems to have got the upper hand (the Benjaminites had inflicted heavy losses on the other tribes in the first two engagements). Only now, with passion spent and a more sober perspective restored, do the claims of brotherhood begin to influence behaviour again (21.6; cf. 20.23, 28). But the damage has already been done: all the Benjaminite women have been slaughtered (20.47-48; 21.16) and because of the oath the six hundred male survivors must die childless and the tribe become extinct.

The realization that Benjamin has in effect been eliminated from Israel at first provokes the same response from the other tribes that their own defeat at the hands of Benjamin had provoked in the previous episode: they assemble at Bethel, weep before Yahweh (this time with a 'great weeping'), inquire of him, and offer sacrifices

(21.2-4; cf. 20.23, 26-28). It is an indication of the radical 'repentance' they have undergone in relation to the Benjaminites (21.6, 15) and of their desire for their rehabilitation. But the wording of the inquiry is noteworthy:

> Why, O Yahweh, God of Israel
> has this come about in Israel
> that one tribe has today been lost to Israel? (v. 3).

The threefold reference to Israel, with Yahweh being addressed as 'God of Israel', implies that the matter in hand is ultimately his responsibility. The inquiry is less a request for information than an oblique form of protest and an attempt by the inquirers to absolve themselves of responsibility. But Yahweh will not be drawn. In the previous episode he chastised them by speaking; in this one he chastises them by remaining silent. He will not be used by them.

But now an apparent solution presents itself in the form of a fortuitous combination of circumstances. A roll-call reveals that the inhabitants of Jabesh-Gilead did not send any contingent to the war, and a second oath sworn at Mizpah—now conveniently remembered— has made all such defaulters subject to the ban (vv. 5-8). A force is despatched at once with instructions to slaughter all the inhabitants of the town except the virgins (vv. 10-11)—a selective application of the ban for which there was Mosaic precedent according to Num. 31.17-18. The present instance, however, is a clear case of using one oath in order to circumvent another: legally justifiable, but morally dubious to say the least. The operation yields four hundred wives, two hundred short of the required total.

Now the most senior and responsible members of the assembly— the elders—bring their minds to bear on the situation (v. 16). At first they can only restate the problem, as though searching for a solution which for the moment eludes them (vv. 16-18). Then at last they hit upon a plan (note the use of הנה [behold] in v. 19a to indicate the sudden burst of inspiration!), possibly suggested by the fact that the camp is now situated at Shiloh (v. 12). They remember that there is a Yahweh festival held in Shiloh each year[35] at which it is customary for the local girls to dance in the vineyards,[36] and they advise the remaining Benjaminites to ambush them, seize the number they require, and carry them off (vv. 19-21). Of course they anticipate a protest from the men of Shiloh but have already thought of a form of words with which to pacify them: the girls have not been captured in battle (that is, there has been no bloodshed), so the men of Shiloh are not bound to conduct a vendetta, and since they have not *voluntarily* given the girls to the Benjaminites they themselves have incurred no guilt (v. 22). It is a clever piece of casuistry which entirely avoids the moral issues involved. In effect the the men of Shiloh are asked to accept the rape as a *fait accompli*, just as Micah had to accept the plundering of his shrine by the Danites (18.22-26).

So, with consummate irony this episode reaches its climax with the elders, זקנים, doing, in principle, the same thing as the old man, זקן (the Levite's host), had done in Gibeah. The rape of the daughters of Shiloh is an ironic counterpoint to the rape of the concubine,[37] as the campaign against Jabesh-Gilead is an ironic counterpoint to the war against Benjamin:

```
┌─The rape of the concubine
│   ┌─Holy war against Benjamin
│   │     Problem: The Oath—Benjamin threatened with extinction
│   └─'Holy' war against Jabesh-Gilead
└─The rape of the daughters of Shiloh
```

The conclusion of the story (21.1-24) turns out to be a highly satirical narrative episode in which the assembly, headed by the elders, resorts to a mixture of force, casuistry and guile to circumvent the oath sworn at Mizpah without actually breaking it. The behaviour of the assembly, like that of the host at Gibeah, is a comedy of correctness. The narrative finally moves to a point of fragile equilibrium, with calm restored, in 21.23-24: Israel has miraculously survived intact!

4.03

In the story of Micah and the Danites the theme was realized principally through the character Micah, and the reversal of his fortunes in the course of the narrative. He figured in all three episodes, and even after he was no longer present in the story his name continued to be mentioned, so that he served as a kind of reference point which shed light on the subsequent behaviour of the Danites. No character has such central significance for the theme of the present story. The Levite at first appears destined to fulfil such a role, but he disappears without trace after his speech to the assembly. We never hear what happens to him. Interest lies not so much in the Levite as a person but in him as the convenor of the assembly. That is, the function of the Levite is to contribute to a critique of the assembly as an institution; once he has fulfilled this purpose he is simply dropped from the story. The same is true of the old man of Gibeah. His function is to contribute to a critique of Israelite hospitality in the period; his personal fortunes are of no intrinsic interest. The same is true of the rapists of Gibeah; for all we know they could have been among the six hundred survivors. This story is essentially a piece of social criticism, and the criticism is of a moral nature. It shows how Israel's hospitality, warfare, justice, and politics were all debased because of the moral blindness and/or perversity of its citizens (including Levites and elders) and the consequent malfunctioning of its institutions. Yahweh's displeasure, and his sovereignty,[38] find expression in the chastisement he brings to bear on the whole community.

5.00 *Chapters 17-21 as the conclusion of the book*

5.01
These chapters complete the book, first of all, in the purely aesthetic sense of giving it a balanced, symmetrical shape: the 'variations' of 3.7-16.31 are preceded by an 'overture' in two parts (1.1-2.6; 2.7-3.6) and followed by a 'coda' in two parts (17.1-18.31; 19.1-21.25). I don't wish to claim too much by pressing the musical analogies, but I trust the appropriateness of 'overture' and 'variations' is apparent from my analysis of these sections. The appropriateness of 'coda' for chapters 17-21 will, I hope, become evident before the end of this chapter if it is not so already.

5.02
These chapters also complete the book in a rhetorical-literary sense. An effect of literary bracketing or closure is produced by the way in which these closing chapters pick up and repeat or complement elements from the introduction. The frequent reference to Judah in these final chapters (17.7, 8, 9; 18.12, 20; 19.1, 2, 18) recalls the prominence given to Judah in 1.1-19; the characterization of Jebus/ Jerusalem as 'a city of foreigners' in 19.10-12 recalls the note in 1.21 about the failure of the Benjaminites to expel the Jebusites; the weeping at Bethel in 20.18, 26 recalls the weeping at Bochim (= Bethel)[39] in 2.1-5; and the account of the forced migration of the Danites in chapter 19 recalls the failure of the Danites to gain a

secure foothold in their allotted territory in 1.34. The most striking instance of such back-reference is, of course the almost word-for-word repetition of 1.1-2 in 20.18:

1.1-2   Who shall go up first for us against the Canaanites to fight against them? Yahweh said, Judah shall go up . . .

20.18   Who shall go up first for us to the battle against the Benjaminites? And Yahweh said, Judah first.

A very similar principle of composition is in evidence here as in the return to Ophrah at the end of the Gideon story or the return to Zorah at the end of the Samson story. The bracketing effect signals the completion of the literary unit and invites us to compare and contrast the circumstances the characters find themselves in at the close of the unit with the circumstances they were in at the beginning of it. (See the quotation from Boling towards the end of §4.05 in Chapter 1.)

5.03

In terms of thematic development, these chapters come after the climax that is reached in the Samson episode, but they resonate thematically with the rest of the book and with the Samson episode in particular. (It is this quality of post-climactic resonance which influenced my 'coda' analogy above.) The refrain which sums up the cultic and moral chaos depicted in these closing chapters as 'every man doing what was right in his (own) eyes' (17.6; 21.25) uses the very same language that is used in ch. 14 to describe Samson's behaviour, first by Samson himself, then by the narrator:

Get her for me, for she is right in my eyes (14.3).

She was right in Samson's eyes (14.7).

In retrospect Samson appears as the typical Israelite of the period, a perspective on him which echoes the implicit identification of Samson with Israel which we found in the Samson story itself. After its elaborate treatment in the Samson episode the theme of knowing or not knowing is restated in the story of Micah and the Danites, and reappears in a more marginal role in the account of the Benjaminite war. The same terminology is applied to the Benjaminites in 20.31-34 as was used of Samson in 16.20: they 'go out . . . as at other times . . . not knowing' that Yahweh is about to hand them over to

their enemies. The way in which Yahweh is shown to respond to
Israel's inquiries in 20.18-25, but not in 21.3 makes the same point as
is made through the handling of the 'calling upon Yahweh' motif in
3.7–16.31: while Yahweh is God of Israel, he cannot be used by
Israel. The vow which leads to the rape of the virgins in chapter 21
recalls Jephthah's vow which led to the sacrifice of his virgin
daughter. The daughters of Shiloh, like Jephthah's daughter, 'come
out . . . with dances', unaware of the fate which is about to overtake
them (21.21; cf. 11.34). In both cases Yahweh remains silent, passive,
withdrawn, in contrast to his active involvement earlier in the
respective narratives. Micah's manufacture of an ephod (17.5)
reminds us of the similar action of Gideon (8.27), and so we could go
on; there are other reminiscences of events that have been narrated
earlier in the book, although most are of only marginal significance
thematically.[40]

These final chapters do, however, bring to a head one issue which
has figured in only a secondary way in the rest of the book, namely,
the danger that Israel's internal situation may become so chaotic that
Israel might, as it were, collapse from within. There is already a
potential for civil war in the 'bitter curse' pronounced on Meroz in
5.23, because its inhabitants 'did not come to the help of Yahweh'.
The civil war motif enters explicitly in the Gideon and Abimelech
stories, and appears again in the Jephthah narrative. In the Samson
episode Judahite and Danite are at loggerheads with one another
(15.11-13), and Israel as such seems incapable of action of any kind.
But the climactic treatment of this motif is clearly the account of the
war against the Benjaminites in chapter 20. Paradoxically it is civil
war which finally produces a unified Israel again—a tragi-comic
conclusion, as Boling has rightly observed.[41]

The forced migration of the Danites in chapter 18 is a pointed
reminder that the programme of conquest and settlement envisaged
at the outset of the book was never fully realized. The reference to
Jebus as 'a city of foreigners' is another reminder (19.12). So, too, is
the rather curious note in 21.12 that Shiloh, where the Israelites were
camped, was 'in the land of Canaan', a phrase which recalls the
frequent mention of Canaan and Canaanites in the introduction (17
occurrences in 1.1–3.6). Elsewhere in the book Canaan is mentioned
only in the Deborah-Barak episode, where the opposition is
specifically 'kings of Canaan' (5.19; cf. 4.2, 23, 24). Kiriath-arba has
become Hebron (1.10), Kiriath-Sepher has become Debir (1.11),

Zephath has become Hormah (1.17), Luz has become Bethel (1.23), and Laish has become Dan (18.29), but ארץ כנען (the land of Canaan) has not become ארץ ישראל (the land of Israel).[42] Israel continues to live in a land it has not fully conquered and resettled. This is precisely the state of affairs which the introduction to the book indicated would be the net result of Israel's persistent apostasy despite all Yahweh's efforts to reclaim it throughout the judges period. In these closing chapters the situation foreshadowed in the judgment speech of 2.20-21 becomes a settled state of affairs. The Danites find a solution to their problem (ch. 28), and Israel as a whole occupies itself with more pressing matters (chs. 19–21), but the ominous note sounded in 18.30—'until the captivity of the land'—intimates that the unresolved problem of apostasy is destined to have even more serious consequences for Israel's tenure in Canaan.

A further intimation of things to come is contained in the setting given to the events narrated in these chapters by the refrain of 17.6, 18.1, 19.1, and 21.25, namely, 'those days in which there was no king in Israel'. But the primary function of this refrain is one of closure. It cuts off the narrative flow of the book by assigning all the events in these closing chapters to the same, broadly defined time or period. The very note of anticipation accentuates this effect of closure since it indicates that with the material presented here one period (or rather the literary treatment of it) is at an end, and another period is about to begin. The effect of closure is further heightened by the way in which the fourth and last occurrence of the refrain falls at the very end of the book.

The second element of the refrain draws attention to the way in which the material in these final chapters complements that in the main body of the book. The leading refrain of 3.7-16.31, 'the Israelites did what was evil in the eyes of Yahweh', finds its counterpart in the 'each man did what was right in his own eyes' of 17.6 and 21.25. The Samson episode provides the link between them:

> *Israel* does what is evil in Yahweh's eyes (chs. 13–16).
>
> *Samson* does what is right in his [own] eyes.
>
> *Every man* does what is right in his [own] eyes (chs. 17–21).

The shift in focus from the sin of Israel to the sins of the individuals and communities which comprise Israel is mediated through the figure of Samson who is both the man, Samson, and the symbol, Israel. The expression 'right in his own eyes' nicely reflects the comedy of correctness which emerges in these final chapters. The two narratives of chapters 17–21 complement those of the main body of the book and so complete the literary treatment of an era.

5.04 Excursus: The references to Judah and the alleged pro- and anti-monarchical tendencies of Judges
The references to Judah in 17.7, 8, 9; 18.12; 19.1, 2, 18; and 20.18 span the two narratives which comprise the conclusion to the book and are one of the unifying elements between them. Both the Levites in these stories have associations with Judah. The Levite of chs. 17–18 is not just a *resident* of Bethlehem-Judah (a fact which is repeatedly drawn to our attention) *but is himself a Judahite* (17.7).[43] He is portrayed as mercenary and as a willing accomplice in the cultic abuses committed by Micah and the Danites. In the second narrative the Levite's concubine is a Judahite and the text keeps this fact before the reader. This lends a certain appropriateness to the oracle concerning Judah in 20.18. But it does not appear that we are meant to see Judah as being accorded any particular honour here as it was in 1.1-2. The oracle in which Judah is nominated contains no promise of victory; the context is one of divine chastisement. Victory is eventually given, but not in a way which reflects any special credit on Judah (contrast 1.3-19). Judah is disciplined along with the rest of Israel; it is not idealized as it was in chapter 1.

Judges begins by presenting Judah in a favourable light, and ends by presenting it in an unfavourable light. It does not seem possible, however, to explain this difference simply in terms of the underlying traditional sources. The respective attitudes to Judah are expressed in the later redactional levels of the text more than in the traditional narrative sources. In particular the contrast between 1.1-2 and 20.18 appears to belong to the literary shaping of the finished form of the work. Furthermore, the change in the characterization of Judah is progressive and not haphazard:

1.1-2	Judah first—victory promised.
1.3-19	Judah embodies ideal of conquering Israel.
3.7-11	Othniel of Judah is ideal warrior-judge.
10.9	Judah, with other tribes, vainly resists Ammonite incursions.

15.9-20	Judah has no more will to fight, and is blind to the divine purpose.
17-18	The Judahite Levite is a willing accomplice in the cultic abuses of the period.
19-20	[The Judahite concubine is ravished] Judah first—but no victory. Judah, along with the rest of Israel, is disciplined by Yahweh.

The way in which Judah is portrayed in the book has implications for the ongoing discussion as to the attitude or attitudes to the monarchy to be found in Judges. It has generally been agreed that inasmuch as the monarchy is approved, it is the Davidic-Judahite monarchy which is in view.[44] It is noteworthy in this connection that Judah is represented favourably in that section of the book (chs. 1-12) which Buber regarded as anti-monarchical, and negatively in chapters 17-21, which he regarded as pro-monarchical.[45] There is no correlation between the protrayal of Judah and the alleged pro-monarchical and anti-monarchical tendencies of the book. In view of this it does not seem possible to argue, as Cundall has done, that the references to Judah which span all the major sections of the work are evidence that a first edition of the work, from the period of David and Solomon, was in effect an apology for the monarchy.[46] Further, the way Judah is handled in the finished form of the book does not seem to indicate that either chapters 17-21 or the work as a whole is simply pro-monarchical or anti-monarchical, and discussions of theme have, in my judgment, been dominated too much by this issue.

5.05

The reference to 'the captivity of the land' in 18.30 is a significant clue to the vantage point from which the narrator views the judges era.[47] So, too, is his insistence in the Samson episode that it is Yahweh, not Dagon who gives his servant Samson into the land of the Philistines, to be taken, blinded and taken down to humiliating servitude in Gaza.[48] So also, is his presentation of Judah in these closing chapters as 'fallen', and under divine discipline along with the rest of Israel (see the excursus in Section 5.04 above). The narrator speaks as one who has seen kingship come and go,[49] as judgeship had come and gone, and recognizes that both, in their time, had a role to play in Yahweh's administration of Israel. The refrain of 17.6, 18.1, 19.1 and 21.25 intimates that kingship will be the subject-matter of a sequel to the present work, and that the positive contribution of kingship will be to bring a measure of order and stability to Israel's internal affairs.[50] But the clear message of the two narratives brought together in these chapters is that no institution can make Israel proof against divine chastisement, and paradoxically, that it is that very chastisement which preserves Israel, not its institutions.

Shiloh will feature in the early career of Samuel, as will Gibeah and the tribe of Benjamin in the career of Saul. Plainly these chapters do not *simply* complete the book of Judges as a literary unit; they also set the scene for what is to follow.[51] But their received position at the end of Judges does, I believe, accurately reflect their primary literary function. They are integrated imtimately with the motifs and themes of the book as a whole. Compositionally they balance the two-part introduction and with it form a literary frame around the connected series of episodes which constitute the central narrative complex. They complete the literary treatment of an era.

PART III

Chapter 6

CONCLUSIONS

6.00

The dominance of Martin Noth's analysis of Deuteronomy–2 Kings in terms of an original Deuteronomic work in which the judges period began with Judg. 2.6sqq. and ended with Samuel's speech in 1 Sam. 12 has strongly disposed subsequent scholarship against giving serious consideration to Judges as a literary unit in its own right. Indeed it is possibly only the market demand for commentaries on the traditional books which has kept alive any scholarly interest at all in the *book* of Judges as such. Also, the ongoing intense scholarly interest in the style and theology of the deuteronomist(s) has disposed most scholars to distinguish sharply between deuteronomic and non-deuteronomic material in Judges, and has militated strongly against an integrated reading of the text. Nevertheless, a serious case has been made by Robert Boling for the redactional unity of the book in its finished form, and certain exploratory synchronic studies have suggested that an integrated reading of the text is possible, and that the book possesses a deeper coherence than has been recognized by most historical-critical scholars. It has seemed worthwhile to me, therefore, to reopen the question of what the book is about (in a thematic sense) by attempting a fresh analysis of it in terms of its 'narrativity'.[1] The time has now come for me to try to make explicit some of the major findings of this analysis.

6.01

The notional starting point of this thesis was a conviction that the book of Judges in its finished form is far more coherent and meaningful than had hitherto been recognized. The grounds for this initial conviction were presented in Part I (Chapters 1 and 2) together with an explanation of the methodological principles which were to inform the subsequent analysis of the book. In Chapter 1 I sought to justify the proposed analysis in principle; in Chapter 2 I tested its feasibility by a literary analysis of the Jephthah story in its finished form. In Part II (Chapters 3-5) I undertook a literary analysis of the entire book in its finished form. The analysis was guided throughout by two basic questions: How precisely is the text structured? and, what does it mean as a complex whole? Basic to the methodology was the assumption that these two questions are inextricably related to one another, although it was with the latter, not the former, that the analysis was ultimately concerned. Chapter 3 dealt with the material which precedes the appearance of the first judge, namely 1.1-3.6; Chapter 4 dealt with the series of episodes concerning the careers of the judges which forms the body of the book, namely 3.7-16.31; Chapter 5 dealt with the final section of the book, namely 17.1-21.25. The conclusions were summarized in Part III (Chapter 6), together with some brief comments on the wider implications of the present study.

The principal findings were (a) that the fundamental issue which the book as a whole addresses is the non-fulfilment of Yahweh's oath sworn to the patriarchs (to give Israel the whole land); (b) that themes related to this fundamental issue—especially Israel's persistent apostasy, and the freedom of Yahweh's action over against Israel's presumption that it can use him—are progressivly developed in the body of the book and receive their climactic treatment in the Samson episode; and (c) that the final chapters resonate with these themes, and, by picking up elements from the introduction, form the work out into a rounded literary unit.

6.02

a. Considerable evidence has been adduced of that 'deeper coherence' to which I referred in the first paragraph of this chapter. This is summarized in some detail in the conclusions to chs. 2-5 and I will not repeat it here. One example, however, may be useful in helping to make clear what I see to be the implications of this coherence for a proper understanding of the book in its finished form. I refer to the way in which the repentance of Israel vis-à-vis Yahweh in the deuteronomic introduction to the Jephthah story (10.6-16) was found to be closely paralleled by the repentance of the Gileadites vis-à-vis Jephthah in 10.17-11.11 which immediately follows. This parallel was found to be an integral part of the thematic structure of the story in its finished form.[2] The implication of this kind of coherence is that the theme of the book cannot be read off from the redactional framework material alone. An integrated reading of the text is necessary if an adequate statement of theme is to be achieved.

b. Such an integrated reading throws into relief the fully personal dimension of the two leading characters in the narrative, God and Israel, and shows how far the book in its finished form is from evincing a simplistic moralism or a mechanical theory of history. Israel is chosen by God but too weak to live up to its calling. This conflict between choice and weakness creates the dramatic tension of the unfolding narrative. Yahweh is angry at Israel's apostasy but cares too much for it to let it disintegrate or be destroyed.[3] The motif of calling upon Yahweh is handled in such a way as to preclude any simple connection between repentance and deliverance. In the face of Israel's persistent apostasy Yahweh does not so much dispense rewards and punishments as oscillate between punishment and mercy. The major judges from Barak to Samson are all set within contrasting perspectives which do not allow us the luxury of simple moral judgments. There is a constant playing-off of the 'knowable' aspects of the divine providence against the contrariness-to-expectation, freedom, and 'unknowability' of Yahweh's actions. My reading of Judges puts me in broad sympathy with the rather striking comment made recently by R. Polzin on the basis of his 'literary interpretation' of Deuteronomy–Judges:

> Contrary . . . to widespread scholarly attitudes about the overly mechanistic attitude of the Deuteronomic History with respect to the retributive aspects of Israelite religion, our compositional analysis has revealed strong evidence of a predominant point of view that critically rejects such a simplistic explanation of Israel's self-understanding vis-à-vis The Lord. The Deuteronomist is, for example, much more obviously united with the basic viewpoint of the Book of Job than scholars, including myself, have heretofore allowed.[4]

I find myself totally out of sympathy with Alter's recent reference to Judges as

> that long catalogue of military uprisings . . . where no serious claims could be made for complexity of characterization or for subtlety of thematic development.[5]

To be fair to Alter, he is making a concession; his point is that *even here* (in Judges), *some* evidence of the kind of complexity and subtlety he has in mind can be found. (The example he gives is the Ehud story pruned of its editorial framework.) My own work indicates that the concession is unnecessary.

6.03
Finally I wish to move beyond what could properly be called conclusions to comment briefly on one or two directions in which my work on Judges seems to be pointing.

The first concerns the structure of the Deuteronomic History in its finished form. This arises from my conclusion that the book of Judges is a literary unit. If the judges era ends where the book of Judges ends, where does the period of the monarchy begin? The closing refrain of Judges indicates that the emergence of the monarchy is the next major item on the narrative agenda, and clearly this figures very centrally in 1 Samuel, which begins with the birth of Samuel and ends with the death of Saul. The second book of Samuel opens with a formula which marks Saul's death as a major landmark in the unfolding narrative: 'Now after the death of Saul . . .'; compare Judg. 1.1, 'Now after the death of Joshua . . .', and Josh. 1.1, 'Now after the death of Moses . . .' The recapitulation of the death of Saul in 2 Sam. 1 after the report in 1 Sam. 31 further underlines its boundary function as the end of one era and the beginning of another. (Compare the recapitulation of Joshua's death at the beginning of Judges [2.6-10] after the report given at the end of Joshua [24.29-31].) In short, it seems to me that one could argue very plausibly that 1 Samuel is a distinct literary unit dealing with the transitional period between the era of the judges and the period of the monarchy. Samuel and Saul are both transitional figures; the monarchy period does not properly begin until Saul is dead and the king of *Yahweh's* choice is established on the throne (see Deut. 17.15). The monarchy period then follows a course similar to that of the judges: first an ideal king (compare David with Othniel the Judahite judge), then a series of variations until finally Yahweh is 'forced' to take the hard decision to *evict* Israel from the land. (Compare his decision at the end of the Judges era not to *give* them the whole land originally promised.)[6]

A second direction in which the present study points is towards a clearer recognition of the marked differences of procedure and perspective which are evident among the various literary units (some at least of which correspond to the canonical books) which comprise the Deuteronomic History in its finished form. The black-and-white moralism which I have *not* found in Judges, *does* seem to be conspicuously present in the books of Kings with their 'good' and 'bad' sovereigns.[7] And the tendency towards a mechanistic historiography which is the natural concomitant of such moralism is accordingly much more evident in the books of Kings than in Judges, but hardly discernible at all in the books of Samuel with their complex portraits of Samuel, Saul, and David. These and other marked differences are perhaps better accounted for in terms of an edited series of books than in terms of a series of more-or-less arbitrary units concealing an originally unified work.[8] And it is perhaps also worth noting here that when Noth published his *Überlieferungsgeschichtliche Studien* in 1943 the scholarly discussion of the alleged distinctive (treaty) form of the book of Deuteronomy itself had not yet begun.[9]

One of the stimuli to my own work was the recognition by Boling and Auld, who worked within the broad parameters of Noth's thesis, that Judges had some of the marks of a rounded literary unit. One of the implications of my work is that it may be time to re-open the question of how the Deuteronomic History as we have it came into existence.

NOTES

Notes to Chapter 1. Rationale

1. A slip for κριτῶν? See Philo, *On the Confusion of Tongues* (*De Confusione Linguarum*) (Loeb Classical Library. Philo, Vol. iv; tr. F.H. Colson and G.H. Whitaker; London: Heinemann, 1932), p. 80 n. 1.

2. Philo, *Confusion of Tongues*, XXVI, pp. 128-20. I have departed from the Loeb translation only in respect of παρελθοῦσα (passes by—Loeb has 'comes to the aid') and ἐν τῇ τῶν κριμάτων ἀναγραφομένῃ βίβλι (in the recorded book of judgments—Loeb has 'in the book of Judges').

3. Philo, *Confusion of Tongues*, XXVIII, p. 149. Translation as in the Loeb edition.

4. I have not attempted an exhaustive study of Philo's citation styles. In *Confusion of Tongues*, however, the introductory quotation from Gen. 11.1-9 is introduced simply by λέγει, 'he [Moses] says'. The treatise contains a further 52 quotations or allusions to Pentateuchal material, only 6 of which are accompanied by an explicit indication of the source; in each case this consists simply of naming 'Moses' or 'the lawgiver' (νομοθέτης) as the source (VII, 23; IX, 24; XII, 50; XII, 57; XXVII, 141; XXVII, 145). In addition two quotations are located 'in the Psalms' (ἐν ὕμνοις—XI, 39; XII, 52), one, from Jer. 15.10, is attributed to 'a chorister of the prophetic company possessed by divine inspiration' (XII, 44), and one, from Zech 6.2, is introduced as 'an oracle [λόγιον] from . . . one of the disciples of Moses' (XIV, 62). No source is indicated for a quotation from Josh. 1.5 (XXXII, 166). The only other scriptural references are the two using βίβλος and quoted above. Philo does not use βίβλος (or βίβλιον) in this way elsewhere in his works, although he did write separate commentaries on Genesis and Exodus (*Questions and Answers on Genesis*, and *Questions and Answers on Exodus*). Nor does he refer elsewhere to the book of Judges or its contents.

5. With the possible exception of a few Hebrew fragments, so far unpublished, which were discovered at Qumran and may be earlier. 4QJdg^a contains part of 6.3-13 and 4QJdg^b preserves the whole of 21.12-25 and a fragment of 16.5-7. The letter from F.M. Cross (who is in charge of their publication) quoted by Robert G. Boling in *Judges: introduction, translation and commentary* (The Anchor Bible; New York: Doubleday, 1975), p. 40, is not very informative.

6. In his *Syntagma*, cited in H.B. Swete, *An Introduction to the Old Testament in Greek* (Cambridge: Cambridge University Press, 1902), p. 191. The two texts are in parallel columns (1) 'ex codice Romano', and (2) 'ex codice Alexandrino'.

7. P.A. de Lagarde. *Septuaginta-Studien, Teil I* (Göttingen: 1891), pp. 14-71 (Judg. 1-5 only).

8. S. Jellicoe. *The Septuagint and Modern Study* (Oxford: Clarendon Press, 1968), pp. 280-83.

9. See, most recently, W.R. Bodine, *The Greek Text of Judges: Rescensional Developments* (Harvard Semitic Monographs, 23; Chico, California: Scholars Press, 1980). Bodine concludes (p. 186) that 'the latter (the B text) constitutes a part of the revision of a form of the Old Greek toward the developing Hebrew text carried out near the turn of the era and known as the καιγε recension, while the former (the A text) represents a later form of text which is influenced primarily by Origen's fifth column'.

10. H.B. Swete, *Introduction*, pp. 201-202.

11. A. καὶ εἶπεν τοῖς ἀνδράσιν Φανουὴλ λέγων ᾿Εν τῷ ἐπιστέφειν με μετ᾿ εἰρήνης κατασκάψω τὸν πύργον τοῦτον.

B. καὶ εἶπεν Γεδεὼν πρὸς ἄνδρας Φανουὴλ ᾿Εν ἐπιστροφῇ μου μετ᾿ εἰρήνης τὸν πύργον τοῦτον κατασκάψω.

Philo ὤμοσε... Γεδεὼν τοῖς ἀνδράσι Φανουὴλ λέγων. ἐν τῷ με ἐπιστρέφειν μετ᾿ εἰρήνης τὸν πύργον τοῦτον κατασκάψω.

12. *Jewish Antiquities* xx.xxi.1.261.

13. *Against Apion* I.8.38-40.

14. *Jewish Antiquities* v.ii.1−v.viii.12. He first surveys the material in 1.1-2.5, then moves directly to the outrage at Gibeah and the resulting civil war in chs. 19-21. He gives a brief account of the northward migration of Dan (chs. 17-18) omitting the parts of this narrative involving Micah's image. He then returns to 3.7 (ignoring 2.6-3.6) and moves systematically through the stories of the individual judges, omitting Tola (10.1-2), and climaxing his account of the age with the Samson story.

15. *Jewish Antiquities* VI.v. 4.84-85. Translation from the Loeb edition except for opening words, for which Loeb has 'After Joshua's death'.

16. *Jewish Antiquities* V.ix.1.318.

17. Judg. 16.12 in *Berakoth* 9.5; Judg. 13.5 in *Nazir* 9.5; Judg. 16.21 in *Sotah* 1.8. See index to H. Danby, *The Mishnah, translated from the Hebrew with introduction and brief explanatory notes* (Oxford: Oxford University Press, 1933).

18. See index to I. Epstein ed. *The Babylonian Talmud;... transl. into English with notes, glossary and indices* (18 vols; London: Soncino, 1935-52).

19. *'Abodah Zarah* is quoted from the 1935-52 edition (see note 18 above); *Baba Bathra* from I. Epstein, ed., *Hebrew-English edition of the Babylonian Talmud* (13 vols.; London: Soncino, 1963-76); and *Soferim* from A. Cohen, ed., *The Minor Tractates of the Talmud... transl. into English with notes, glossary and indices* (2 vols.; London: Soncino, 1965).

20. See Moshe Greenberg's similar comments in relation to Exodus in his introduction to *Understanding Exodus* (Vol. II, part I of the Melton Research

Centre Series, The Heritage of Biblical Israel; New York: Behrman House Inc., 1969), p. 2.

21. *Schriften der Königsberger Gelehrten-Gesellschaft. Geisteswissenschaftliche Klasse, 18*, pp. 43-266, quoted below from *The Deuteronomistic History* (JSOT Supplement Series, 15; Sheffield: JSOT Press, 1981) being a translation of the better known 2nd edition, *Überlieferungsgeschichtliche Studien* (Tübingen: Max Niemeyer Verlag, 1957), pp. 1-110.

22. *The Deuteronomistic History*, p. 8.

23. *The Deuteronomistic History*, p. 52.

24. *The Deuteronomistic History*, p. 121 n. 29.

25. 'The Background of Judges 17-18', *Israel's Prophetic Heritage: essays in honour of James Muilenburg* (eds. B.W. Anderson and W. Harrelson; London: SCM, 1962), pp. 68-85.

26. 'The Background of Judges 17-18', p. 82 n. 35. Noth sees the narrative as a product of the northern royal court designed to contrast the dubious origins of the shrine of Dan with the positive reform measures taken by Jeroboam I to purify the shrine later in order to make it one of the two great national sanctuaries of the North.

27. 'The Background of Judges 17-18', p. 79.

28. (Bonner Biblische Beiträge, 21; Bonn: Peter Hanstein).

29. *Das Königtum in der Beurteilung der deuteronomistischen Historiographie: eine redaktionsgeschichtliche Untersuchung* (Annales Academiae Scientiarum Fennicae, Ser. B, Tom. 198; Helsinki: Suomalainen Tiedeakatemia, 1977).

30. *Das Königtum*, pp. 27-29.

31. In particular from his *Prophetie und Geschichte: eine redaktionsgeschichtliche Untersuchung zum deuteronomistischen Geschichtswerk* (FRLANT, 108; Göttingen: Vandenhoeck und Ruprecht, 1977).

32. *Probleme biblischer Theologie: Gerhard von Rad zum 70. Geburtstag* (ed. H.W. Wolff; München: Chr. Kaiser Verlag), pp. 494-509.

33. *Das Gesetz und die Völker*, p. 506. For Smend Judg. 2.10 was the direct continuation of Josh. 24.31 in the original Deuteronomic History, Josh. 24 (to v. 31) being an original part of that work and Josh. 23 a later insertion by DtrN. Contrast Noth in 4.01 above.

34. Repeating Josh. 24.28-31 (with appropriate alterations) in Judg. 2.6-9 in order to preserve, in essence, the original connection between Josh. 24.28-31 and Judg. 2.10ff. (see note 33 above). *Das Gesetz und die Völker*, pp. 506-507.

35. *Das Gesetz und die Völker*, pp. 508-509. Smend attributes to this reviser the introduction into the original Deuteronomic History of the concept of 'the remaining nations'. The success of Joshua and his generation against the nations of Canaan was due to their strict adherence to 'the book of the law [of Moses]' (Josh. 1.8; cf. 23.6). However at Joshua's death there still remained some 'nations' (גוים) (Josh. 23.4) and land (Josh. 13.2ff.) to be

216   The Book of the Judges

conquered and success in doing this depended on continued obedience to the law (Josh. 23.6ff.). Israel failed to exhibit such obedience (Judg. 1.1–2.5) and so the 'remaining nations' were left permanently in Canaan as a punishment (Judg. 2.20-21).

36. With reference to Josh. 23 see note 33 above.

37. *Das Gesetz und die Völker*, p. 509.

38. *Prophetie und Geschichte*. See n. 31 above.

39. Whereas Smend had worked with Joshua–Judges Dietrich focused exclusively on Kings. Using methods similar to those of Smend, he argued that DtrG had contained very few prophetic traditions and that most had been inserted by DtrP, either by utilizing older traditions or by composing his own material. The promise and fulfilment schema in Kings, emphasized by von Rad, was taken to be the contribution of DtrP. Thus for Dietrich the two later redactions by DtrP and DtrN were no minor ones but included rather major additions, both of older traditions and of new compositions. By comparing the language and style of these three redactions with other Israelite literature Dietrich concluded the DtrG had written around 580 BC, DtrP about ten years later, and DtrN another ten years later.

40. The surprisingly rapid acceptance of Dietrich's analysis has been documented in a recent dissertation by Gerald E. Gerbrandt: 'Kingship According to the Deuteronomistic History' (Union Theological Seminary in Virginia, ThD, 1980). Gerbrandt cites, in addition to Timo Veijola (see below) Tryggve Mettinger, Ernst Würthwein, Helmut Hollenstein, Otto Kaiser, and Wolfgang Roth as being in fundamental agreement with Dietrich's proposals. To quote Gerbrandt, Würthwein and Hollenstein in particular 'suggest that this is the direction Deuteronomistic studies will take, and Kaiser's introduction points in a similar direction' (p. 17).

41. *Die ewige Dynastie. David und die Entstehung seiner Dynastie nach der deuteronomistischen Darstellung* (Annales Academiae Scientiarum Fennicae, Ser. B, Tom 193; Helsinki: Suomalainen Tiedeakatemia).

42. Each cluster of passages is related to a lead text: 1 Kgs 1-2 (ch. 2), 1 Sam. 25 (ch. 3), 1 Sam. 20.12-17, 42b (ch. 4) and 2 Sam. 21-24 (ch. 5).

43. In the concluding chapter 6, 'Synthese und Konsequenzen', the views of the redactors are described. I quote here from the synopsis in *Old Testament Abstracts* 1.2 (1978) p. 199: 'DtrG idealizes David and his dynasty. He sees in the king both the *nāgîd* and the servant of the LORD. The monarch is exemplary in piety and justice, and his house is the legitimate and enduring dynasty. DtrP presents the king as sinful yet ready to repent. The ruler is never titled 'the servant of the LORD' while prophets are so designated. A future for the royal house is not envisaged. Finally, DtrN allows both place and future to David's house in as far as its members are obedient to the law. Thus history, prophecy, and law, three important constituents of the religion of ancient Israel, have together shaped the Deuteronomistic David tradition and created a manifaceted image.'

44. See n. 29 above.

45. The texts examined are: Judg. 17-21 (ch. 2); 1 Sam. 7.2-17 (ch. 3); 1 Sam. 10.17-11.15 (ch. 4); 1 Sam. 8 (ch. 5); 1 Sam. 9.1-10.16 (ch. 6); 1 Sam. 12 (ch. 7); Judg. 8.22-23 and 9.7-21 (ch. 8).

46. In fact only the work of DtrG and DtrN is found in the texts studied. The views of these two Deuteronomists as found in these texts are characterized by Veijola as follows (I quote here from the synopsis in *Old Testament Abstracts* 1.2 [1978] p. 200): 'The basic Deuteronomist uses traditions which in outlook are similar to his own and describes the rise and role of kingship in keeping with Deut. 17.14-20. In as far as kings came to rule according to that law they are divinely called and legitimated (as 'the Judges' had been before them) . . . The nomistic Deuteronomist, on the other hand, condemns kingship as the result of the people's disobedience and as the rejection of the LORD's kingship, the positive estimate of David notwithstanding.'

47. ' . . . der Richter ein *Retter* ist, der das Volk von äusseren Feinden befreit. Es ist nach DtrG nicht seine Aufgabe, gegen kultische oder andere Delikte *innerhalb* des Gottesvolkes einzuschreiten' (p. 29). Cf. the detailed analysis of the 'promonarchial notices' on pp. 15-17.

48. 'Damit lässt er gleichzeitig erkennen, dass er die kultischen Angelegenheiten dem Verfügungsbereich des Königs unterordnet, vollends in Übereinstimmung mit der Konzeption, die in der späteren Geschichtsdeutung des DtrG eine wesentliche Rolle spielt' (p. 27).

49. Veijola refers (p. 16 n. 5) to a seminar presentation in which Smend held that in Deut. 12, vv. 13-28 (in the singular) were original, while vv. 1-12 (in the plural) consisted of two later additions, by DtrG (vv. 8-12) and DtrN (vv. 1-7) respectively.

50. Pp. 17-27.

51. Pp. 18-19.

52. Pp. 21-22.

53. Pp. 28-29.

54. J. Alberto Soggin, *Judges: a commentary* (Old Testament Library; Philadelphia: Westminster, 1981).

55. See 'In Those Days There Was No King in Israel', *A Light Unto My Path: Old Testament Studies in Honour of Jacob M. Myers* (eds. H.M. Bream, R.D. Heim, and C.A. Moore; Philadelphia: Temple University Press, 1974), pp. 33-48; *Judges*, pp. 29-30; and 'Response', *JSOT* 1 (1976), pp. 47-52.

56. *Judges*, p. 36.

57. Boling spells out the extent of his indebtedness to Richter in 'In Those Days', p. 34. Cf. *Judges*, p. 36.

58. F.M. Cross, Jr, 'The Structure of the Deuteronomic History', *Perspectives in Jewish Learning* 3 (1968), pp. 9-24. Cf. Boling, 'In Those Days', p. 34 and *Judges*, pp. 30-31, 35.

59. With both the A and B texts of the LXX. Cf. Boling, *Judges*, p. 62, and

'The Oak of Weeping' near Bethel in Gen. 35.8.

60. *Judges*, pp. 184-85.

61. *Judges*, p. 31.

62. *Judges*, p. 64, and cf. p. 36: 'To the exilic (Deuteronomistic) redactor is left the addition of the bulk of ch. 1 (in itself a configuration of some of the oldest material in the book)'.

63. A.G. Auld, 'Judges 1 and History: a Reconsideration', *VT* 25 (1975), pp. 261-85.

64. 'Judges 1 and History', p. 265.

65. 'Judges 1 and History', p. 285.

66. *Judges*, p. 35: 'The disaster of 721 only heightened one of Deuteronomy's enduring concerns—to find provision for jobless rural Levites at the central Yahweh sanctuary (Deut. 18.1-8). Provision for the Levites presents, in fact, the most notable discrepancy between the Deuteronomic platform of the reform and its implementation as reported in Kings and Chronicles. That discrepancy became a source of controversy that now provides an important key to the redactional history of the Book of Judges; compare the contrasting characterizations of the two Levites in chs. 17 and 19.'

67. *Judges*, p. 36.

68. But he does have the support of Noth for his view that chs. 19-21 as a unit are secondary to chs. 17-18. See the end of section 4.01 above.

69. For Veijola, following Dietrich, the basic Deuteronomic History was itself exilic. See n. 39 above.

70. *Judges*, p. 278.

71. 'Response', p. 49.

72. H.-W. Jüngling, *Richter 19—Ein Plädoyer für das Königtum: Stilistische Analyse der Tendenzerzählung Ri 19,1—30a; 21,25* (Analecta Biblica 84; Rome: Biblical Institute Press, 1981). Jüngling finds the setting for the final redaction of the whole unit, 19-21, to be the exilic or post-exilic period in which it served to instruct the community (on the basis of ancient precedent) how a sinning brother is to be disciplined (excommunicated and restored) in a context where 'there is no king in Israel'. See esp. pp. 244-46.

73. *Judges*, pp. 37-38.

74. A.G. Auld, 'Review of Boling's *Judges*. The Framework of Judges and the Deuteronomists', *JSOT* 1 (1976), pp. 41-46, esp. p. 41.

75. 'One cannot but agree with Boling, even if in a different spirit, that the repetition of the oracular device and the primacy of Judah in 1.1-2 and 20.18 "is something quite out of the ordinary"' ('Review of Boling's *Judges*', p. 45). Compare his analysis of the literary interdependence of these two passages in 'Judges 1 and History', pp. 267-68.

76. 'Review of Boling's *Judges*', p. 45.

77. See Richard D. Nelson, *The Double Redaction of the Deuteronomistic History* (JSOT Supp. 18; Sheffield: JSOT Press, 1981).

78. Jo Cheryl Exum, 'Literary Patterns in the Samson Saga: an Investigation

of Rhetorical Style in Biblical Prose' (PhD Dissertation; Columbia University, 1976).

79. D.F. Murray, 'Narrative Structure and Technique in the Deborah-Barak Story, Judges iv 4–22', *Supplements to Vetus Testamentum* 30 (1979), pp. 155-89.

80. 'A Literary Appreciation of the Book of Judges', *Tyndale Bulletin* 18 (1967), pp. 94-102 (95).

81. 'A Literary Appreciation of the Book of Judges', pp. 94, 96.

82. 'A Literary Appreciation of the Book of Judges', p. 95. A similar assumption of 'authorship' underlay Noth's original analysis of Deut.-2 Kings: 'Dtr. was not merely an editor but the author of a history which brought together material from highly varied traditions and arranged it according to a carefully conceived plan' (*The Deuteronomistic History*, p. 10). This statement occurs in the preliminaries to Noth's study.

83. 'A Literary Appreciation of the Book of Judges', p. 95.

84. 'A Literary Appreciation of the Book of Judges', p. 97.

85. Kenneth R.R. Gros Louis, 'The Book of Judges', *Literary Interpretations of Biblical Narratives* (eds. K.R.R. Gros Louis, J.S. Ackerman, T.S. Warshaw; Nashville: Abingdon, 1974), pp. 141-62.

86. The author compares Judges with the *Odyssey*, which also uses traditional stories in an epic framework. He argues that questions which are always implicit in the study of the *Odyssey*—Why these heroes? Why these particular stories? Why in this particular order?—are equally applicable to Judges (p. 142).

87. Gros Louis either overlooks or ignores vv. 5-7, another mini-narrative embedded in the chapter.

88. *Moses and the Deuteronomist. A Literary Study of the Deuteronomic History, Part One: Deuteronomy, Joshua, Judges* (New York: Seabury Press).

89. In a footnote (p. 214 n. 6) Polzin states that his work in the present volume 'owes much' to the work of a number of Russian scholars belonging to the 'formalist' and 'sociological' schools (Voloshinov, Bakhtin, Uspensky) and that he has 'benefited greatly' from the rhetorical insights of Wayne Booth and the frame-analysis insights of Erving Goffman.

90. A full explanation of the jargon and methodology of 'compositional analysis' can be found in Boris Uspensky, *A Poetics of Composition: the Structure of the Artistic Text and Typology of a Compositional Form* (tr. V. Zavarin and S. Wittig; Berkeley: University of California Press, 1973).

91. See the first quotation in n. 93 below.

92. Polzin sees a similar 'recapitulation' at the beginning of Joshua: 'Largely by means of a number of literal or paraphrasing repetitions of utterances from Deuteronomy, Joshua 1 recapitulated the central position of the Book of Deuteronomy and applied it to the period following the death of *that* book's main hero, Moses' (p. 147, my emphasis). Cf. Judg. 1.1a with Josh. 1.1a.

93. E.g. p. 200: 'If the book's first chapter began with an effective psychological portrait of the process whereby Israel, after Joshua's death, progressively went from certainty to confusion . . . the book's finale [chs. 19–21] now completes with a flourish the paradoxical picture of confusion within certainty, obscurity in clarity, that has occupied its pages from the start'; or p. 202, ' . . . here [chs. 19–21] the narrator is intent upon intensifying the doubt and confusion in Israel with which he began his story in Judges 1'.

94. D.W. Gooding, 'The Composition of the Book of Judges', *Eretz-Israel, Archeological, Historical and Geographical Studies, Vol. 16; H.M. Orlinsky Volume* (Jerusalem: Israel Exploration Society, 1982), pp. 70-79.

95. Gooding ignores areas of agreement, as well as the ways in which later critics refined the analyses of scholars whose work preceded their own. Contrast my own treatment of the relevant redaction-critical studies in sections 4.01–4.06 above.

96. See p. 79 n. 23 for the author's justification of this procedure.

97. Polzin's study is perhaps the most systematic in terms of method, but only one chapter (58 pages) is devoted to Judges. The 'minor judges' are ignored.

98. As in empiricist historiography, in which history consists of just 'one damned thing after another' (F. Jameson, 'Marxism and Historicism', *New Literary History* XI.I (1979), p. 51).

99. J. Muilenburg, 'Form Criticism and Beyond', *JBL* 88 (1969), p. 7.

100. Vladimir Propp, *Morphology of the Folktale* (2nd edition, revised and edited with a preface by L.A. Wagner, and a new introduction by A. Dundes; Austin and London: University of Texas Press, 1968). The original Russian edition was published in 1928; *The Historical Roots of the Fairy Tale*, by the same author, was first published eighteen years later in 1946. In his introduction to the *Morphology* Propp states, 'We shall insist that as long as no correct morphological study exists, there can be no correct historical study'.

101. *Morphology*, p. 89.

102. Claude Lévi-Strauss, 'The Structural Study of Myth', *Structural Anthropology* (Garden City, New York: Basic Books, 1963), pp. 202-31.

103. A.J. Greimas, *Sémantique structurale* (Paris: Larousse, 1966) and *Du Sens* (Paris: Sevil, 1970).

104. Ferdinand de Saussure, *Course in General Linguistics* (eds. C. Bally, A. Sechehaye; tr. W. Baskin; London: Peter Owen, 1960). First French edition, 1915.

105. E.g., in English, J.D. Crossan, *The Dark Interval: Towards a Theology of Story* (Niles, Illinois: Argus, 1975) and D. Patte, 'Structural Network in Narrative: The Good Samaritan', *Structuralism, An Interdisciplinary Study* (ed. S. Wittig; Pittsburgh Reprint, 3; Pittsburgh: Pickwick, 1975), pp. 77-98.

106. E.g. the three essays, on 1 Sam. 13-31, Numbers 11-12, and 1 Kings 17-18 respectively in D. Jobling, *The Sense of Biblical Narrative* (JSOT Supplement Series, 7; Sheffield: JSOT Press, 1978).

107. This remains true even in the work of Roland Barthes who does not, like most structuralists, *subordinate* surface structure to deep structure. See the comments on Barthes's distinctive style of structuralism and Barthes's own analysis of Gen. 32.23-33 in R. Barthes *et al.*, *Structural Analysis and Biblical Exegesis* (tr. A.M. Johnson Jr; Pittsburgh Theological Monograph Series, 3; Pittsburgh: Pickwick Press, 1974).

108. Such sensitivity is evident, for instance in W. Richter's *Traditions-geschichtliche Untersuchungen zum Richterbuch* (2nd edn; Bonner Biblische Beiträge, 18; Bonn: Peter Hanstein Verlag, 1966), and Boling's *Judges*, but conspicuously absent from C.A. Simpson's *Composition of the Book of Judges* (Oxford and New York, 1957).

109. Compare here the helpful, if brief, analysis of the relationship between 'theme' and authorial intention in D.J.A. Clines, 'Theme in Genesis 1-11', *CBQ* 38 (1976), pp. 484-87.

Notes to Chapter 2. Sounding

1. Jephthah has likewise been of central interest to scholars interested in either the sources of the book or the office of 'judge' or both. The major literature is reviewed in H.N. Rösel, 'Die "Richter Israels". Rückblick und neuer Ansatz', *Biblische Zeitschrift* 25 (1981), pp. 180-203.

2. Or, 'The Israelites again did . . .' Boling considers that only the former alternative is justifiable since 'only with the addition of the particle עוד does the verb [the hiphil of יסף] mean "to do again"' (*Judges*, p. 85). Cf. Polzin, *Moses and the Deuteronomist*, p. 177. Within Judges the hiphil of יסף is used with עוד in 9.37, 'Gaal again spoke . . .'; 11.14, 'Jephthah sent messengers again . . .'; and 20.28, 'Shall we go out again to battle . . .'; and without עוד at 2.21, 'I will not continue to drive out . . .' (cf. 10.13). But contrast 20.22, 'The Israelites . . . again formed the battle line . . .' (no עוד), and 20.23, 'Shall we again draw near for battle?' (no עוד). In 10.13 (no עוד) the similarity to 2.21 makes 'I will not continue to deliver you' more probable than 'I will not deliver you again', although it is not possible to be dogmatic. Similarly, against Boling and Polzin, dogmatism is not possible in 10.6 and parallels. Questions of distinctively 'deuteronomic' usage are not strictly relevant to the present study, but I note in passing that a similar inconsistency appears in the book of Deuteronomy (cf. Deut. 18.6 and 26.68, which use עוד, with Deut. 13.11 [12], which does not). No use of the hiphil of יסף comparable to that in Judg. 10.6 and parallels appears in the deuteronomic formulae of the books of Kings.

3. The geographical setting of the dialogue in 10.10-16 is unspecified. A

change of setting is indicated by the activity of the Israelites in 10.17b.

4. My demarcation of episodes corresponds to that proposed in Polzin, *Moses and the Deuteronomist*, pp. 177-81. An alternative stucture is proposed by Phyllis Trible in 'A Meditation in Mourning: The Sacrifice of the Daughter of Jephthah', *Union Seminary Quarterly Review* xxxi (1981), p. 69. For Trible the 'Introduction' to the story is 10.17–11.3. With most scholars she brackets out 10.6-16 as 'Theological Preface' and does not treat it as an integral part of the narrative.

5. For a note on the translation and a brief explanation of the principles I have followed in displaying the text see p. 9.

6. With Boling and Freedman; see Boling, *Judges*, pp. 191-92. That is, the eighteenth year of the Ammonite oppression. The syntax is anomalous, but it seems clear that 'in that year' בשנה ההיא refers to the year of the crisis detailed in 8b-9c while שמנה עשרה שנה for 'eighteenth year' is paralleled in the expressions for the thirteenth and fourteenth years in Gen. 14.4-5. The LXX [B] produces a smoother reading but obliterates the force of 'in that year' שנה by weakening it to 'at that time' καιρός.

7. In its OT usage the term 'to cry out' (זעק) does not of itself imply repentance as shown by W. Brueggemann in 'Social Criticism and Social Vision in the Deuteronomic Formula of the Judges', *Die Botschaft und die Boten: Festschrift für Hans Walter Wolff zum 70. Geburtstag* (eds. J. Jeremias and L. Perlitt; Neukirchen, 1981), pp. 108-109. It may refer to a formal complaint against or protest against injustice, in which case it is an appeal to a higher authority against an offender (e.g. Gen. 4.10, Isa. 5.7); it may be simply a cry of desperation, hoping for deliverance (e.g. Deut. 22.24); or it may be a general outcry against an unbearable situation in which it is not a plea addressed to anyone, but simply an undirected grieving (e.g. Isa. 14.31). For full references see Brueggemann. Cf. Richter, *Die Bearbeitungen*, pp. 18-20, who argues that the association of צעק/זעק with confession of sin is a late deuteronomistic development.

8. With the comments by Richter and Boling cited below cf. Soggin, *Judges*, p. 203 and J.D. Martin, *Judges* (Cambridge Bible; Cambridge: Cambridge University Press, 1975), p. 135.

9. Not merely 'in the way'. The Hebrew is בדרך. On the use of ב after קצר see further below.

10. *Moses and the Deuteronomist*, p. 177. Polzin does not himself draw the comparison with 16.16.

11. Literally, 'his [Yahweh's] soul'.

12. I use sq. and sqq. instead of f. and ff. to avoid confusion with f as used to denote a line within a verse.

13. The Niphal of זוק/צעק always denotes a summons to battle and implies a 'caller', that is, a leader. Within Judges see 6.34, 35; 7.23, 24; 12.1; 18.22, 23. Cf. Josh. 8.16; 1 Sam. 13.4; 14.20; 2 Kgs 3.21. The Niphal of אסף is less precise. It *may* be synonymous with זעק/צעק but is not necessarily so. Cf.

Judg. 6.33 with 2.10 and 16.23. The middle sense is frequent, as in Exod. 32.26; Josh. 10.5, Amos 3.9, etc.

14. There it was virtually synonymous with ישראל considered as a corporate personality. Cf. 10.6a with 10.7a.

15. העם שרי גלעד (the people, the captains of Gilead) in 18a is anomalous and has probably arisen through the combination of variants, in this case שרי עם גלעד (the captains of the people of Gilead) (LXX^A) and שרי גלעד (the captains of Gilead) which is still reflected in MT and LXX^B. With Boling (*Judges*, 197) I follow LXX^A. Thus the עם גלעד (people of Gilead) is the Gileadite militia—a sub-unit within the בני ישראל—and the שרים (captains) are their (military) leaders. Cf. Sisera who is general שר of Jabin's army in 4.2. Similar uses of שר occur at Gen. 21.22; 26.26; 1 Sam. 12.9; 1 Kgs 22.31, 32, 33. For other instances of עם as 'people bearing arms' see BDB and note particularly בעם (among the people) in Judg. 5.9 and עמו (his people) in Judg. 11.20.

16. Presumably in Gilead (cf. Gen. 31.49) rather than Benjamin (Josh. 18.26 and elsewhere).

17. 'Gilead' in 1c appears to be a substitute for his father's actual name, presumably unknown to the narrator.

18. Thus Jephthah already learns the power of words, 2d-f.

19. טוב, mentioned here and again in v. 5, also recalls the words of the Israelites to Yahweh in 10.15c: 'Do whatever is good (טוב) in your sight'. Is Yahweh already moving behind the scenes?

20. אנשים ריקים literally, 'empty men' (3c). Cf. 9.4 where the opprobrium 'reckless' is added. ריקים in itself does not specifically imply moral obliquity, but rather a lack of the qualities which command success in the leading of a regular life, and also, possibly (as suggested by the usage of the adverbial form ריקם, 'with empty hands') a lack of material goods such as property, and social status: C.F. Burney, *The Book of Judges with Introduction and Notes* (London: Rivingtons, 1918), p. 308. Cf. the description of the men who attached themselves to David in similar circumstances, 1 Sam. 22.2. Indeed, Jephthah's early career anticipates that of David in a number of respects: his flight, his life in exile, and the circumstances of his rise to power, first over a part of Israel, then over the whole.

21. Cf. 6.12 where the emphasis is on prowess in battle with Ruth 2.1 where it is on wealth and the social status which (normally) goes with it.

22. J. Gray, *Joshua, Judges and Ruth* (The Century Bible, New Edition; London: Nelson, 1967), p. 332.

23. This, rather than the more general meaning, 'ruler' (Isa. 1.10 etc.) is warranted by the context. See Josh. 10.24 where the 'leaders (קצינים)' are ranking officers within Joshua's military organization. Boling, *Judges*, p. 198.

24. Compare the account of Jephthah's expulsion in v. 2. Simpson (*Judges*, p. 46) finds the two accounts contradictory and assigns them to different

hands. Soggin (*Judges*, pp. 206-208) finds them 'clearly difficult to reconcile' and takes v. 7 as more reliable on the grounds that v. 2 is secondary, the ensuing narrative saying nothing about the restitution of Jephthah's family rights.

Neither Simpson nor Soggin takes sufficient account of the quite different narrative functions of the two accounts. The first (v. 2) is presented as the narrator's own dispassionate account of what happened. Its primary function is informational. The second 'account' is in fact an accusation in the form of a rhetorical question, delivered with obvious passion and with an eye to its effect on the elders. Its function is primarily rhetorical, and the narrator does not accept direct responsibility for its contents: it is what *Jephthah* said to the elders (7a).

In terms of narrative function, therefore, the narrator's version in v. 2 has, *prima facie*, a stronger claim to be taken at face value. The fact that there is no subsequent mention of the restitution of Jephthah's family rights is not surprising in view of his appointment as 'head of all the inhabitants of Gilead' (11b): the greater includes the lesser.

Even in absolute terms, the two versions are not necessarily contradictory: may not the elders have adjudicated in legal proceedings relating to inheritance? Cf. W. Richter, 'Die Überlieferungen um Jephtah, Ri 10,17–12,6', *Biblica* 47 (1966), p. 495: 'Man kann die Unebenheit psychologisch motivieren: Jephtah mache in der Hitze der Heidenschaft einen Vorwurf, der nicht die ganz richtigen Adressaten trifft.'

25.   Cf. the heads (ראשים) of the twelve tribes in Numbers 1.4-16 and 13.1-16; cf. also Deut. 1.13; 5.20 (23). H.N. Rösel, 'Jephtah und das Problem der Richter', *Biblica* 61 (1980), pp. 251-55, draws a distinction between קצין, 'military commander' and major judge, and ראש, 'civil governor' or the like. In the post-war era Jephthah reigns as 'Richter' not as 'Retter'. Cf. also Boling, *Judges*, pp. 195, 198.

26.   The captains appear to act without reference to the elders in 10.17-18 and vice-versa in 11.4-10. The same lack of co-ordination is reflected in v. 11. There seems to be no clear authority structure or agreed way of proceeding (except between Jephthah and the elders).

27.   The לכן of 8a in the MT is puzzling. Perhaps we should read לא כן, 'Not so', with LXX^A (so Boling, *Judges*, p. 198). But in that case what is denied (as indicated by the change of verbs) is that they have merely 'come' to Jephthah, expecting help without admission of guilt. 8b as a whole, in any case, involves a tacit admission that they have been wrong.

28.   שוב אל is, of course, one of the standard expressions for repentance in the Old Testament: 1 Kgs 8.35, 48; 2 Chron. 6.38; Neh. 1.9; Jer. 3.10; Hos. 7.10; Jer. 3.1; Hos. 5.4; 2 Chron. 30.6; Isa. 44.22; Hos. 14.3; Joel 2.13; Zech. 1.3; Mal. 3.7; etc. Less frequent are שוב עד: Deut. 4.30; 30.2; Amos 4.6, 8, 9, 10; Hos. 14.2; Jeol 2.12, and שוב על: 2 Chron. 30.9.

29.   Cf. the rise of Odysseus and his triumph over the suitors in the *Odyssey*.

30.   See note 38 below. A different rule was understood to apply to Israel's relationships with the 'seven nations' of Canaan (Deut. 7.1-5). Accordingly Joshua is not said to have opened up any dialogue with them.

31.   Compare Lot's economic appraisal of the Jordan Valley, from a different vantage point, in Gen. 13.10.

32.   G.F. Moore comments that the disputed territory as defined by Jephthah 'extends eastward to the desert (v. 22) leaving no place at all for Ammon': *A Critical and Exegetical Commentary on Judges* (2nd edn; International Critical Commentary; Edinburgh: Clark, 1908), p. 294.

33.   Cf. Num. 21.26; 1 Kgs 11.7, 13; 2 Kgs 23.13; Jer. 48.7, 13, 46 with 1 Kgs 11.5, 33; 2 Kgs 23.13; 1 Kgs 11.7.

34.   The reference to Chemosh in v. 24 and the prominence of Moab throughout are commonly explained diachronically in terms of an adaptation of material which originally referred to negotiations between Israel and *Moab*. Various forms of this basic thesis are to be found in, for example, the following: Moore, *Judges*, p. 283; O. Eissfeldt, *Die Quellen des Richterbuches* (Leipzig: J.C. Hinrichs, 1925), p. 76; Burney, *Judges*, pp. 298-305; M. Wüst, 'Die Einschaltungen in die Jiftachgeschichten, Ri 11.13-26', *Biblica* 56 (1975), pp. 464-79; Richter, 'Die Überlieferungen um Jephtah', pp. 522-47; and Soggin, *Judges*, pp. 211-13.

Against this prevailing view Boling (*Judges*, pp. 201-205) draws attention to the absence of the kind of reflective glossing that accompanies such redactional activity elsewhere in the book (e.g. 1.36), and the intelligibility of the whole in its present context. The only clearly secondary phrase is the total 'three hundred years' in v. 26. He defends 'Chemosh' in v. 24 on the grounds that it was the technically correct deity for Jephthah to invoke for diplomatic purposes, an attention to detail in keeping with the technical character of the argument as a whole. Compare the claims that Cyrus of Persia makes for the benefactions to him of Marduk, chief deity of Babylon. Boling recognizes that Ammonite sovereignty over Moab is assumed.

35.   As recognized by Boling; see n. 34 above.

36.   Contrast Adonibezek (king of Jerusalem?) 1.5-7; Cushanrishathaim, king of Aram-naharaim (3.8); Eglon, king of Moab (3.12) and Jabin, king of Canaan (4.2).

37.   The argument being advanced here does not depend upon the priority of the Numbers account. The point being made is simply that Jephthah speaks as the custodian of an *Israelite* tradition which is attested elsewhere in the Old Testament and therefore known to the reader of the story. On the priority of the Numbers account vis-à-vis that of Judges 11 see the debate between Van Seters (who denies it) and Bartlett (who defends it): J. Van Seters, 'The Conquest of Sihon's Kingdom: A Literary Examination', *JBL* 91 (1972), pp. 182-97; J.R. Bartlett, 'The Conquest of Sihon's Kingdom: A Literary Re-examination', *JBL* 97 (1978), pp. 347-51; Van Seters, 'Once Again—The Conquest of Sihon's Kingdom', *JBL* 99 (1980), pp. 117-19. In

terms of style the account in Judges 11 is more tightly written, more technically oriented, and less antiquarian and moralistic in tone than its Numbers counterpart.

38. Jephthah speaks only of 'Israel' sending messengers since the term Israel has already been used by his opponent while the name 'Moses' would probably have little or no significance for him. In the parallels in Numbers 'Moses' sends the messengers at 20.14 and 'Israel' at 21.21. Jephthah is perhaps more pragmatic and less concerned with theological principle than Moses (cf. Judg. 11.24 with Deut. 2.16-19).

39. For a form-critical study of this entire section see C. Westermann, *Basic Forms of Prophetic Speech* (Philadelphia: Westminster, 1967), pp. 111-15.

40. Note Jephthah's words in 12.2, which refer back to the present context: 'I was an איש ריב', that is, 'a man with a complaint' or 'a legal adversary'. J. Limburg, 'The Root ריב and the Prophetic Lawsuit Speeches', *JBL* 88 (1969), pp. 291-304, esp. p. 298.

41. For 'words before blows' as an ancient morale-boosting technique within the Hebrew tradition cf. David's encounter with Goliath. In the Greek tradition cf. the *Iliad* throughout.

42. Cf. the attempt of the Israelites themselves to secure Yahweh's help in 10.10-16. They confess their guilt vis-à-vis Yahweh. Here Jephthah establishes Israel's innocence vis-à-vis Ammon. Both alike appeal to the special relationship between Yahweh and Israel ('our god', 10.10c; 11.24b) and hence his stake in their national interests.

43. Presumably East Manasseh, north of the Jabbok, though if ויעבר (passed on) in 29c refers to a (re)crossing of the Jordan it may include West Manasseh as well.

44. The anomalous עבר בני עמון of 29d is explicated by 32a. 29b seems to require the meaning 'he passed through' Gilead and Manasseh even though the usual construction for this is עבר ב (but cf. Isa. 33.21). עבר with the accusative meaning 'to go across/travel to' a place, as in 29c, is not so unusual (cf. Judg. 18.13, Amos 6.2; 5.5; Isa. 23.6, etc.), although we may have expected שוב אל in this context (but see my comment below on the significance of the fourfold repetition of עבר). The text may well have undergone some disturbance, but Moore (*Judges*, p. 298) exaggerates when he states that 'it is not possible to form any satisfactory notion of these movements or of their object'. See my own further comments below and compare also Boling's translation and notes (*Judges*, pp. 206-207).

45. *Judges*, p. 81.

46. W. Richter, 'Zu den Richtern Israels', *ZAW* 77 (1965), pp. 40-72, esp. 61-68. Contrast H.C. Thomson, who argues that it refers to 'seeking the will of Yahweh' since Deborah judges Israel by obtaining and giving to them Yahweh's decision (משפט) in a similar situation (4.5): 'Shophet and Mishpat in the Book of Judges', *Transactions of the Glasgow University Oriental*

Society 19 (1961-62), pp. 74-85, esp. p. 78.

47. The translation 'he became judge' favoured by early commentators and most recently advocated by Soggin (*Judges*, pp. 45-46) is without warrant in usage. The view that it is a generalization 'he vindicated Israel' (Moore, *Judges*, p. 88; Burney, *Judges*, p. 66) does not commend itself either. The first-order generalizations of this kind are in v. 9: Yahweh 'raised up' a saviour who 'saved' them. These generalizations are then explicated in v. 10: he 'raised up' Othniel by endowing him with his spirit, and Othniel 'saved' Israel by 'judging' and 'going out to war'. Neither of the alternatives I have rejected has the support of the LXX which has the aorist εκρινε in both the A and the B text.

48. The sequence of verbs is the same as in Judg. 3.10: Samuel judged (שפט) the Israelites (בני ישראל) (v. 6) who then went out (יצא) against the Philistines (v. 11). Samuel, unlike Othniel, did not take to the field himself.

49. 'Natural' if not legal; that is, the right to humane treatment if not to equal legal standing with his 'legitimate' brothers. Such a concern for humane treatment of those without legal rights underlies the teaching concerning the 'stranger' (גר) in the Torah.

50. I assume that Jephthah's accusation against the elders is not without some foundation, at least in Jephthah's mind. See n. 24 above.

51. היוצא אשר יצא specifies neither species (man or animal) nor gender.

52. Cf. Moore (*Judges*, p. 299) who, however, overstates the case and hence resolves an ambiguity which properly belongs to the building of suspense: 'that a human victim is intended is, in fact, as plain as words can make it; the language is inapplicable to an animal, and a vow to offer the first sheep or goat that he comes across—not to mention the possibility of an unclean animal—is trivial to absurdity'. Contrast Boling (*Judges*, p. 208) who, in addition to the ambiguity of the language, refers to the more or less standard plan of Iron Age houses, such as to accommodate livestock as well as family.

53. Compare the situation in which the king of Moab offers his son and heir as a burnt offering in 2 Kgs 3.26-27.

54. Trible ('A Meditation in Mourning', pp. 60-61) reads too much into 29a when she says, 'Jephthah himself does not evince the assurance that the spirit of Yahweh ought to give. Rather than acting with conviction and courage, he responds with doubt and demand.' Jephthah is not responding to Yahweh, but still trying to prevail upon Yahweh to respond to *him*.

55. Ironically, as Sisera was laid low by Jael (5.27). Cf. 2 Sam. 22.40 where the same verb is used of laying low enemies in battle.

56. I follow BDB (see under ב.I.7) where בעכרי is taken to involve the idiomatic use of *Beth essentiae* as in בעזרי in Ps. 54.6 (not 'Yahweh is among/ one of my helpers' but 'Yahweh is my essential/chief helper'). Cf. Burney, *Judges*, p. 321: 'the supreme cause of my trouble'. On the strength of the verb

עכר cf. Gen. 34.30; Josh. 6.18; 7.25; 1 Sam. 14.29; 1 Kgs 18.17-18.

57. Contrast Abraham in Genesis 22.

58. Cf. Trible, 'A Meditation in Mourning', p. 63.

59. See also note 57 above. Both Gen. 22 and Judges 11 feature a father faced with the prospect of sacrificing an 'only' child (יחיד; Gen. 22.2; Judg. 11.34c). In Gen. 22 the obligation to do so is divinely imposed; Jephthah incurs the obligation primarily through his own voluntary act (the vow). Does no substitute appear in Jephthah's case because that substitute (Jephthah hoped to sacrifice someone or something else) has already been imposed in the form of his daughter? Is she the 'ram caught in the thicket' by divine providence? We simply do not know. At any rate the outcome is precisely the opposite of that in Genesis 22: not 'descendants as the stars of heaven' (Gen. 22.17) but no descendants at all (Judg. 11.34). For the suggestion that the story of Jephthah's vow is a 'mirror image' of the testing of Abraham I am indebted to E.R. Leach, 'The Legitimacy of Solomon: Some Structural Aspects of Old Testament History', *Archives Européennes de Sociologie*, 7 (1966), pp. 58-101, esp. p. 67. The validity of the detailed comparisons made by Leach has been challenged by B. Nathhorst in *Formal or Structural Studies of Traditional Tales: the usefulness of some methodological proposals advanced by Vladimir Propp, Alan Dundes, Claude Lévi-Strauss and Edmund Leach* (Stockholm: 1969), esp. pp. 68-69. In my own judgment the comparison is of heuristic value even though it cannot be used to establish firm conclusions. The primary context for interpreting the episode of the vow is the Jephthah narrative as a whole.

60. The one, of course, implies the other, and the words of the vow can mean nothing other than that he literally sacrificed his daughter. On the history of interpretation see Moore, *Judges*, pp. 304-305, and for a fairly detailed presentation of the case for a 'spiritual' interpretation (he dedicated her to Yahweh in perpetual virginity) see C.F. Keil and F. Delitzsch, *The Book of Judges* (Commentary on the Old Testament in Ten Volumes, 2; trans. J. Martin; Grand Rapids: Eerdmans, 1973), pp. 388-95.

61. Cf. Trible, 'A Meditation in Mourning', p. 66.

62. Contrast Martin, *Judges*, p. 146: '*It became a custom*: This is the point at which this section of the Jephthah narrative (11.29-40), with its emphasis on the fate of this virgin daughter, has been aiming. It is an attempt to explain by means of a legend about the sacrifice of a virgin, an annual four-day festival in Israel.' Episode III does offer an explanation of the custom, but as is clear from its literary structure and its context in the wider Jephthah narrative, it does so only incidentally.

63. Taking ותהי as a 'neuter-feminine' as in Ps. 69.11, 'It became reproaches unto me'. On the use of the feminine in a neuter sense see G-K, §122q. Trible ('A Meditation in Mourning, p. 66), following König, renders it as a true feminine, 'She (Jephthah's daughter) became a tradition in Israel'. The weakness of this view is that it involves a 'special' usage of חק (a person

= a tradition) without parallel in the OT while the context provides a 'fixed' activity such as חק customarily refers to (v. 40). In fact the troublesome 39d is exegeted by 40a-c which immediately follows: 'It became a custom in Israel, *that is*, the Israelite women went out year by year etc.' For the almost certain reason for the false verse division of the MT see Burney, *Judges*, p. 325.

64. Judg. 5.11 and 11.40 are the only two certain occurrences in the OT (*t^enāh* in Ps. 8.2 is sometimes emended to *tānāh*, e.g. RSV, JB). Ugaritic usage verifies the meaning, 'to repeat, recite' (A Weiser, 'Das Deboralied: eine gattungs- und traditionsgeschichtliche Studie', *ZAW* 71 [1959], pp. 67-97).

65. The LXX translator(s) were apparently unfamiliar with תנה. They render it according to the general sense of the context as δώσουσιν (show forth) in 5.11 and as θρηνεῖν (to mourn) in 11.40. The ancient versions in general agree with the LXX in 11.40.

66. An exception to the 'particular-general' relationship between vv. 37-38 and vv. 39c-40c.

67. Suggestions that the activity of the Israelite women in Judg. 11.40 was 'really' something other than this (e.g. a fertility cult) or that it became such generally rely on extra-biblical 'parallels'. They could form part of an interpretation of the Jephthah story as a literary composition only if they found confirmation in the text itself. As far as I can see this is not the case. For a brief but helpful bibliography of the relevant literature see Trible, 'A Meditation in Mourning', p. 72 n. 44.

68. I owe this apposite reference to Sirach, again, to Trible ('A Meditation in Mourning', p. 65) whose sensitive analysis of 11.29-40 in particular has considerably influenced my own appreciation and understanding of this part of the Jephthah story. I have noted some of my disagreements with her above, especially notes 4, 54, 62. The full text of Sirach 44.8-9 is apposite:

> Some there are who have left a name behind them to be commemorated in story.
> There are others who are unremembered;
> they are dead, and it is as though they had never existed,
> as though they had never been born
> or left children to succeed them (NEB).

69. They go צפונה (1b)—to Zaphon, one of the 'cities of Gilead' according to Josh. 13.27. Cf. LXXA. 'Northwards' (LXXB) would seem to be topographically impossible. Boling (*Judges*, p. 212) suggests that the Ephraimites may have met Jephthah at Zaphon during one of his tours as a circuit riding judge (cf. 11.29 and 1 Sam. 7.15-17).

70. Cf. 14.15.

71. Cf. Boling (*Judges*, p. 150): 'they argued vigorously with him'.

72. Of course he avoids any explicit reference to the vow; that was a private affair and one he would rather forget. עבר ... עבר in 1d, 3c echoes the fourfold עבר of 11.29-32.

73. See note 40 above.

74. With LXX and OL against the MT, which has 'in the cities of Gilead'. Cf. Boling, *Judges*, p. 213.

75. The portrayal of Yahweh as silent and withdrawn in relation to Jephthah contrasts with his explicit involvement, from the very beginning, in the careers of Othniel, Ehud, Barak and Gideon (3.9-10; 3.15; 4.6-7; 6.11-12). Note in particular the extent of his involvement with Gideon in 6.11-7.23.

76. Similar restraint is present in the presentation of minor characters, but complexity and ambivalence of motivation is lacking: Jephthah's daughter (a foil for her father) is wholly good; the captains of Gilead are caricatures, etc.

77. Compare §4.01 of Chapter 1, and note 1 to Chapter 2.

Notes to Chapter 3. Overture

1. That is, more intelligible in its own right without reference to what is outside it. See, for example, the story of Saul and the witch of Endor in 1 Sam. 28. It opens with a statement to the effect that Samuel had died and was buried (v. 3a). This has already been told in the book (1 Sam. 25.1) in its proper chronological place; it is mentioned here for the second time as a piece of background information, making the story more independent in its context. J. Licht, *Storytelling in the Bible* (Jerusalem: Magnes, 1978), p. 38.

2. So e.g. Moore, *Judges*, p. 5; A.E. Cundall, *Judges* (London: Tyndale, 1968), p. 51; F.F. Bruce, *Judges* in *The New Bible Commentary Revised* (ed. D. Guthrie *et al.*; London: IVP, 1970), p. 50. The effect is to distance the words from the content of ch. 1 (which is held to refer to events which actually took place prior to Joshua's death) and to ease the tension with 2.6-10 where Joshua's death is said to be reported in its proper chronological position. However, the words have the form and syntactical function of a time-clause and not of a heading. The fact that similar open-ended expressions were used by the rabbis as titles of biblical books (בראשית, in the beginning = Genesis etc.) is hardly relevant because of the comparative lateness of the practice, and especially because such titles were derived from the words of the text; that is, they were an integral part of the text before they were used as headings.

3. See note 41 below.

4. In accordance with its general OT usage בתחלה here means 'first in time', not 'first in rank'. Judah is not accorded hegemony over the other tribes, but only the honour of being the first to strike a blow for Israel. Cf. Gen. 13.3; 2 Sam. 17.9; Dan. 8.1; Gen. 14.21; 43.18, 20; Dan. 9.21. Judg. 20.18 is arguably a special case and will be discussed at the appropriate point

later in this study. D. Karl Budde, *Das Buch der Richter* (Freiburg: Mohr, 1897), p. 3.

5. אח 'brother', is used in a more general sense in 20.23, 28 and 21.6 where Benjamin is the 'brother' of the 'Israelites'. It is not certain that the more particular relationship I have suggested is in view in 1.3, but likely in my judgment. Cf. Moore, *Judges*, p. 12. The point is not essential to my interpretation of the passage.

6. Against Auld, who holds that the association with Simeon is 'unmotivated' (*Judges 1 and History*, p. 268).

7. Other, less relevant elements of the Hormah tradition are to be found in Num. 14.45; Deut. 1.44; Num. 21.1-3; Josh. 12.14, 15.30.

8. Possibly with the exception of certain treasures to be dedicated to Yahweh, as in Josh. 6.16-19. Cf. Boling (*Judges*, p. 58) who suggests that the ban was originally used 'as a way of building up the treasury in the emerging covenant league, the accumulation of booty marked for the King, Yahweh'. The only other occurrence of חרם in Judges is at 21.11 where the ban is used selectively against Jabesh-Gilead as a means of securing wives for the surviving Benjaminites!

9. On the probable place of departure for the upward movement (and hence the locale for the dialogue of vv. 1-2) see below on v. 16.

10. As well as being programmatic, this combination of terms is probably intended to indicate the comprehensiveness of Judah's activity over against the selectiveness of the material which follows. Cf. Josh. 10.40.

11. The NEB treats ויביאהו as indefinite and renders it as an English passive, 'He was brought to Jerusalem and died there'. The implication is that the king's own supporters brought him *home* to Jerusalem to die, a reading advocated by Auld (*Judges 1 and History*, pp. 268-69) and various early critical scholars (see Moore, *Judges*, p. 1). The present context will not permit such a reading, however. The king is captured by the Judahites and their allies (v. 6) and he is ruler of Bezeq, not Jerusalem (v. 5). He is captured and mutilated by the Judahites and their allies who take him with them in their advance against Jerusalem (perhaps as a spectacle to terrorize its inhabitants?). He dies there in their custody. As a narrated event this is quite distinct from the narrative concerning Joshua and Adoni-zedeq in Joshua 10: the kings have different—if similar—names; the 'Israelite' assailants are different in the two cases; and there is mention of neither an enemy alliance in Judges 1 nor of mutilation in Joshua 10.

12. D.M. Gunn, *The Story of King David: Genre and Interpretation* (JSOT Supplement Series, 6; Sheffield: JSOT Press, 1978), pp. 51-54, 56-62. Gunn identifies the pattern in the instances I have cited here from 1 and 2 Samuel. He accounts for the pattern in terms of an originally oral mode of composition. The application to the present text is entirely my own.

13. Cf. the use of אלהים by the Midianite in 7.14 in contrast to יהוה in the following verse. I am not claiming that the variation of the divine names

always has such a narrative function.

14. Cf. 9.56-57 where, likewise, retribution is attributed to אלהים. In both cases the mention of 'seventy' victims underscores the heinous nature of the crime committed.

15. The burning of the cities is associated with the ban (חרם) in each case in Joshua (cf. the deuteronomic legislation of Deut. 13.16-17). The ban is not specifically mentioned in Judges 1.8 but may fairly be assumed (cf. v. 17). Compare, within Judges, the action of the Danites against Laish/Dan (18.27) and the action of the Israelites against Gibeah and other Benjaminite cities (20.48). See also n. 8 above.

16. Hebron is in fact at a higher elevation than Jerusalem. The presentation in terms of two major movements is schematic only.

17. The emphasis is original. Joshua 14.15 has ושם תברון לפנים קרית ארבע האדם הגדול בענקים הוא.

18. According to Josh. 11.21-22 Joshua eradicated (כרת) the Anakim from Hebron and from the Judean hills in general, though some survived in Gaza, Gath and Ashdod. The reappearance of Anakim at Hebron after the withdrawal of Israel (Josh. 10.43) is plausible from a narrative point of view, but unexplained. More problematical is the claim in Josh. 11.21 that Joshua utterly destroyed (חרם) Hebron and its inhabitants, since Sheshai, Ahiman and Talmai are specifically Hebronite Anakim in the tradition (Num. 13.22), and it is these in particular which reappear at Hebron in Judg. 1.10 (cf. Josh. 15.13-14, Judg. 1.20). But possibly this is attaching too much precision to the use of traditional names.

19. E.g. Deut. 9.2: 'a people great and tall, the sons of the Anakim, whom you know, and of whom you have heard it said, Who can stand before the sons of Anak?' (RSV). Cf. Num. 13.32, 33.

20. The semantic range of נכה is wide, even in specifically military contexts (see BDB). When used unqualified in listing casualties (as in 4c, 'they struck in Bezeq 10,000 men') it appears to mean 'to put out of action' (by killing or severely wounding). Used, again unqualified, as a general statement of the outcome of a battle (as here in 10c, and also in 5c, 'they struck the Canaanite and the Perizzite') it certainly means 'to defeat' but not necessarily 'to annihilate' (see 2 Kgs 13.25; Gen. 14.5-7, 17). More commonly it is supplemented by more specific terms which indicate the nature and extent of the damage inflicted, as in v. 8 of our present text.

21. Again (cf. 10b above) what looks like an antiquarian gloss actually performs an important narrative function. After the mention of Debir in 11a it prepares the way for a reference to the same town as Qiriath-sepher in the direct speech of 12a. It obviates the need for an anachronism (Debir) in 12a.

22. The subject of וילד is יהודה as in 10a. The intervening ויכו (10c) also has the same subject despite its plural form (LXX^A has a singular verb here). Comparison with the parallel in Josh. 15.15 in which Caleb is the subject

(but the verb is עלה, not הלך) has led to the suggestion that v. 20 of Judges 1 (cf. Josh. 15.13-14) is misplaced and should occur after v. 10 and before v. 11: C.H.J. de Geus, 'Richteren 1.1—2.5', *Vox Theologica* 36 (1966), p. 37; J. Van Seters, *In Search of History: Historiography in the Ancient World and the Origins of Biblical History* (New Haven and London: 1983), p. 339. But this is to ignore the fact that it is quite specifically *Judah's* progress which is being traced schematically in vv. 9-19. See my further comments below on v. 20.

23. Contrast 'Judah' and 'Judahites' in the preceding verses. The 'Judah' who speaks in v. 3 is not an individual person, as the context makes clear.

24. 'The sons of Judah came near to Joshua in Gilgal, and Caleb . . . said to him . . .' This is the same progression from 'Judah' to Caleb as leading representative of Judah as in v. 11 of Judges 1. Cf. Nahshon, *the naśi'* of Judah, Num. 1.7, 16; 2.2; 10.4.

25. Both Kenizzites. 'Son of Kenaz, Caleb's Younger brother' is ambiguous. Othniel is either Caleb's younger brother (LXX[A]) or his nephew (LXX[B]). The intricate genealogical data of 1 Chron. 4.13-15 appears to represent an independent tradition and is even more difficult to interpret.

26. Cf. Jephthah's victory in 11.32-34, on which see my comments in Chapter 2 above.

27. Cf. Josh. 14.12. Achsah shows the same enterprising spirit as her father!

28. A particular point is made of the fact that Othniel is *younger* than Caleb (13a). The ageing Caleb depends on younger men for leadership in the field in the most demanding military operations. But cf. v. 20.

29. She first takes the initiative in relation to Othniel: 'She urged him to ask her father . . .' (146). There is no need to emend this (with LXX and most scholars) to 'he urged her . . .' since what immediately follows explains how she rather than Othniel actually does the asking. Caleb asks Achsah, 'What's the matter?' (14d) and thereby invites *her* to be the spokesman. She then takes up the matter directly with her father and extracts from him more than he had intended to give. Cf. Y. Kaufman, *The Book of Judges* [Hebrew] (Jerusalem: Kiryat Sepher, 1962), p. 80.

30. MT בנגב 'in the Negeb . . .' is not entirely free from suspicion. LXX reads במורד (*at the descent* of Arad). In any case the proper name Arad (and Zepath Hormah in the next verse) identifies the wilderness in question as the southern wilderness rather than the one which borders on the Dead Sea. Further, the anticipatory use of נגב in 9c strengthens the case for retaining it in v. 16. Cf. Burney, *Judges*, pp. 15-17.

31. It is possible that a catchword principle has played some part in the inclusion of the Kenite note at this point.

32. See the standard commentaries on, in particular, מדבר, בני קני יהודה בנגב ערד (cf. note 29 above), and העם. On העם see my further comments below.

33. In this respect vv. 16 and 17 are a contrasting pair, both dealing with the effects of Judah's penetration into the Negeb.

34. The text does not explicitly say that Hobab eventually agreed, but this is implied by the way the journey begins directly after Moses has had the last word (vv. 32-33).

35. 'Hobab, son of Reuel, the Midianite, Moses' חתן' (v. 29). The tradition has 'Jethro' and 'Reuel' variants (Exod. 2.16, 18; 3.1; 18.1); it also has 'Midianite' and 'Kenite' variants (Num. 10.29; Judg. 1.16), but it is clearly the same clan which figures in them all—חתן משה establishes the continuity. In all probability the Kenites were also Midianites by political affiliation: Boling, *Judges*, p. 57; R. de Vaux, 'Sur l'Origine Kenite ou Midianite du Yahvisme', *Eretz Israel* 9 (1969), p. 29.

36. Budde, *Richter*, p. 9; Moore, *Judges*, pp. 32, 34-35, and, most recently, Soggin, *Judges*, p. 19. This reading is attested in Moore's 'N' group of LXX MSS and the Sahidic. However the loss of the 'missing' letters in the MT cannot be explained in terms of any familiar type of scribal error. It appears more likely to me that העמלקי was itself an early emendation made under the influence of 1 Sam. 15.6 and/or Num. 24.20-22.

37. A *waw* having been lost by haplography, and the article then supplied in compensation. Budde, *Richter*, p. 9.

38. Cf. Hobab's reluctant words in Num. 10.30: 'I will go (הלך) to my own land and to my people (מולדתי').

39. *The Book of Judges*, p. 82 (my translation).

40. It is similarly identified, outside the Deuteronomic History, in 2 Chron. 28.15. While an 'original' reference to the תמר of Ezek. 47.19 and 1 Kgs 9.18 is sometimes alleged (and hence to an entry of the Kenites from the south) it is generally recognized that the reference in the finished form of the text is to Jericho. Martin, *Judges*, pp. 22-23; Boling, *Judges*, p. 57.

41. The associations with the conquest and the 'messenger of Yahweh' make it clear that it is *the* Gilgal of Josh. 5.10-15 which is intended—against Kaufmann, who thinks the מלאך יהוה of 2.1 is a prophet and identifies the Gilgal of 2.1 with 'the Gilgal which is close to Bethel' in 2 Kgs 2.1-2. See n. 39 above.

42. The position of 19cd at the end of the unit is significant. Like an admission reluctantly made, it is held over until all the possibilities for positive comment have been exhausted.

43. The LXX (A + B) is negative: 'did not take possession of' (ouk εκληρονομησεν)—probably a harmonizing emendation. Auld, *Judges 1 and History*, p. 272.

44. It is theoretically possible that the MT is correct at this point, giving the impersonal sense 'it was not possible to drive out . . .' (G-K §1141; cf. Amos 6.10) but no exact parallel exists. Mitchell Dahood has suggested that MT's *lo*'; is defective for *la'a*, 'to be weak, unable' (cf. Gen. 19.11; Exod. 7.18): 'Scriptio defectiva in Judges 1,19', *Biblica* 60 (1979), p. 570. Scholars

generally assume, on the basis of Josh. 15.63; 17.2 the haplography of יכל (most recently, Boling, *Judges*, 58)—a reading supported by the LXX (A + B).

45. I use 'Canaanite' in the general sense of 1c, not in the more restricted sense of 4b (' . . . the Canaanite and the Perizzite'). The Danites are hard-pressed here by the Amorites (34–36), not by the Philistines as they are in the Samson stories. Cf. Y. Kaufmann, *The Biblical Account of the Conquest of Palestine* (trs. M. Dagut; Jerusalem: Magnes, 1953), p. 83.

46. The oracle of v. 2 has delivered הארץ (the land) into Judah's hand. And compare Joshua's words to the northern tribes in Josh. 17.18: 'you shall dispossess the Canaanite *even though he has chariots of iron* and is strong' (my emphasis). Within Judges the Barak-Sisera story of ch. 4 will demonstrate how ineffective iron chariots are against Yahweh.

47. The Targum adds, 'after they had sinned'. One anonymous Greek commentator (see Moore, *Judges*, p. 38) writes, 'they were unable, not because of powerlessness, but because of laziness'.

48. A circumstance which makes Judah's attack on it understandable—a fortified Canaanite city on its northern border would be a serious threat to its own security. The oracle of 1.2 did not limit the promise of victory over the Canaanites to Judah's own allotted territory (note הארץ in 2c, and cf. 3.11; 5.31; 8.28; 2.1, 2) though the distribution of the land (presupposed in the narrative) makes it natural that Judah's efforts should be concentrated there. Besides the attack on Jerusalem on its northern border, Judah is shown to extend its activity also (by agreement) into Simeon's territory on its southern flank. Kaufmann unnecessarily limits the meaning of הארץ in 2c in saying that it must be understood here as referring to *Judah's* land (ארצו). He is right, however, in the light of 1c ('who will go *first* . . . ?') to comment that Judah's victory is intended to be 'a sign and banner for the whole land' (*The Book of Judges*, p. 72).

49. In spite of its plural form the most natural subject for ויתנו (they gave) in 20a is the יהודה (Judah) of vv. 10–19 (cf. בני יהודה [men of Judah] in vv. 8–9). Alternatively ויתנו could be treated as impersonal and rendered by an English passive (so NEB: 'Hebron was given to Caleb as Moses directed . . .'; cf. RSV). In either case it is the victory of v. 10 which opens the way for Caleb to occupy his 'special possession'. Contrast Josh. 15.13-14, which knows only of Joshua giving (verb singular) Hebron to Caleb—'a portion . . . among the sons of Judah'—and Caleb's occupation of it. See note 22 above.

50. The note views the co-existence of Benjaminites and Jebusites as present ('to this day') and not merely as past. The 'parallel' in Josh. 15.63 also has 'to this day', but has Judahites instead of Benjaminites and apparently refers to the continued presence of Jebusites in Jerusalem after David had established himself there (2 Sam. 5.6ff.; 24.17-18). Judg. 1.21 could be taken to reflect a 'present' prior to this; so (by implication) Martin, who comments: 'This difference [Judahites instead of Benjaminites in Josh. 15.63] is no doubt due to the fact that at a later historical period Jerusalem

became the capital of Judah' (*Judges*, p. 26). But there is no need to ascribe the two versions of the note to two distinct periods in this way (with the implication of a very early date for Judg. 1.21). If David did not expel the Jebusite inhabitants of Jerusalem presumably he did not expel its Benjaminite inhabitants either. Judg. 1.21 may indicate that the continued association of Benjaminites with Jebusites in Jerusalem was viewed as a scandal by the more zealous Judahites of a later time. According to Josh. 15.63 the Judahites '*could* not' expel the Jebusites; according to Judg. 1.21, the Benjaminites '*did* not' expel them. Both versions of the note seek to absolve Judah of responsibility for this intercourse with Canaanites (in the nation's capital, no less!) but they do it in different ways. Boling attributes the 'to this day' of Judg. 1.21 to a sixth-century redactor: 'this appears to be a redactional use of the formula which addresses the tradition to a time when Judah and Benjamin are all that is left of Israel, i.e. late seventh to early sixth century' (*Judges*, p. 59). He finds preserved in Josh. 15.63; Judg. 1.8, 21 evidence of equally unsuccessful attempts by Judah and Benjamin to occupy what was essentially a border city (*Judges*, p. 56). The narrator of Judges 1 does not take such a disinterested view!

51.   Cf. Auld, *Judges 1 and History*, p. 267: 'The mention of Josephites in both 22sq. and 35 suggests that for one compiler at least all the northern tribes could be conveniently subsumed under this name—just as Qenites and Qenizzites are casually mentioned in the first part of the chapter alongside Judah and Simeon'. The same usage of 'Judah' and 'house of Joseph' occurs in Josh. 18.5, and cf. 2 Sam. 19.20; 1 Kgs 11.28.

52.   Cf. Auld, *Judges 1 and History*, p. 276 (with reference to vv. 22-26): 'It would be idle to speculate just how much or how little the editor added to his source—however he was presumably responsible for at least גם הם in 22. And that observation may provide confirmation on two other points: that there is a correspondence between this passage and the beginning of the chapter, 22 thus marking the opening of the second part of the chapter; and accordingly that the correcting additions to the first part of the chapter conclude with 21'.

53.   Note the disjunctive syntax in 19c-d and 21a, in contrast to the flow of narrative verb-forms in vv. 3-19b, interrupted only by the peaceful interlude at v. 16. Cf. n. 66 below.

54.   The MT of 22b is supported by LXX [B] but not by LXX [AL], and OL which read 'Judah' instead of 'Jahweh'. Their combined witness is weighty and cannot be dismissed out of hand. In favour of the MT is the clear literary structure of the chapter 'Judah' and 'Joseph' are dealt with separately in parallel sections. Budde holds that an original יהושע was changed first to יהודה and then finally to יהוה after the separate Judah section (vv. 1-21) was added (*Richter*, p. 11). However that may be the MT is perfectly intelligible as it stands and is arguably the intended 'finished' form of the text. There is no compelling reason to emend it (cf. Moore, *Judges*, pp. 41-42).

55. The same kind of change occurs in vv. 11sqq., on which see my earlier comments above.

56. Cf. S.B. Gurewicz, 'The Bearing of Judges i–ii.5 on the Authorship of the Book of Judges', *Australian Biblical Review* 7 (1959) pp. 37-40. On p. 37 he observes that the capture of Bethel is given prominence in the second half of the chapter 'probably because of the action of the man who showed them the way into the city'.

57. The inclusive sense in which 'land of the Hittites' is used in Josh. 1.4 is clearly not applicable here. Almost certainly the reference is to the locality of the seven city states in Syria which perpetuated the name 'Hittite' for several centuries after the fall of the empire. Cf. the references to 'the kings of the Hittites' in 1 Kgs 8.28f.; 11.1; 2 Kgs 7.6. The MT of 2 Sam. 24.6 should probably be emended to read (with LXX^L), 'Kadesh, in the land of the Hittites' (see BH).

58. The site of Luz is unknown, but Israel had commercial and military links with 'the kings of the Hittites' during the monarchy period. See n. 57 above.

59. So J.P. Fokkelman in his very perceptive stylistic and structural analysis of Gen. 28.10-22 in *Narrative Art in Genesis: Specimens of Stylistic and Structural Analysis* (Amsterdam: Van Gorcum, 1975), ch. 2, esp. p. 69.

60. This is, of course, not to call in question the archaeological evidence that 'Bethel (i.e. Luz) is known to have been destroyed in the latter half of the thirteenth century by a terrific conflagration that left a layer of ash and debris several feet thick' (John Bright, *A History of Israel*, 2nd edition; London: SCM, 1972), p. 128). The observation I make here is a purely literary one. Archaeology knows nothing of 'new Luz', but our narrative does!

61. It is more customary to compare 1.22-26 with the battle for Ai in Josh. 7–8 and to suggest that both narratives refer to the same event: Bright, *History of Israel*, p. 128. The reasons are partly archaeological (Ai was destroyed in the third millennium and not re-occupied until after the Israelite conquest) and partly literary-critical—the mention of Bethel with Ai at a number of points in Josh. 7–8 (7.2; 8.9, 12, 17; cf. 12.9). Spies are used in both stories, but otherwise (in terms of plot structure and motifs) there is no resemblance between them. Within Joshua it is the Jericho story which offers the most striking parallel to the Bethel story of Judges 1.

62. Cf. the company she keeps in Heb. 11.31 and Jas. 2.25!

63. It could be argued that the pledge of חסד in Joshua 2 likewise induces Rahab to co-operate (by maintaining her silence). At least this is how the spies seem to view it (2.14, 20). But this reflects the nervousness of the spies, or perhaps an attempt by them to preserve their dignity (by seeming to be in charge) rather than the realities of the situation. Rahab has already committed herself irrevocably to the Israelite cause; she would have nothing

to gain by revealing her act of treason to the authorities.

64. Between the Joseph tribes in the narrower sense and the Galilean tribes lies the line of unconquered Canaanite cities listed in 27a.

65. The place-names in vv. 34-35 indicate that it is Dan's allotted territory (גורל) of Josh. 19.40-45 which is in view here, not its later settlement in the far north.

66. Disjunctive syntax returns, and now predominates, giving the series of notes in vv. 27-35 a staccato effect. Cf. n. 53 above.

67. Cf. Moore, *Judges*, p. 47; Burney, *Judges*, p. 25. The weaker sense, 'did not utterly dispossess them' (as in RSV, NEB would require לא הוריש הורישו; cf. Amos 9.8.

68. The semantic range of יאל hiphil is wide, including, in its OT usage, 'to be willing, to be pleased, to decide, to undertake, to determine' (see BDB). It occurs again in Judg. 17.11 in the context of an amicable agreement. The context of hostility in Judges 1 makes the stronger sense the probable one, particularly in view of v. 35. The Canaanites do not 'agree' to tributary service; it is imposed on them when Israel is strong enough to do this (28ab). Cf. Moore, *Judges*, p. 47.

69. The full expression, מס עבד, occurs in Josh. 16.10 (cf. 17.13, which is parallel to Judg. 1.28, and Gen. 49.15).

70. Using the generalizations 'Israelites' and 'Canaanites' for 'house of Joseph, Manasseh etc.' and 'Canaanites, Amorites', respectively.

71. Contrast 1 Kgs 9.21 where 'to this day' *is* used in connection with the conscription of Canaanites as forced labour by Solomon.

72. So Budde, *Richter*, p. 12; Moore, *Judges*, p. 45; Gray, *Judges* , p. 154; Martin, *Judges*, p. 27.

73. Cf. Kaufmann, *The Conquest of Palestine*, p. 83.

74. Admittedly it is בני ישראל (Israelites) rather than simply ישראל (Israel) in 1.1. But cf. the use of ישראל in 2.7, 10, 14, 22, and throughout the book in general.

75. So Kaufmann, *The Conquest of Palestine*, pp. 83-84. The corvée system of the early monarchy was different in both conception and effect. It included both Israelites and Canaanites and was remembered as a decisive ground for the secession of the northern tribes (1 Kgs 12). My own argument does not depend upon the historicity of Judges 1, but cf. Boling (*Judges*, pp. 60-61): '... the kings of the tenth century must have had some precedent, and it would be remarkable if Israelites, many of whom had been recruited from the ranks of forced labourers, did not make use of the same system when faced with the problems of geographical expansion'. The corvée system is well attested as a Canaanite institution in the Ras Shamra texts (references in Gray, *Joshua*, p. 154). Solomon appears to have adapted it to his own purposes.

76. Cf. Boling, *Judges*, p. 65.

77. The expression is not entirely free from textual uncertainty. LXX[AL] has

'the border of the Amorite, the Edomite', . . . and cf. S^h. Note the explicit reference to Edom in the parallel in Num. 34.3. האמרי (the Amorite) could have displaced האדמי (the Edomite) by a simple scribal error, but since האמרי provides the raison d'être for the note in its present context either the change (if there was one) was deliberate or the error (if there was one) preceded the inclusion of the note in Judges 1. The same border is referred to whichever term is used; only the point of view changes.

78. The place name 'Akrabbim' in particular, plus the similar use of the verb עלה, 'to go up' (cf. Josh. 15.4) leave little room for doubt that v. 36 refers to the same border as these other texts. It is the ideal border between 'the land of Canaan' (which Yahweh had allocated to Israel) and Edom (which he had not). Commentators are divided on how to take הסלע, 'Sela'. Is it Petra (cf. 2 Kgs 14.7), or the rock in the wilderness of Zin referred to in Num. 30.8, 10, or some other landmark unknown to us? The puzzling מעלה ' upward', in the final position, plus comparison with Josh. 15.3-4, suggests that v. 36 is a fragment. But see n. 80 below.

79. A similar effect is produced in 21.12 when Shiloh is said to be 'in the land of Canaan'.

80. Against Boling (*Judges*, p. 61) I would maintain that it does not disturb the literary structure of the chapter.

81. I use this neutral translation of מלאך יהוה here because the identity of the messenger is problematic and because the text itself does not draw attention to the question of his identity (contrast 6.22; 13.6, 16-22). Only the *function* of the messenger is important; he is the means by which Yahweh (on this occasion) addresses his words of indictment to Israel. Targum Jonathan and the medieval Jewish commentators understand the messenger to be a prophet, a view still advocated by Kaufmann, *The Book of Judges*, p. 92 (cf. Haggai 1.13; 2 Chron. 36.15-16). Certainly the messenger behaves like a prophet, addressing the assembled Israelites in the form of a covenant lawsuit. (The Angel of Yahweh, by contrast, typically speaks only to individuals and does not use the speech forms of classical prophecy). Further, the MT has a gap after ויאמר 'and he said', in 1b and LXX^B has 'Thus says the Lord' in this position. However if *a* messenger of Yahweh (= a prophet) were in view, normal grammatical usage would seem to require the indefinite form מלאך ליהוה 'a messenger of Yahweh' rather than מלאך יהוה in 1a. Also 'a prophet' and '*the* messenger of Yahweh' are clearly distinguished from one another in 6.7-10/11-24. With reference to 2.1-5 Boling suggests that 'an old story of one incident involving Yahweh's heavenly envoy has here absorbed something of the character of the prophetic covenant lawsuit' (*Judges*, p. 62). After the specification of 'means' in 2.1-5 and 6.7-10 the bald 'Yahweh said' of 10.11 contributes to the sense of climax which is achieved in the angry confrontation which takes place there.

82. Contrast, as examples of keywords which, are primarily thematic,

πνεῦμα (spirit) in Rom. 8 and πίστις (faith) in Heb. 11.

83. Why does Bochim have the article in 1a but not in 5a? Boling translates 1a very literally, 'Yahweh's envoy went up from The Circle to The Weepers', and infers that 'the beginning of ch. 2 presupposes for its setting an occasion of public lamentation', and that 'the first chapter was added to the book to explain why the Israelites were weeping at the outset of ch. 2' (*Judges*, pp. 53, 66). But this is to attach too much significance to the article on הבכים and to ignore the explicit connection which is made in v. 4 between the weeping and the words of the messenger. Both Bochim and Gilgal have the article in 1a, the latter in accordance with the normal OT practice for this word. Of its 46 occurrences in the MT it has the article 44 times (34 with ה, and indicated by the masoretic pointing a further 10 times). Only in Josh. 5.9 and 12.33 does it not have the article, and of these only the former refers to the same Gilgal as Judg. 2.1. Where it balances Gilgal in the expression מן הגלגל אל הבכים (from Gilgal to Bochim), Bochim has the article (1a). Where it stands alone in the stereotyped formula, 'they called the name of that place Bochim' a normal anarthrous form is used (cf. Gen. 33.17; Josh. 7.26; 2 Sam. 5.20; 1 Chron. 14.11; 2 Chron. 20.26 etc.). Even Gilgal conforms to the normal pattern when it occurs in this same stereotyped formula (Josh. 5.9). No special significance, in terms of either the history of the text or in terms of narrative function, is to be attached to the variation between הבכים and בכים. The difference is purely stylistic.

84. See the final paragraph of section 1.10 above.

85. It is possible that 2.1 contains a veiled allusion to the transference of the ark from Gilgal to Bethel, where it is said to be located in 20.26-27. But the focus of the narrative is on the indictment of Israel by Yahweh, not on the movement of the ark or the establishment of a new amphictyonic centre. On the probable identification of Bochim as Bethel see the excursus at section 1.18 below.

86. Cf. Exod. 34.11-12 and 13 respectively.

87. Cf. Joshua's ברית with the Gibeonites, also involving forced labour (Josh. 9). Joshua, of course, was deceived into thinking they were *not* 'inhabitants of the land'.

88. Cf. Lilley, 'A Literary Appreciation of the Book of Judges', p. 97.

89. Cf. Lev. 26.42-44; Exod. 3.16-17.

90. Cf., again, Lilley, 'A Literary Appreciation of the Book of Judges', p. 97.

91. The MT לצדים (sides) appears to be defective for לצנינים בצדיכם (thorns in your sides); cf. Num. 33.55.

92. 'The speech of the angel is a cento of quotations and reminiscences' (Moore, *Judges*, p. 61). This may perhaps account for the anomalous tense of אעלה, literally, 'I will bring you up', in 1c which may be a 'quotation' of Exod. 3.17a.

93. Cf. n. 85 above.

94. Both the A and B recensions have 'from Gilgal to the [place of] weeping, and to Bethel, and to the house of Israel...' Against this, comparison with Josh. 18.1 has suggested to some that the Bochim referred to in the MT must have been in the vicinity of Shiloh (for references see Moore, *Judges*, p. 58). But the alleged parallel with Josh. 18.1 is extremely tenuous. Cf. Kaufmann, *The Book of Judges*, p. 92.

95. Contrast the normal *disjunctive* syntax of the flashbacks at 1.16 and 11.1.

96. Either vv. 6-10 were the original continuation of Josh. 23 (so Noth), or the author has quoted from Josh. 24.28f. without emending the syntax (cf. Kaufmann, *The Book of Judges*, p. 94).

97. Most commentators simply treat 2.6ff. as a 'second', 'deuteronomic', or 'proper' introduction to the book/period, separating it from what precedes by a major sectional heading (so Soggin, *Judges*, p. 36; Gray, *Judges*, p. 255; Moore, *Judges*, p. 62; Martin, *Judges*, p. 32).

98. Cf. Keil and Delitzsch, *Judges*, p. 267.

99. At Shechem (cf. Josh. 24.28-31), where Joshua had challenged the Israelites to choose between Yahweh and other gods (v. 15) and confirmed their choice to serve only Yahweh by making a 'covenant' with them (v. 25). But contrast Kaufmann, *The Book of Judges*, p. 94, who thinks that the changes made in the text at Judges 2 indicate that an earlier dismissal from the camp at Gilgal is in view, after which, at the end of his life, Joshua reassembled the Israelites at Shechem (Josh. 23.1-2). This makes better sense of 'all the days of Joshua' in v. 7a, but this same expression occurs in Josh. 24 (v. 31) and the similarities between the two passages are so extensive that the attempt to make them refer to different occasions is forced and unconvincing.

100. Cf. Richter, *Die Bearbeitungen des 'Retterbuches'*, pp. 29-31, who argues against the view that AB and A'B' are variants with essentially the same meaning derived from different sources.

101. Further instances of this somewhat unusual use of יצר occur in Gen. 32.8; 1 Sam. 30.6; 2 Sam. 13.2; Job 18.7; 20.22; Prov. 4.12; Isa. 49.19.

102. 'Groaning' cannot simply be equated with 'crying out to Yahweh' here, especially in view of the precise formula used in the book for the latter. Cf. the distinction in Exod. 2.23. Cf. also the 'groanings' (נאקות) of the slain in Ezek. 30.24.

103. Cf. Richter, *Die Bearbeitungen des 'Retterbuches'*, p. 34 (with reference to v. 17): 'Der Vers sieht die Richter (singulär) als Lehrer, Unterweiser, auf die man hört, weil sie den Weg weisen, den die Väter gingen, nämlich die Befolgung der Gebote Jahwes. Der Richter erschiene also wie ein dtr Prediger.'

104. Compare the way the Israelites 'turn quickly from the way' in Exod. 32.8; no sooner is the commandment given than it is broken. Cf. Richter, *Die Bearbeitungen des 'Retterbuches'*, p. 34.

105. Cf. the apostasy before *and* after the death of Gideon in 8.22-35.

106. Contrary to Boling (*Judges*, p. 74) the speech continues to the end of v. 22. The change of subject in 23a marks the change to indirect speech. The commentary on Yahweh's speech begins at that point and continues to the end of 3.6. (See note 110 below.)

107. Cf. Westermann, *Basic Forms of Prophetic Speech*, Chapter D (pp. 169-98): 'The Announcement of Judgment Against Israel (JN)'.

108. I choose this expression advisedly. The language of the speech stops short of an explicit repudiation of the promise. Contrast 1 Sam. 2.30: I promised that your house . . . would minister before me for ever; but now the Lord declares, 'Far be it from me . . .'

109. Cf. Kaufmann, *The Book of Judges*, p. 98: 'Because Israel broke the covenant law of the Lord, the Lord will break his covenant promise to give them the whole land of Canaan' (my translation).

110. MT's וימת (and he died) at the end of v. 21 is awkward and probably not original. It is omitted in the OL. The LXX has in its place 'in the land; and he left [them] to test . . .', leaving it unclear whether the subject of 'he left (αφηκε)' is Joshua or Yahweh. LXX is probably not original either (see Moore, *Judges*, p. 75), and, in any case, the explicit change of subject does not come until 23a, 'Yahweh left these nations'. It is here that the change to indirect speech is made and the commentary on Yahweh's speech begins (see note 106 above). If v. 23 refers to a future rather than a past testing of Israel then v. 23 (did not deliver them into the hand of *Joshua*) becomes unintelligible. Hence Richter (*Die Bearbeitungen des 'Retterbuches'*, p. 38) following Budde (*Richter*, p. 24) emends יהושע (Joshua) to יהוה (Yahweh, cf. BH) without any support from the texts and versions. This reading also leads to a contradiction between v. 22 and vv. 20-21, because according to vv. 20-21 Yahweh did not expel the nations because of the sins of Israel, while according to v. 22 he did not expel them in order to test Israel.

Both the syntax and the general sense of the passage in the MT point to the reading which I have adopted above. Cf. also Kaufmann, *The Book of Judges*, p. 99, and M. Weinfeld, 'The Period of the Conquest and of the Judges as seen in the Earlier and the Later Sources', *VT* 17 (1967), p. 100. למען נסות (in order to test) of 22a is to be connected in sense with אשר עזב יהושת (that Joshua left . . .) and not with לא אוסיף להריש (I will not henceforth drive out . . .). The intervening וימת is to be read as equivalent to במותו, 'when he died'. The rather compressed language of Yahweh in v. 22 is then recapitulated and clarified in v. 23. Both verses refer to the nations being left *originally* (at the time of Joshua's death) as a test.

111. Cf. v. 22 where it is Joshua who leaves the nations as a test, but only as Yahweh's agent. See n. 110 above.

112. See n. 108 above, and the related remarks in the relevant part of section 1.24 above.

113. P. Ricoeur, 'The Narrative Function', *Semeia* 13 (1978), p. 185.

114. Jephthah's daughter represents an ironic inversion of this motif. She

'brings low' a male hero in the hour of his triumph (11.35) without realizing what she does.

115. Cf. the observations made by Gros Louis, referred to on p. 30f. above.

116. In both respects 2.6—3.6 orients us to what follows in a much more overt way than 10.6-16 does to the Jephthah narrative. 10.6-16 contains no outline of the plot and only the merest intimation of the theme. Functionally 10.6-16 is more comparable to 1.1—2.5 than to 2.6—3.6.

117. Cf. Yehuda T. Radday, who characterizes the book of Judges as, among other things, 'a vindication of the God of Israel who did not fulfil his promise of a swift conquest' ('Chiasm in Joshua, Judges, and Others', *Linguistica Biblica* 27/28 [1973], p. 11).

Notes to Chapter 4. Variations

1. See Chapter 2, n. 2 above.

2. See §5.05 of Chapter 1. Gooding counts 8.33 as an occurrence of the formula.

3. Cf. Gooding, 'The Composition of the Book of Judges', p. 79.

4. The round figures (years of peace) in 3.7-16.31 may be the work of an editor who constructed a more wide-ranging chronological scheme extending as far as the 480 years of 1 Kgs 6.1. See Richter, *Die Bearbeitungen des 'Retterbuches'*, pp. 132-41 (with copious references to the relevant literature). Outside Judg. 3.7-16.31, however, the relevant chronological references are scattered and unsystematic, and no explanation of how the figure of 480 was arrived at is free from serious difficulties. If a lucid scheme on this scale ever existed it belonged to an earlier form of the Deuteronomic History than that which we now have. Within Judges only 3.7-16.31 has a detailed chronology.

5. See the standard commentaries. He has been variously identified as a Babylonian Cassite (cf. Gen. 10.8), a Nubian, an Edomite, an Asiatic usurper in Egypt (so Malamat), a Midianite (cf. Num. 12.1; Hab. 3.7), a chieftain of a tribe related to the Midianites who had migrated north and settled in Syria (so Kaufmann), and a surviving chieftain of the southern (Judean) hills (so Boling). The Edomite hypothesis commands widest support (read אֲרָם, 'Edom', for אֲרָם, 'Aram', and delete נַהֲרַיִם, '-naharaim', as a gloss), but no consensus exists. See my comments below on the significance of the name in its literary context.

6. The first-order generalizations are in v. 9; they are explicated in v. 10. The saviour is Othniel; he saved Israel by judging and going out to war. Judging here should probably be taken to involve an element of proclamation, as in 2.17 (cf. Samuel's judging of Israel in the context of the Philistine crisis in 1 Sam. 7).

7. 11b implies that peace lasted for the whole of Othniel's lifetime (cf.

2.18), but it does not necessarily imply that Othniel lived for the whole period of peace. Cf. Kaufmann, *The Book of Judges*, p. 104.

8. On my reckoning (see Section 3.01 above) the one-word line ויושיעם, literally 'and he saved them', of 9c is positioned centrally in the unit; eight lines precede it and eight follow. For the rationale behind the division into lines see Chapter 2, n. 5. Syntactically ויושיעם is in parenthesis, since 9d is in apposition with מושיע (a saviour) in 9b. Although it repeats the idea of ישע (to save) it is emphatic rather than tautological:

> Yahweh raised up a saviour to the Israelites
> —and he saved them—
> Othniel ben Kenaz ...

The subject could be מושיע (= Othniel) or יהוה (= Yahweh). The difference is immaterial since Othniel is Yahweh's agent.

9. See note 25 to Chapter 3.

10. In the text as we have it Othniel, as his father-in-law Caleb was, is a survivor from an earlier period (see 2.10). In 1.12-15 he is a young man. On his apparent longevity see n. 7 above. Contrast Roland de Vaux, who comments (from a tradition-critical perspective) that 'this Othniel ... [whom we know from 1.12-15] did not belong to the period of the Judges, but to that of the settlement of the tribes' (*The Early History of Israel, to the Period of the Judges* [tr. D. Smith; London: Darton, Longman and Todd, 1978; originally published in French, 1971], p. 807).

11. Cf. similar name-plays in Ishbosheth, Molech, Tabal (Isa. 7.6) etc.

12. Cf. Boling, *Judges*, pp. 80-81.

13. Martin Buber has claimed that the first twelve chapters of Judges contain a series of seven antimonarchical stories and that the thesis of these twelve chapters is spelt out explicitly in 8.23: 'I will not rule over you, and my son will not rule over you—Yahweh will rule over you' (*The Kingship of God* [3rd edition; tr. R. Scheimann; London: Allen and Unwin, 1967], pp. 66-77).

14. L. Alonso Schökel, 'Erzählkunst im Buche der Richter', *Biblica* 42 (1961), pp. 148-58.

15. This form of address is not inevitable in the situation. Contrast the more customary and polite use of אדני (my lord) in 1 Sam. 24.8; 26.17; 29.8; 2 Sam. 4.8; 13.33 etc.

16. Clearly a reference to Jericho (see Section 1.10 of Chapter 3 above) although the city itself was probably unoccupied at the time in which the story is set. F.F. Bruce suggests that what is indicated is a temporary occupation of the oasis at 'Ain es-Sultan (*Judges*, p. 260). Control of the lower Jordan valley is what is at stake; the Israelites have been forced back and confined to the hills (v. 27). The descriptive title, 'City of Palms', together with Eglon's fatness and his cool upper chamber opens up for us 'the vast differences between the lives of the Moabites and the conquered

Israelites—inside versus outside, cool versus hot, fatness versus barrenness, palms versus hills' (Gros Louis, '*The Book of Judges*', p. 147).

17. As in the use of מנחה for a cereal offering (Lev. 2.1 etc.). The use of a cadre of bearers suggests its bulk. Cf. C.E. Armerding, *Judges*, in *A Bible Commentary for Today* (eds. G.C.D. Howley *et al.*; London: Pickering and Inglis, 1979), p. 346.

18. E.M. Good, *Irony in the Old Testament* (2nd edition; Sheffield: Almond Press, 1981), pp. 33-34.

19. Robert Alter, *The Art of Biblical Narrative* (New York: Basic Books, 1981), p. 40.

20. שמן is generally used of 'fatness' in an agricultural sense: Gen. 49.20; 1 Chron. 4.40; Neh. 9.25, 35; Isa. 30.23; Ezek. 34.14, 16; Hab. 1.16. Judg. 3.29 is the only place I know of where it is applied to human beings. See further below.

21. For בריא as an antonym of רזה see Ezek. 34.20. For the corresponding use of שמן see Num. 13.20.

22. Boling (*Judges*, p. 85) renders שמן as 'plump'. Alter (*The Art of Biblical Narrative*, p. 41) renders it by 'lusty' but notes that it can also mean 'fat'. Soggin (*Judges*, p. 49) renders it more traditionally as 'able-bodied'. LXX^A has μαχατάς (warlike); LXX^B has λιπαρός (well-oiled, fat).

23. Verse 30 contains the final occurrence of the key word יד (hand), a further connection between the murder of Eglon and the slaughter of his troops:

v. 15	Ehud is restricted in his right יד
v. 16	The Israelites send tribute by his יד
v. 21	Ehud reaches with his left יד
v. 28	'Yahweh has given Moab into your יד'
v. 30	So Moab was laid low under the יד of Israel.

The stock expressions of vv. 28 and 30 are nuanced by their narrative context. Cf. Alonso Schökel, 'Erzählkunst', pp. 149sqq.

24. Alter, *The Art of Biblical Narrative*, pp. 40-41.

25. Cf. Robert C. Culley, 'Structural Analysis: Is it Done with Mirrors?', *Interpretation* 28 (1974), pp. 165-81. Culley includes the story of Ehud and that of Jael (4.17-24) in an analysis of plot structure in six 'deception stories' taken from the OT.

26. Left-handed; probably, in this case, because of a literal deformity of the right hand. See the discussion of איש אטר יד ימינו ('a man restricted in his right hand', v. 15) in Soggin, *Judges*, p. 50.

27. The repetition of 'hand' (יד) in the last two lines of v. 15 ('he was a man restricted in his right hand, and the Israelites sent tribute by his hand') suggests that his suitability for the task consisted precisely in his physical abnormality. The choice of Ehud could not be construed by Eglon as a provocation.

28. 'The dagger or short sword (חרב) is . . . short enough to hide under his

clothing, long enough to do Eglon's [sic] business without the killer's having to be unduly close to his victim, and double-edged to ensure the lethalness of one quick thrust' (Alter, *The Art of Biblical Narrative*, p. 39).

29. Cf. E.G. Kraeling, 'Difficulties in the Story of Ehud', *JBL* 54 (1935), pp. 206-207. The assumption that Eglon knew about Ehud's movements, although we are not told this, is reasonable in view of the compressed narrative style. Whatever their precise identity the פסילים mark the limits of Eglon's effective control; once Ehud passes the פסילים in v. 26 he has 'escaped' and can openly muster the Israelite militia. The double mention of the פסילים in vv. 19 and 26 respectively forms a literary bracket around Ehud's private mission.

30. See n. 23 above on the key word יד.

31. In addition LXX[A] and LXX[B] specify, in v. 30, that he 'judged'. The lack of this in the MT is attributed by Boling to haplography (*Judges*, p. 87). If the episode is read in the light of 2.16-19 Ehud must, in any case, be regarded as a judge who saved Israel and not simply as a saviour.

32. The use of the definite article in בן הימיני (the Benjaminite) suggests that he is presented as typical—the Benjaminite par excellence. Compare the seven hundred Benjaminites of 20.16, likewise 'restricted in their right hands'. Cf. Boling, *Judges*, p. 86.

33. The ancient versions do not agree in their rendering of the hapax מלמד. Some render it 'goad', others 'plough-head' or 'plough-beam'. 'Goad' still commends itself to most scholars. See the discussion by A. Van Selms in 'Judge Shamgar', *VT* 14 (1964), p. 306. He draws attention to the use of the word in the Mishnah, e.g. *Sanhedrin* 10.28: malmēd šěhū mᶜlammēd, 'called malmēd because it teaches (the ox)'.

34. Compare the 600 warriors sent by the tribe of Dan to conquer Laish (18.11). The number 600 is commonly used of an organized military force under a commander: 1 Sam. 13.15; 14.2; 27.2; 2 Sam. 15.18; 18.2. Cf. Van Selms, 'Judge Shamgar', p. 305.

35. The ואחריו היה (and after him was . . .) of this note has no exact stylistic parallel in the notes of 10.1-5 and 12.8-15, where אחריו (after him) follows either ויקם (there arose) or וישפט (there judged). The notes about David's mighty men in 2 Sam. 23.9, 11 (their feats are similar in kind to Shamgar's) appear to offer a closer parallel. In them ואחריו stands first, with the meaning 'next in *rank* to', but it is not followed by היה. No exact stylistic parallel exists in the OT, the nearest being the negative ואחריו לא היה (after him there was not . . .) in 2 Kgs 18.5, where succession in time is clearly signified. I follow the general consensus in taking Shamgar as successor to Ehud rather than as his contemporary in spite of the problem posed by ואהוד מת in 4.1. These words are parenthetical, 'the Israelites continued to do what was evil in the sight of Yahweh (Ehud being dead) . . .' and strictly speaking imply no more than that Ehud was the last figure under whom any significant recovery from apostasy took place. They are ommitted in LXX[A].

For comment in terms of the history of the text see the standard commentaries.

36. Yahweh here reviews the series of deliverances which have preceded his confrontation with the Israelites in 10.10-16, extending from the exodus ('from Egypt') to the deliverance under Gideon ('from Amalek and Maon [= Midian, LXX]', see 6.3). 'From the Philistines' is preceded by 'from the Ammonites', allies of Eglon in the Ehud episode (3.13), and followed by 'from the Sidonians', the coalition of northern Canaanites and Sea Peoples who are the oppressors in the Barak episode. See W.J. Moran, 'A Study of the Deuteronomic History', *Biblica* 46 (1965), p. 228. On the chronological difficulties with regard to this mention of the Philistines see Van Selms, 'Judge Shamgar', pp. 297-306.

37. The most thorough discussion is by Van Selms in 'Judge Shamgar'. But see also F.C. Fensham, 'Shamgar ben 'Anath', *JNES* 20 (1961), pp. 197-98; E. Danelius, 'Shamgar ben 'Anath', *JNES* 22 (1963), pp. 191-93; P.C. Craigie, 'A Reconsideration of Shamgar ben Anath (Judg. 3.31 and 5.6)', *JBL* 91 (1972), pp. 239-40.

38. This reference in 5.6 sets 'the days of Shamgar ben Anath' in a rather more sombre light than 3.31. It looks back to the situation before the victory achieved by Deborah and Barak, when the Canaanites and their allies who occupied the fortified cities in the Jezreel Valley were able to interrupt the flow of trade and communication between north and south, so vital for the well being of the Israelite tribes. In the days of Shamgar ben Anath the Israelites were barely able to survive. Shamgar may have 'saved Israel' by repelling an incursion into the hills; it took Deborah to rouse the Israelites sufficiently for an assault on the plain.

39. For a discussion of the relevant historical questions see A. Malamat, 'Hazor, "The Head of all those Kingdoms"', *JBL* 79 (1960), pp. 12-19. The hegemony accorded to Hazor here recalls the earlier greatness of the city in the Mari period (cf. Josh. 11.10). In the Armarna letters the ruler of Hazor, unlike most other rulers, is called 'king (šarrum)' and, uniquely, refers to *himself* as a king in a letter to Pharaoh (El-Amarna 227, 1.3). Judges 4 seems to envisage a situation in which Hazor retains a nominal headship (a vestige of its former greatness) while effective power lies with an alliance between Canaanites and Sea Peoples centred in the Jezreel Valley. On the vexed literary question of the relationship between the present text and Joshua 11 see the standard commentaries.

40. The chapter is generally regarded as a conflation of two separate battle accounts (see standard commentaries) but it makes good sense read as a unity. Cf. J.S. Ackerman, 'Prophecy and Warfare in Early Israel: A Study of the Deborah-Barak Story', *BASOR* 220 (1975), p. 7.

41. Note the word-play, 'God subdued (ויכנע) . . . Jabin king of Canaan (מלך כנען)', also noted by J. Blenkinsopp in 'Ballad Style and Psalm Style in the Song of Deborah', *Biblica* 42 (1961), p. 64 n. 4. Buber refers to the

'almost paean-like . . . threefold repetition of the contrast of the sons of Israel with the representative of heathen monarchism, grown to symbolic greatness' (*Kingship of God*, p. 70).

42. Canaanites to the far north (Jabin of Hazor), like Israelites to the far south (Judah) do not participate directly in the battle, although according to 4.31 the fighting subsequently spreads northwards. On the possibility that the twelfth-century settlement at Hazor was a consequence of the battle at the Kishon see B. Lindars, 'The Israelite Tribes in Judges', *Studies in the Historical Books of the Old Testament* (VT Supp., 30; ed. J.A. Emerton; Leiden: Brill, 1979), p. 109.

43. 'The Deborah-Barak Story', p. 163.

44. The Samson episode is set in the south, but as in chapter 1, Dan is schematically associated with the northern tribes in anticipation of its ultimate location in the north.

45. 'The Deborah-Barak Story', p. 183.

46. 'Erzählkunst', p. 164.

47. Cf. Alter, *Biblical Narrative*, p. 41. Both תקע and יתד (Jael *drove* the *tentpeg*) will recur at a crucial point in the Samson story, when Samson is on the brink of being overcome by Delilah: Delilah will fasten (תקע) Samson's hair with a pin (יתד) (16.14).

48. 'Erzählkunst,' p. 166.

49. His motives for so doing are not indicated in the narrative. Barak's hesitation is further spelled out in LXX: 'for I never know what day the Yahweh angel will give me success', suggesting that he desires her presence as a source of oracular inquiry; cf. Boling, *Judges*, p. 96. But Deborah's response clearly indicates that *she* considers his casuistic response to Yahweh's command improper, and the narrative as a whole supports this point of view.

50. Cf. Barnabas Lindars, who shows how Jael became the model for Judith, whose story in turn influenced the retelling of the Jael episode in Pseudo-Philo's *Biblical Antiquities* ('Deborah's Song: Women in the Old Testament', *BJRL* 65/2 [1983], pp. 173-74).

51. Cf. Polzin, 'Moses and the Deuteronomist', p. 163.

52. Cf. Blenkinsopp, 'Ballad Style and Psalm Style in the Song of Deborah', p. 64, who thinks that Deborah's call to battle in 4.14 'may have provided the grounds for a revisor to fill out and transpose into a more explicitly religious key the accompanying ballad'.

53. For references see Blenkinsopp, 'Ballad Style and Psalm Style in the Song of Deborah', and Lindars, 'Deborah's Song', pp. 158-75. Both consider that an original war ballad has been adapted for liturgical use by the addition of hymnic elements which have obscured its clear stanzaic structure. The hymnic elements are identified and set aside to prepare the way for a literary analysis of the original ballad.

54. See note 53 above. But contrast A. Globe, 'The Literary Structure and

Unity of the Song of Deborah', *JBL* 93 (1974), pp. 493-512, who argues that ANE practice in the second millenium suggests that this 'mixture' of styles was in fact the rule, not the exception, and that the song in substantially its present form is from about 1200 BCE.

55. 'A Structural and Literary Analysis of the Song of Deborah', *CBQ* 40 (1978), pp. 143-66.

56. P. 144 n. 4. This is the only point at which Coogan shows any interest in the original as distinct from the finished form of the song. Did the verse prove an embarrassment to his neat stanzaic analysis?

57. Coogan (pp. 152-53) points to an inclusive use of עַם (people) in vv. 9 and 13, and to a similarity of compositional structure between vv. 9-13 and vv. 2-8 (stanza I). But עַם is a very common word, occurring elsewhere in the song at vv. 2, 11, 14, 18 and the parallel structure to which he points is not at all obvious, and, on his own admission, 'not entirely symmetrical'.

58. Not literally, of course, since the battle itself is past; it is being relived imaginatively in the song. The singing of the song is, in itself, a kind of liturgical re-enactment of the battle and the events associated with it. A thoroughgoing liturgical interpretation was proposed by A. Weiser in 'Das Deboralied', in which he argued that the song was composed for a cultic ceremony at a later date. In this way he was able to explain why the song mentions many tribes who are not mentioned in connection with the battle itself in chapter 4. But the fact that the list of tribes in vv. 14-18 does not correspond to the later lists of twelve tribes strongly favours the traditional view that it refers to those who actually took part in the battle or failed to do so, and this is certainly the sense required by the present literary context. The difference from chapter 4 must remain an anomaly or be explained in some other way, as, for example, by Ackerman in 'Prophecy and Warfare', p. 7: 'Why are only the northern tribes mentioned in the summons to Barak? Because the tribes south of the Esdraelon valley, among whom Deborah now lived, apparently respected her authority and were ready for battle (cf. Judg. 5.14). The problem was in mustering the tribes north of the Esdraelon, and Barak was commanded to do that.'

59. Martin Buber, *The Prophetic Faith* (New York: Harper and Row, 1960), p. 9, called attention to the repetition of 'Israel' and of 'Yahweh' in the entire poem. Israel occurs eight times, all in stanzas I (six times) and II (twice); in 8d and 9a it is used as a catchword to link these two stanzas. 'Yahweh' occurs ten times in stanzas I and II, but only three times elsewhere (Coogan, 'The Song of Deborah', p. 156). Cf. Blenkinsopp, 'Ballad Style and Psalm Style', p. 76.

60. So NEB, and Boling, *Judges*, p. 102. Cf. Soggin, *Judges*, p. 82 ('glorious achievements') and see the discussion of the word in Gray, *Judges*, p. 283.

61. Cf. Coogan, 'The Song of Deborah', p. 161.

62. Cf. Coogan, 'The Song of Deborah', p. 154.

63. The second stanza opens with an exclamation of praise which is

practically the same in form and content to that which opened the first (cf. v. 9 with v. 2). Cf. Blenkinsopp, 'Ballad Style and Psalm Style', p. 66.

64. Cf. Lindars, 'Deborah's Song', pp. 169-70. A similar effect is produced, on a much larger scale, by the long review of the troops in the *Iliad*, Book 2. See also n. 58 above.

65. Cf. Lindars, 'Deborah's Song', p. 170. Zebulun has also been mentioned in v. 14, a further indication of the limits of the stanza. For the 'heights', which also exist on the plain and have strategic value, see Boling, *Judges*, p. 113.

66. Cf. Lindars, 'Deborah's Song', p. 170.

67. Probably a reference to Sisera and his allies, the local kings of neighbouring Canaanite cities (Gray, *Judges*, p. 289). Kings as such are not mentioned in the description of the battle in the prose narrative (4.14-16) but Sisera is linked with Canaanite kingship as general of 'Jabin king of Canaan' (4.2).

68. Cf. Exod. 15.3-11.

69. Cf. Blenkinsopp, 'Ballad Style and Psalm Style', p. 73.

70. Cf. Lindars, 'Deborah's Song', p. 170. The stars are considered the source of rain in Canaanite mythology as noted by Blenkinsopp in 'Ballad Style and Psalm Style', p. 73, citing 'NT II, 41.

71. Cf. Lindars, 'Deborah's Song', p. 171. Jael, unlike the inhabitants of Meroz *did* 'come to the help of Yahweh against the mighty' (v. 23b).

72. Blenkinsopp, 'Ballad Style and Psalm Style', p. 75.

73. Both Coogan and Lindars refer to the equally ironical ending of the ballad of *Sir Patrick Spens*:

> O lang, lang may the ladies stand
> Wi thair gold kems in their hair
> Waiting for thair ain dier lords
> For they'll se thame na mair

74. Cf. the similar conclusion reached by Lindars in 'Deborah's Song', esp. pp. 160 and 175. But Lindars's observations are made with reference to the hypothetical original (ballad) form of the song, not its finished form. See n. 54 above.

75. With Boling (*Judges*, pp. 124-25) I take בני קדם (Easterners) in 6.3 as a summarizing appositive: Midian and Amaleq, that is, the Easterners. Cf. 8.10c, 11a. Both Midian and Amaleq are regarded in the Torah as ancient enemies of Israel, victory over whom is closely connected with the figure of Moses (Exod. 17.8-16; Deut. 25.17-19; Num. 31). The reappearance of these ancient enemies prepares the way for the Mosaic role in which Gideon will be cast in 6.11–8.3.

76. Cf. A. Malamat, 'The War of Gideon and Midian: A Military Approach', *PEQ* (1953), p. 61, who argues that the breach made in the Canaanite defence system under Deborah and Barak actually opened the

way for foreign invasions. The Israelites had not yet attained the high material level nor the advanced political organization which would have enabled them to take the place of the Canaanites in defending the northern part of the country.

77. 'Ox, ass, and sheep' represent, collectively, the sum total of economically valuable animals and hence are special objects of destruction by enemies (1 Sam. 15.3; 22.19; Josh. 6.21) or of coveting and theft (Exod. 20.17; 22.3, 8, 9). We may take it then that this expression in Judg. 6.4 refers to the utter destruction of Israel's economic base.

78. 'As far as the approach to Gaza' (v. 4a). According to two well-attested traditions within the OT, represented in Judges by 1.18 and 1.19 respectively, Israel had some military successes in the 'Gaza strip' but never established effective control there, even in the golden age of Joshua (Josh. 11.2; cf. 10.41 and Gen. 10.19). 'As far as the approach to Gaza' must therefore be taken to mean 'until one passes beyond the southwestern limits of Israelite settlement'. From the plain the raiders penetrated deeply into the highlands as well.

79. Literally 'was brought very low before Midian'. Although the lexical connections are slight the situation is strongly reminiscent of that projected in the curses of Deuteronomy 28: Israel will be brought very low (Deut. 28.43); a nation of strong (עז) countenance (cf. Judg. 6.2, ותעז) will eat the fruit of Israel's cattle and land, and leave (שאר; cf. Judg. 6.4) neither corn, wine, nor oil, or increase of oxen, flocks and sheep, until Israel is destroyed, (Deut. 28.50-51).

80. Both איש נביא (lit. a man, a prophet) and אשה נביאה (a woman, a prophetess) are unique in the OT. The only expression which offers any comparison to איש נביא is הנער הנביא (the young man, the prophet) in 2 Kgs 9.14, but this is used resumptively to distinguish Elisha's apprentice (mentioned earlier) from the prophet himself, and not absolutely, as איש נביא is used in Judg. 6.8. In every other instance where a prophetess is mentioned the expression used is simply נביאה (prophetess) without אשה (woman).

81. Gideon had already crossed the Jordan according to the closing words of 7.25. But 8.1-3 is nevertheless, in terms of plot-structure, the completion of the action which had taken place west of the Jordan, not a part of the new developments now to take place east of it. Hence the resumption from the crossing of the Jordan in 8.4. The LXX avoids the difficulty by rendering מעבר לירדן as 'from beyond the Jordan'.

82. The appeal here of course is to 'Elohim'; the name 'Yahweh' is not revealed until chapter 3.

83. The five essential elements of the paradigm have been identified by W. Richter as the noting of the affliction, the commission, the objection, the promise of strength, and the sign. Richter finds these five elements in both the alleged E and J strands of Exod. 3sq., in Judg. 6.11-17, and in 1 Sam. 9.1–10.16 (*Die sogenannten vorprophetischen Berufungsberichte* [Göttingen:

Vandenhoeck & Ruprecht, 1970], esp. pp. 138-39). Cf. also W. Beyerlin, who argues that the historical data of an original story about the clan of Abiezer (still discernible in 8.4-21) have been worked over by a later narrator in such a way as to transform them into a typical example of salvation history based squarely on the exodus traditions: Gideon is a new Moses; Yahweh saves Israel in holy war; Yahweh alone is Israel's king ('Geschichte und heilsgeschichtliche Traditionsbildung im Alten Testament: ein Beitrag zur Traditionsgeschichte von Richter vi-viii', *VT* 13 [1963], pp. 1-25). For a critical review of Beyerlin's article see B. Lindars, 'Gideon and Kingship', *Journal of Theological Studies* n.s. 16 (1965), pp. 315-26.

84. This is a key expression in Exodus 3, involving as it does a transparent word-play on the divine name, יהוה, about to be revealed (Exod. 3.14).

85. The angel of Yahweh here is in effect Yahweh himself in manifestation as a comparison of vv. 11, 12, 21, 22 and 23 with vv. 14 and 16 makes clear.

86. Cf. Elijah's exposure of Baal on Mt Carmel.

87. Cf. Jephthah, 11.1. Boling renders גבור חיל 'aristocrat' in 6.12 and 'knight' in 11.1. Jephthah, unlike Gideon, was already renowned for his fighting ability (*Judges*, pp. 128, 196).

88. Cf. Gray, *Judges*, p. 298, who comments that this expression 'possibly refers to the courage of Gideon in having secured a harvest in spite of Midianite raids, and in venturing to thresh it, or it may refer to his strength of character in questioning the conventional greeting . . .' Boling's proposal (*Judges*, p. 131), following Freedman, to read the pronoun suffix on בכחך as an emphatic *kaph* ('in the strength of this one [i.e. Yahweh]'), is unwarranted.

89. The text of 6.5-6 is clearly in a disordered state. The original distinction must have been between those who knelt and scooped the water to their mouths by hand, and those (the 300) who put their faces to the water and lapped like dogs. Boling (*Judges*, p. 145) gives a highly plausible explanation of how the present confusion in the MT arose. It is not clear whether the 300 were chosen because they showed less fear, or less aptitude (the choice of the latter would ensure that Yahweh got even greater credit for the victory), or simply because they were simply the smaller group (so Martin, *Judges*, p. 94). All three views have had their advocates (see the discussion in Soggin, *Judges*, pp. 136-37) but the second, advocated by Boling and favoured by Soggin, seems the most probable.

90. The dream symbolism reinforces, for Gideon and the reader, the point of the water test in 7.1-7: Yahweh will achieve a great victory with the most unpromising material. Boling (*Judges*, p. 146) renders צלול לחם שערים by 'mouldy barley bread', relating צלול to Ar. *ṣalla* 'to become dry, cracked, putrid'.

91. There has been no mention of a battle at Tabor in the preceding narrative although the seven years of hostilities referred to in 6.1-5 provide ample opportunity for one. I suspect, with Boling, that the question in 8.18

'is intended to be as startling as it sounds' (*Judges*, p. 157). The explanation for Gideon's behaviour is held over until the climax so that it might strike us with particular force.

92. See 1 Sam. 23.6,9; 30.7, where David uses the ephod which was in the custody of Abiathar the priest to inquire of Yahweh. Presumably 'ephod' here refers to the high-priestly ephod complete with its breastplate containing the Urim and Thummim. But this is exceptional. The OT traditions generally associate the ephod with divine government in the period of Moses and Joshua rather than with the period of the monarchy (see especially Num. 27.21). Kings characteristically consult prophets rather than the ephod. The ephod which Gideon erects is a symbol of divine government according to the old Mosaic ideal. After erecting it he retires from public life (8.29). I am unconvinced by G. Henton Davies's argument that Gideon in fact accepted the offer of kingship and 'sought to show his royal position by the possession of an ephod' ('Judges VIII 22-23', *VT* 12, 2 [1963], pp. 151-57).

93. Just as Abimelech emphasized his close ties with the men of Shechem against Jerubbaal, so Gaal emphasizes his close ties with them against Abimelech. The important place which the Gaal episode plays in this symmetry of retribution is generally overlooked by those who argue that it is an interpolation which interrupts the flow of the narrative (see the standard commentaries). A.D. Crown, 'A Reinterpretation of Judges IX in the Light of its Humour', *Abr Nahrain* 3 (1961-62), finds a further ironical comparison between the two scenes in the unusual wording, ב ויעברו, in v. 26: 'Gaal and his brothers appear to be in transit and "pass through" Shechem on their travels. They too are nothing but vain and worthless fellows: Abimelech is simply hoist with his own petard' (p. 95).

94. Cf. L. Ginzberg, *The Legends of the Jews*, IV (Philadelphia: The Jewish Publication Society of America, 1928), p. 41: 'But God is just. As Abimelech murdered his brothers upon a stone, so Abimelech himself met his death through a millstone', citing *Tan.* B I, 103. Further the 'one woman' (אשה אחת) of 9.53 answers to the 'one stone' (אבן אחת)' of 9.5 etc. Abimelech suffers a similar fate to Sisera. The woman of Thebez is a veritable second Jael.

95. Eugene Maly has argued that 'the meaning of the original fable . . . was clearly not directed against kingship itself but against those who refused, for insufficient reasons, the burden of kingship' ('The Jotham Fable—Anti-monarchical?', *CBQ* 22 [1960], p. 303). Barnabas Lindars has accepted Maly's proposal and suggested that the fable may have originated in a Canaanite city state of the conquest period when local landowners were more concerned to protect their own estates than to take responsibility for territorial claims which could no longer be sustained ('Jotham's Fable—A New Form-critical Analysis', *JTS* 24 [1973], p. 365). However, the majority view remains that the fable probably arose in early Israel among those who

saw kingship as an institution with no positive function (F. Crüsemann, *Der Widerstand gegen das Königtum* [Wissenschaftliche Monographien zum Alten und Neuen Testament, 49; Neukirchen Vluyn: Neukirchener Verlag, 1978], pp. 19-32). But even granting that the original intention of the fable was to denigrate the institution of kingship it does not follow that this is how it functions in its present literary context. The speech as a whole does not attack kingship as such but the foul play associated with Abimelech's rise to power (9.19-20). The fable is used to pour scorn on Abimelech, whom Jotham never addresses directly, by contrasting his absurd pretensions with the modest refusal tendered by men better than himself (such as Gideon and his sons?), and also, via v. 15b to prepare the way for the pronouncement of Jotham's curse in v. 20.

96. The phrase באמת ובתמים occurs in v. 16 and is repeated in v. 19 for emphasis. The same combination of terms occurs elsewhere within the OT only in the covenant formula of Josh. 24.14 (Boling, *Judges*, p. 174).

97. As a rhetorical device the fable allows the speaker who has an unpopular point to make to gain a hearing for himself by approaching his subject obliquely and in an interesting manner. Cf. Lindars, 'Jotham's Fable', p. 361; and Richter, *Traditionsgeschichtliche Untersuchungen*, pp. 296-99, where the sociological-political functions of fable are discussed with particular reference to the fable of 2 Kgs 14.9.

98. Cf. Ginzberg, *Legends of the Jews*, VI, p. 201 (citing *Aggadat Bereshit* 26, 52-53): 'The ingratitude of the Israelites who permitted Abimelech to murder the children of their benefactor Gideon was counted unto them as though they had forsaken God; ingratitude is as grave a sin as idolatry'.

99. Cf. 2.17: 'They would not listen to their judges . . . they turned *quickly* out of the way . . .' (my emphasis). See my comments on 2.16-19 in Section 1.23 of Chapter 3.

100. Other more sinister interpretations of Gideon's conduct are possible and have been cogently argued: Gideon's refusal in 8.23 is in reality a veiled acceptance and his manufacture of the ephod a cynical prostitution of religion to political ends, corrupting it in the process, a scenario which becomes conspicuous by repetition in the later Deuteronomic History. There is an opacity in the text which teases us and makes us suspect that there is more here than meets the eye. But the narrator himself adopts a more generous perspective on Gideon. See note 92 above.

101. Cf. Polzin, *Moses and the Deuteronomist*, p. 175: 'Fairness and honesty (*'emet w^{e}tāmim*) (9.16, 19), may be capable of illuminating the issues of retributive justice; they are relatively useless in clearing up the mystery of what happened to Israel in the period of the judges. Not the least aspect of that mystery consisted in the realization that, in all fairness and honesty, Israel should not have survived.'

102. Cf. G.E. Gerbrandt, *Kingship According to the Deuteronomistic History*, pp. 171-86.

103. Cf. Boling, *Judges*, p. 187, who holds that the syntax of the notice *requires* such an interpretation.

104. So Moore, *Judges*, p. 310; Burney, *Judges*, pp. 290, 334; Boling, *Judges*, pp. 215-16; and Soggin, *Judges*, p. 223. Josephus took it as the Judean Bethlehem, as did Rashi, Kimchi, and Levi ben Gershon, who identified Ibzan with Boaz the ancestor of David.

105. Cf. Gooding, 'The Composition of the Book of Judges', p. 79 n. 23.

106. Cf. Boling's comment that vv. 6-16 of ch. 10 'form a theological introduction to the second half of Judges' (*Judges*, p. 193).

107. The Spirit has already begun to move Samson before he goes down to Timnath and becomes infatuated with a Philistine girl—an infatuation which we are explicitly told was 'from Yahweh'. It is the Spirit which empowers him to kill the lion, a deed which sets off a chain reaction which leads, via the riddle and the resulting feud with the Philistines, to the slaughter at Ramath-lehi. Samson sees himself as merely seeking just redress for personal wrongs he has suffered and desires an end to the feud (15.7, 8, 11b), but he finds that withdrawal is impossible; the Philistines are intent on capturing him and destroying him and will stop at nothing to accomplish their end.

108. I am indebted for these observations about the formal design of the narrative to J. Cheryl Exum, 'Aspects of Symmetry and Balance in the Samson Saga', *JSOT* 19 (1981), pp. 3-29.

109. A much more detailed account of the symmetry between these two movements is given by Cheryl Exum in the article referred to in n. 108. She also sees structural parallels *within* the first movement, between chs. 14 and 15.

110. For details see J. Cheryl Exum, 'Promise and Fulfilment: Narrative Art in Judges 13', *JBL* 99 (1980), p. 44 n. 2 (citing Richter). Exum also gives a very useful annotated listing of the relevant literature in notes 1 and 3 of the same article (pp. 43 and 44 respectively).

111. Cf. the comparison made by Delilah in Milton's *Samson Agonistes*, lines 981-990:

> In Ekron, Gaza, Asdod, and in Gath,
> I shall be named among the famousest
> Of women . . .
> Not less renowned than in Mount Ephraim
> Jael, who with inhospitable guile
> Smote Sisera sleeping, through the temples nailed.

112. Cf. Boling, *Judges*, p. 230, and note Isa. 7.18: 'the bee (דבורה) which is in the land of Assyria [i.e. the Assyrian king]'.

113. שמשון (Samson) appears to be derived from שמש (sun), as דגון (Dagon) is derived from דג (fish). On the connections frequently postulated by the older commentators between the Samson story and solar myth, see Burney, *Judges*, pp. 391-408.

114. Cf. Boling, Judges, p. 232: 'The Samson stories swarm with reminiscences and allusions to virtually all the great protagonists from Deborah to Barak ... This can scarcely be accidental.'

115. Entitled simply 'Samson' and read at a seminar in the Biblical Studies Department at the University of Sheffield in 1982.

116. Cf. Exum, 'Symmetry in the Samson Saga', p. 10: '... the birth account of ch. 13 balances the death account in ch. 16, thereby establishing a symmetrical relationship between the beginning and the end of the narrative. Notice also that both of these chapters are constructed around a fourfold asking and answer discourse, 13.11-18; 16.4-22.'

117. See the standard commentaries and note Boling's plausible reconstruction of the text on the basis of LXX(AL) (*Judges*, p. 222).

118. James L. Crenshaw, 'The Samson Saga: Filial Devotion or Erotic Attachment?', *ZAW* 86 (1974), p. 501.

119. I refer to the words of Manoah in Milton's *Samson Agonistes*, lines 1495-1501:

> And I persuade me God had not permitted
> His strength again to grow up with his hair
> Garrisoned round about him like a camp
> Of faithful soldiery, were not his purpose
> To use him further yet in some great service,
> Not to sit idle with so great a gift
> Useless, and thence ridiculous, about him.

120. The curiosity can perhaps be explained in terms of the special circumstances, namely, the Nazirite in question is not yet born. But from a purely literary point of view the distinction gives the razor rule a separate status which draws our attention to it.

121. Cf. J. Blenkinsopp, 'Structure and Style in Judges 13-16', *JBL* 82 (1963), pp. 65-76, who finds in the order of the prescriptions in Judges 13 'evidence of a thought-out plot' which unfolds in the body of narrative through the violation of the prescriptions in three stages, culminating in the cutting of the hair. But not everything in the present form of the story can be accommodated to such a plot-description, as Blenkinsopp himself admits; he eliminates the whole of 15.1-16.3 as secondary. Cf. also his earlier article, 'Some Notes on the Saga of Samson and the Heroic Milieu', *Scripture* 11 (1959), pp. 81-89. Edward L. Greenstein in 'The Riddle of Samson', *Prooftexts* 1/3 (1981), pp. 237-60, argues that the gap between the breaking of the first two prescriptions and the breaking of the third gives the narrator time to underline the forbearance of God who continues to stand by and invigorate Samson 'so long as he clings to the one last strand of the Naziriteship, the prohibition against shaving'.

122. Cf. Samson's lament in Milton's *Samson Agonistes*, lines 63-64:

> God, when he gave me strength, to show withal
> How slight the gift was, hung it in my hair.

But peace! I must not quarrel with the will
Of highest dispensation, which herein
Haply had ends above my reach to know:
Suffices that to me strength is my bane
And proves the source of all my miseries . . .

123. 'And it came to pass after this that he loved a woman in the valley of Sorek, and her name was Delilah' (16.4). In the paper I referred to in n. 115 above, Gunn points out that although the Timnite was 'right in his eyes' and his tenderness was demonstrated in his attempt at reconciliation, the word 'love' is reserved for Delilah, and that matching this 'love' of Samson is Delilah's quintessential 'womanness' (we are not told her nationality, as we were with the Timnite, nor her occupation, as we were with the prostitute of Gaza; she is simply 'a woman').

124. Cf. Crenshaw, 'The Samson Saga', p. 501.

125. Cf. Exum, 'Symmetry in the Samson Saga', p. 13, who comments with particular reference to chapter 14: ' . . . while going down impels the narrative forward, coming up in conjunction with going down forms an inclusion around it, vv. 1-2 and 19-20. The same may be said of chs. 14-16 as a whole (note the inclusion formed by 14.1-2 and 16.31)'.

126. Compare Samson's extradition by the Judahites in the first cycle (15.11-12). Both extraditions return Samson from a place of withdrawal to a place where he fulfils his divine calling.

127. On the relationship between the legislation in Numbers 6 and Naziriteship in pre-exilic times see Burney, *Judges*, pp. 342-43. The similarities between the ritual prescriptions in the two texts strongly suggest that the author of Judges 13 was familiar with the institution as reflected in Numbers 6. With Samson as a life-long Nazirite compare Samuel ('a razor shall not come upon his head', 1 Sam. 1.11) and the Nazirites referred to in Amos 2.11-12 who are coupled with prophets and spoken of as raised up by Yahweh to their vocation.

128. The quotation is from the same article referred to in n. 113 above.

129. Cf. Boling, *Judges*, p. 83.

130. Cf. Gooding, 'The Composition of the Book of Judges', p. 73: 'There could not, then, be a more vivid contrast between Othniel the first judge and Samson the last: Othniel's wife was his incentive to drive out the Gentiles, Samson's wives were his incentive to live among, rather than drive out, the Philistines . . .'

131. Cf. Exum, 'Symmetry in the Samson Saga', p. 9: 'It bears asking whether the appearance of this formula at the end of each cycle is an indication that the Deuteronomistic historian was aware of the parallelism of the accounts and accordingly provided symmetrical notices about Samson's term of office as judge'.

132. Cf. Boling, 'In Those Days There Was No King in Israel', p. 40, where he comments with reference to 16.31 that here 'the historian

appended a repetition of the judge formula, appropriately revised in perfect tense (only here in the book): "he *had been* judge..."' See also his comments in *Judges*, pp. 240-41, 252-53, where he argues that the old 'pragmatic edition' of the book ended with Samson's 'enlistment' as a judge at 15.20 and that this was supplemented in the 'deuteronomistic edition' by an account of Samson's *career* as judge, concluding with 16.31.

133. 'Symmetry in the Samson Saga', p. 7.

134. The use of עבד (servant) could simply be a piece of conventional politeness of Samson's part, but the context hardly suggests this, and the word is not so used anywhere else in Judges. Samson has already been separated to God for the fulfilment of a specific mission (cf. the use of עבד יהוה [servant of Yahweh] with reference to Joshua in 2.8). At the very least Samson speaks better than he knows. See Boling, *Judges*, pp. 71, 239.

135. Cf. the words of the chorus in Milton's *Samson Agonistes*, lines 1687-89:

> But he, though blind of sight,
> Despised, and thought extinguished quite,
> With inward eyes illuminated...

Gunn (see n. 115 above) compares Samson to Sophocles' Oedipus and Shakespeare's Gloucester.

136. So reads the MT. Moore comments (*Judges*, p. 362): 'the greatest evil he could inflict on them would be but partial retribution for the loss of his sight... There is a grim humour in the words as we read them in the MT, which is altogether in character and may very well be original.' The versions read either 'in one last act of vengeance...' or 'at once...' 'One' and 'two' appear again in the next verse where Samson takes hold of the two pillars, one with his right hand and one with his left.

137. Cf. J.B. Vickery, 'In Strange Ways: The Story of Samson', in *Images of Man and God: Old Testament Short Stories in Literary Focus* (ed. B.O. Long; Sheffield: Almond, 1981), p. 73: 'The desire of the hero and the purpose of the Lord are one: deliverance from bondage is the achievement of both and of the one through the other'. For 'deliverance from bondage' I would substitude 'the downfall of Dagon and his worshippers'.

138. *Samson Agonistes*, line 164.

139. Cf. E.L. Greenstein, 'The Riddle of Samson', *Prooftexts* 1/3 (1981), pp. 237-60. Greenstein argues that the riddle formula (what appears to be x can later be recognized as y) pervades the entire narrative of Samson' and provides the key to its interpretation. The 'solution' which he proposes to the narrative as a whole considered as a riddle is 'What appears to be Samson is the people of Israel; what appears as the Naziriteship of Samson is the Israelite covenant' (p. 247).

140. Cf. Vickery, 'In Strange Ways', p. 62. Although he does not press the analogy as far as Greenstein (see n. 139 above) Vickery, too, notes 'the

parallelism of individual behaviour and national fate' in the Samson story, so that Samson is not only Samson, but also 'the figure of Israel'.

141. As pointed out by Exum in 'Symmetry in the Samson Saga', p. 8, and p. 27 (n. 13).

142. See, for example, Exod. 33.20.

143. So Exum in 'Symmetry in the Samson Saga', p. 27 n. 13, who comments that 'the motif of knowing and not knowing draws attention to the mysterious ways of Yhwh, who works for Israel's benefit through and even in spite of the human participants with their limited vision'.

144. So, David Gunn. See n. 115 above.

145. The messenger appears to the woman when she is alone (v. 9) in spite of Manoah's request that he appear to 'us' (v. 8). Manoah takes centre stage only to have attention redirected to the woman. For details see Exum, 'Promise and Fulfilment'.

146. See n. 115 above.

147. The '40 years' of 13.1 overshoots the end of the Samson story, but see n. 4 above.

148. Richter has argued that the two formulae נתן ביד (to give into the hand of) and מכר ביד (to sell into the hand of) are distinct from one another in the way they are used in the former prophets, the former being associated with raids and plundering, while the second is used consistently for military subjugation: *Die Bearbeitungen des 'Retterbuches'*, pp. 29-30. So, e.g., in Judges נתן ביד is used with reference to the Midianite raids (6.1) but מכר ביד is used for the subjugation to Cushan-rishathaim in 3.7-8. But the use of נתן ביד with reference to the Philistine oppression in 13.1 is problematical for Richter's case. Both expressions occur in Judg. 2.14. See above, Chapter 3 n. 100.

149. Contrast Abimelech, who remains a human appointee, pure and simple.

150. At best one can imagine only an uneasy truce during Jephthah's six years of rule after the civil war of 12.1-6. Cf. Boling, *Judges*, p. 216.

151. See Sections 1.02 and 6.091 above.

152. Lilley, 'A Literary Appreciation of the Book of Judges', p. 98.

153. Boling, *Judges*, p. 215.

154. See Section 4.01 of Chapter 1 above. Characteristic elements of the framework pattern of the major episodes appear in 10.6, 7, 10 and 11.33; elements 2, 3, and 4 of the pattern characteristic of the short notices appear in 12.7.

155. See Section 6.02 above.

156. I owe this observation to an unpublished paper entitled 'Hidden Objects and Games in the Book of Judges', by E.T.A. Davidson of the State University of New York.

157. Cf. Greenstein, 'The Riddle of Samson', p. 249, who notes that the root זנה (to play the harlot) which is used metaphorically in 2.17 and 8.33

with reference to Israel's pursuit of other gods is used literally with reference to Samson's going to a harlot in 16.1.

Notes to Chapter 5. Coda

1. On the inversion of narrative elements compare Boling, 'No King in Israel', p. 42.

2. The same phenomenon appears in the plot structure of the Deborah-Barak story. I owe the definition of 'nodal point' which I use here to Murray ('The Deborah-Barak Story', p. 159). See also the quotation from Martin Noth in n. 18 below.

3. The text as it stands is not entirely coherent. With most commentators I restore 'but now I will return it to you' from the end of v. 3 to follow 'I took it' in v. 2.

4. Heb. פסל ומסכה, 'a graven image and a molten image', a hendiadys. Also in v. 4, where the singular verb, ויהי (and it was . . .), confirms that a single object is on view. The splitting open of this hendiadys in 18.17 may simply be a stylistic device. The resulting envelope construction encloses 'ephod and teraphim', the pair first introduced in 17.5. Cf. Boling, *Judges*, pp. 256, 264.

5. Deut. 27.15! Also Exod. 20.4; 34.17.

6. Reminiscent of the 'eleven hundred of silver' which appears in 16.5, the sum which each of the lords of the Philistines offers to Delilah as a bribe.

7. An ironical name indeed for an idolator! The same form of the name occurs in 1 Kgs 9.22 (Micaiah ben Imlah). Another form, מיכיה (K) occurs in Jer. 26.18 with reference to Micah the Morashite. Cf. מיכאל, 'Who is like El?' (Num. 13.13; Dan. 10.13; 1 Chron. 5.13 etc.).

8. Cf. Alter, *The Art of Biblical Narrative*, p. 63: 'A proper narrative event occurs when the narrative tempo slows down enough for us to discriminate a particular scene'. Biblical scenes, in this sense, characteristically feature dialogue.

9. Either from his accent (southern, like their own) or because they know him personally (cf. 1 Sam. 26.17). The Samson story has drawn our attention to the close connection between the tribes of Dan and Judah (15.9ff.). Cf. the identification of Ephraimites by their accent in 12.6.

10. With Boling (*Judges*, pp. 261-62) I take the unusual syntax of Micah's speech as a reflection of his agitated state of mind rather than as a considered rhetorical device.

11. Cf. the 'six hundred men' of 20.47—a further link between the two narratives of these closing chapters of the book.

12. Compare Abraham Malamat, who has studied the typology of the two accounts in detail and concluded that 'they are individual models of different

scale, following a basic pattern which evolved for biblical narratives of campaigns of inheritance' ('The Danite Migration and the Pan-Israelite Exodus-Conquest: a Biblical Narrative Pattern', *Biblica* 51 [1970], pp. 1-16). My quotation is from p. 16.

13. I comment more fully on this important point in Section 5.03 below.

14. Or possibly, 'with Aram', reading אָרָם for אֲרָם. Cf. the parallel expression in 18.7, where LXX[A] has μετὰ Συρίας (with Syria). The point is not that the town had no contact with the outside world but that it had no defensive alliances with neighbouring states.

15. See further in Section 5.05 below.

16. Ignoring the suspended nun of מנשה (Manasseh).

17. It is a concession not made in the polemic of 1 Kgs 12.31.

18. Cf. Polzin, *Moses and the Deuteronomist*, p. 197.

19. Compare and contrast M. Noth, 'The Background of Judges 17-18', p. 79. In relation to 17.6 and 18.1a Noth comments that 'they have been placed in their present location by someone who comprehended the interior structure of the narrative'. But he argues that the placement of 19.1a and 21.25 at the extremes of the second narrative is evidence that they are secondary to the similar comments in chs. 17-18, and were taken over from there when the complexes 17-18 and 19-21 were joined together. The general point he is making about the redactional history of the text may well be correct, but this particular reason for it fails to appreciate the difference of plot structure to which I have referred.

20. The second episode will provide a different, contrasting perspective on the same events. See further below.

21. The MT is admittedly suspect, since no exact parallel to the construction זנה על is attested. However, ωργίσθη 'became angry [with]' of LXX[A], favoured by most commentators, is regularly rendered by חרה אף in Judges (2.14, 20; 3.8; 6.39; 9.30; 10.7; 14.19) and it is difficult to see how the MT of 19.2 could be a corruption of this. The επορευθη απ αυτου ('she deserted him') of LXX [B] appears to be an interpretation of the MT rather than a translation of an alternative text. See Moore, *Judges*, p. 409.

22. Cf. Boling, *Judges*, p. 274: 'MT is interpretive. As Israelite law did not allow for divorce by the wife, she became an adulteress by walking out on him.' A similar understanding of the MT is reflected in the Jewish commentators. For references see Moore, *Judges*, p. 409.

23. The extensive verbal parallels between the present scene and that in Gen. 19.4-8 are detailed by Burney in *Judges*, p. 444. The analogy is one which we are almost certainly meant to draw and which is, in any case, inescapable when Judges is read in its canonical context. See also n. 27 below.

24. This puzzling feature of the text does serve, however, to underscore the allusion to the episode in Sodom. The offer of the host's daughter

anticipates the proffer of the virgin daughters of Shiloh. Cf. S.D. Currie, 'Biblical Studies for a Seminar on Sexuality and the Human Community, I. Judges 19-21', *Austin Seminary Bulletin* 87 (1971), p. 15.

25. In view of the offer made by the host in v. 24, the words 'the man took his concubine . . .' in v. 25 *could* be taken to mean, 'the host took the Levite's concubine . . .' But the opening words of v. 25 ('but the men would not listen to him . . .') make this unlikely in my judgment. The host has been rebuffed. What follows is not the host doing what he promised, as, for example, 'the man took his virgin daughter and the concubine and . . .', but the Levite, whose fate now seems to be sealed, making a last-ditch attempt to save himself. With the concubine actually in their hands the mob, as creatures of appetite rather than reason, settle for immediate gratification. Cf. Boling, *Judges*, p. 276, who comments that 'the man' of v. 25 is probably the Levite, whose story is being told. Other protagonists—the father-in-law, the master of the house—are regularly identified by some such title'; and Moore, *Judges*, p. 418: 'the Levite gives up the woman to save himself'.

26. That is, here, an *ad hoc* meeting of representatives of the various tribes to deal with a pressing matter of common concern (20.1; 21.10, 13, 16). Compare the similar function of the עדה in Josh. 22.12-34. As an institution the assembly, in this sense, was rendered obsolete by the monarchy. But the related concept (characteristically associated with the term קהל) of all Israel gathered by God as a theocratic state, was of course an ideal which persisted and flourished after the collapse of the monarchy. The verb נקהל (niphal of קהל) appears in 20.2, and the noun קהל in 21.5, 8. The collocation of עדה and קהל in these chapters is taken by most commentators as evidence of a late date. But עדה is the primary term and it is the assembly as a pre-monarchical institution which is principally in view.

27. Cf. the similar action performed by Saul in 1 Sam. 11.6-7 under the impulse of 'the Spirit of God'. Those who are summoned respond as one man because 'the fear of Yahweh' has fallen upon them. Currie ('Seminar on Sexuality') adduces evidence from comparative material to elucidate the significance of this kind of summons. He concludes that 'the gesture combines appeal for help, claim of obligation outstanding, and threat of reprisal against non-responders' (p. 17).

28. The Levite is a caricature judge-figure. Boling (*Judges*, p. 277) sees here 'a calculated inversion of elements in the story of Lot', of whom the locals complained: 'This fellow came to sojourn, and he would play the judge!' (Gen. 19.9 RSV). See n. 23 above.

29. Or at least as polluted and of no further use to himself.

30. Cf. Polzin, *Moses and the Deuteronomist*, pp. 200-202.

31. So, Polzin, on p. 201 of *Moses and the Deuteronomist*.

32. He tells of his visit to Bethlehem because he wishes to present himself as travel-weary, but he does not mention the reason for the visit because this might raise questions about the good character of himself and/or his

concubine. The deferential 'for me and for your handmaid' (v. 19) is calculated to win the host's favour while conveying minimal information. The MT's 'I am going to *the house of the Lord*' (v. 18) is entirely in keeping with the Levite's desire to create a favourable impression, but is not supported by the LXX, which reads '... to my house'. The Levite particularly stresses their self-sufficiency in provisions; all they need is a roof.

33. Cf. the characteristics of holy-war narrative listed by Gerhard von Rad in *Der Heilige Krieg im alten Israel* (4th edn; Göttingen: Vandenhoeck & Ruprecht, 1965), pp. 6-14.

34. An analogy, at the personal level, is to be found in the legislation regarding the avenging of blood in Num. 35.19sq. While it was ultimately the responsibility of the community as a whole to punish the slayer, the chief responsibility fell on the גאל (redeemer) who was kinsman to the victim. The Judahite Levite has, in effect, called upon the assembled Israelites to assist him in avenging the death of his concubine.

35. Cf. Elkanah's annual pilgrimage to Shiloh, 1 Sam. 1.3.

36. An early hint of irregularities at the Shiloh sanctuary? Cf. the vintage festival at Shechem associated with the cult of Baal-berith (9.27; cf. 8.33; 9.4).

37. The 'daughter' motif is a further link between the two incidents (19.24; 21.21). See n. 24 above.

38. Cf. Boling, who on p. 45 of his 'No King in Israel' comments that the purpose of these final chapters is 'to affirm the present rule of Yahweh in the midst of chaos'.

39. See Section 1.18 in Chapter 3 above.

40. The left-handed Benjaminites of 20.16 are reminiscent of Ehud (3.15). Zorah and Eshtaol figure in both the Samson and Micah stories (13.25; 16.31; cf. 18.2, 8.11) as does the motif 'eleven hundred of silver' (see n. 6 above). The Levite's attempt at reconciliation (19.3) recalls that of Samson (15.1). With the פסל (idol) of 17.3, 4 etc. compare (and contrast) the פסילים (idols) of 3.19, 26.

41. 'No King in Israel', p. 44; *Judges*, pp. 37-38.

42. Cf. Malamat's comments in 'The Danite Migration', pp. 14-16, on the renaming of conquered sites—a phenomenon found throughout the conquest traditions .

43. As indicated by the phrase ממשפחת יהודה (of the family of Judah). To the question, how can the young man be at once a Levite, a Judahite of Bethlehem, and a resident alien there (גר שם), the standard commentaries propose various solutions: e.g., read גר שם as 'Gershom' (cf. 18.30); take 'Levite' as indicative of the man's occupation rather than his tribal affiliation; and so on. Soggin (*Judges*, p. 266) deletes ממשפחת יהודה as a gloss, thereby removing the difficulty posed by גר שם, for which he retains the MT pointing. But he admits that ממשפחת יהודה is the *lectio difficilior*

and it is in fact retained by (among others) Budde, Burney, Moore, Boling, Gray, Cundall, and Martin.

44. An apparent exception is Martin Noth's suggestion that the kingship which is positively evaluated in 17.6 and 18.1 is that of Jeroboam I ('The Background of Judges 17–18', pp. 81-82). But this is an attempt to recover an *original* meaning which has been obscured by the gloss of v. 30 and the insertion of the story into its present literary context. Noth argues that the narrative in these chapters is a product of the northern royal court, and that the critique of the old Danite sanctuary with its corrupt Levitical priesthood was intended to justify the measures taken by Jeroboam I to transform it into a royal sanctuary, including his appointment of non-Levites as priests. See also n. 19 above.

45. *The Kingship of God*, pp. 66-84.

46. A.E. Cundall, 'Judges—An Apology for the Monarchy?', *Expository Times* 81 (1970), pp. 178-81.

47. Cf. W.J. Dumbrell, 'In Those Days There was No King in Israel; Every Man Did What Was Right in His Own Eyes: The Purpose of the Book of Judges Reconsidered', *JSOT* 25 (1983), p. 29: 'Most naturally the "captivity" would refer to the exile of the North in 722 BC, all the more so since the removal of the northern priesthood seems to have been part of the Assyrian deportation policy (2 Kgs 17.27) and we know that the Danite sanctuary was still flourishing in Amos's day (Amos 8.14). If the comment of 18.30 does refer to 722 BC, it was doubtless made at a very much later remove and thus quite possibly after the fall of Jerusalem. Equally well, a reference to a "captivity" could, as a comment by a southern redactor, refer absolutely to 586 BC, rather than 722. In either case the notation would seem to stem from an "exilic" period . . .' It is taken as a reference to the Assyrian deportations of either 734–732 (2 Kgs 15.29) or 721 (2 Kgs 17.5-6) by, among others, Rashi, Moore, Gray, Boling, Martin, and Soggin. The note in 18.31 has led some commentators to suggest a captivity of Dan co-incident with the fall of Shiloh (e.g. Kimchi, Keil-Delitzsch, Burney). However, as Soggin has pointed out (*Judges*, pp. 276-77) the destruction of the Shiloh sanctuary is of uncertain date, and, in any case, the comment in 18.31 simply notes when Micah's image was in use at Dan and does not necessarily imply a destruction of the Danite sanctuary co-incident with that of Shiloh (cf. Dumbrell, 'The Purpose of the Book of Judges', p. 29, and Noth, 'The Background of Judges 17–18', p. 85). The only exact stylistic parallel to עד גלות הארץ, 'until the-carrying- away-into-captivity of the land' (using the infinitive construct) is עד גלות ירושלים in Jer. 1.3: 'until the-carrying-away-into-captivity of Jerusalem'.

48. David Pennant, of Trinity College, Bristol, has drawn my attention to the similarity between the blinding of Samson at the end of the judges period and the blinding of Zedekiah at the end of the monarchy period.

49. Cf. Boling, *Judges*, pp. 278, 293; 'No King In Israel', pp. 41-44; and

Dumbrell, 'The Purpose of the Book of Judges', pp. 29-32.

50. Exactly the opposite of what Abimelech's disastrous reign produced! But see my comments in Chapter 4 on the Gideon-Abimelech episode. I have consistently argued in my analysis of chapters 1-16 (a) that none of the stories in these chapters is primarily concerned with the issue of kingship (it does not figure at all in the climactic Samson episode), and (b) that while kingship appears in an unfavourable light in chapters 1-12 it is not rejected in principle. Cf. with reference to Deut.-2 Kings as a whole, Gerbrandt, *Kingship in the Deuteronomistic History.* See also the excursus in my Section 5.04 of this Chapter. In order to maintain his thesis that the monarchy question is central to Judges, Buber had to eliminate from consideration 'the sketchy sections', 'general reflections' (by which he seems to have meant most of the introduction to the book!), the speeches at 2.1-5 and 6.7-10, and all the notices about the so-called minor judges (*Kingship of God*, p. 69). He could find no thematic significance at all in the Samson episode, which was simply a hinge between the two 'books' (anti- and pro-monarchical respectively) of which Judges was composed (*ibid.*, p. 68).

51. Compare the Joseph story at the end of Genesis. It brings the patriarchs down into Egypt and so sets the stage for the exodus, and in that sense can be seen as a bridge between the patriarchs and Moses. But it is also integrated intimately and functionally with the events and theological motifs of the preceding Genesis material and serves as its artistic and theological culmination: B.T. Dahlberg, 'The Unity of Genesis', *Literary Interpretations of Biblical Narratives, Volume II* (ed. K.R.R. Gros Louis, with J.S. Ackerman; Nashville: Abingdon, 1982), pp. 126-44. Compare also 1 Kings 1-2, which completes the so-called Succession Narrative, but also sets the stage for the subsequent treatment of the reign of Solomon.

Notes to Chapter 6. Conclusions

1. Compare, with reference to Hans Frei's *The Eclipse of Biblical Narrative*, J. Barton, *Reading the Old Testament: Method in Biblical Study* (London: Darton, Longman and Todd, 1984), p. 163.

2. See Sections 3.00-4.04 and 8.00 of Chapter 2 above.

3. Cf. Zvi Adar, *The Biblical Narrative* (Jerusalem: 1959), pp. 278-80.

4. *Moses and the Deuteronomist*, p. 160.

5. *The Art of Biblical Narrative*, p. 37.

6. Cf. also the fate suffered by Zedekiah in 2 Kgs 25.7 (at the end of the monarchy period) with that suffered by Samson in Judg. 16.21 (at the end of the judges era). See n. 48 to Chapter 5 above.

7. I am aware that the kings are assessed theologically and not solely or even primarily in strictly moral terms. I use the term 'moralism', for want of a better expression, to refer to the classification of the kings as doers of הַיָּשָׁר (right) or הָרַע (wrong).

8. Cf. G. Fohrer, *Introduction to the Old Testament* (tr. D. Green; London: SPCK, 1970), pp. 194-95.

9. Mendenhall's original observations about parallels between the structure of Hittite treaties and certain Old Testament texts were published in *Biblical Archaeologist* 17 (1954), pp. 26-46, 50-76. The application to Deuteronomy was made by M.G. Kline, *Treaty of the Great King* (Grand Rapids: Eerdmans, 1963), and by K.A. Kitchen, *Ancient Orient and Old Testament* (London: IVP, 1966), pp. 90-102. For a review of more recent discussions of the structure of Deuteronomy see A.D.H. Mayes, *Deuteronomy* (New Century Bible; London: Oliphants, 1979), pp. 29-55. Mayes himself holds that Deuteronomy in its finished form is a farewell speech by Moses (his testament) rather than a treaty document as such, but that in the final stage of deuteronomistic editing (subsequent to its incorporation into the Deuteronomic history) it 'took on the characteristics of covenant (or treaty) law under the influence of ideas, forms and expressions derived from the extra-biblical treaty tradition' (p. 30). Of particular interest is his observation that chs. 1-3, which culminate in the command to Moses to commission Joshua as his successor and chs. 31-34, which describe the commissioning of Joshua and the death of Moses, constitute a literary frame around the central section of the book (p. 42).

BIBLIOGRAPHY

Only works which are mentioned in the book have been included in this bibliography.

Ackerman, J.S., 'Prophecy and Warfare in Early Israel: A Study of the Deborah-Barak Story', *BASOR* 220 (1975), pp. 5-13.

Adar, Zvi, *The Biblical Narrative* (Jerusalem: 1959).

Alonso Schökel, L., 'Erzählkunst im Buche der Richter', *Biblica* 42 (1961), pp. 148-58.

Alter, Robert, *The Art of Biblical Narrative* (New York: Basic Books, 1981).

Armerding, C.E., *Judges*, in *A Bible Commentary for Today* (ed. G.C.D. Howley *et al.*; London: Pickering and Inglis, 1979).

Auld, A.G., 'Judges 1 and History: A Reconsideration', *VT* 25 (1975), pp. 261-85.

— 'Review of Boling's *Judges*. The Framework of Judges and the Deuteronomists', *JSOT* 1 (1976), pp. 41-46.

Barthes, R., *et al.*, *Structural Analysis and Biblical Exegesis* (tr. A.M. Johnson Jr; Pittsburgh Theological Monograph Series, 3; Pittsburgh: Pickwick, 1974).

Bartlett, J.R., 'The Conquest of Sihon's Kingdom: A Literary Re-examination', *JBL* 97 (1978), pp. 347-51.

Barton, J., *Reading the Old Testament: Method in Biblical Study* (London: Darton, Longman and Todd, 1984).

Beyerlin, W., 'Geschichte und heilsgeschichtliche Traditionsbildung im Alten Testament: ein Beitrag zur Traditionsgeschichte von Richter vi-viii', *VT* 13 (1963), pp. 1-25.

Blenkinsopp, J., 'Ballad Style and Psalm Style in the Song of Deborah', *Biblica* 42 (1961), pp. 61-76.

Bodine, Walter Ray, *The Greek Text of Judges: Recensional Developments* (Harvard Semitic Monographs, 23; Chico, California: Scholars Press, 1980).

Boling, Robert G., 'In Those Days There Was No King in Israel', *A Light Unto My Path: Old Testament Studies in Honor of Jacob M. Myers* (eds. H.N. Bream, R. Heim, C. Moore; Philadelphia: Temple University Press, 1974), pp. 33-48.

— *Judges: Introduction, Translation and Commentary* (The Anchor Bible; New York: Doubleday, 1975).

— 'Response', *JSOT* 1 (1976), pp. 47-52.

Bright, John, *A History of Israel* (2nd edn; London: SCM, 1972).

Brown, F., Driver, S.R., and Briggs, C.S., eds., *A Hebrew and English Lexicon of the Old Testament* (Oxford: Clarendon, 1907 and reprints).

Bruce, F.F., *Judges*, in *The New Bible Commentary Revised* (eds. D. Guthrie *et al.*; London: IVP, 1970).

Brueggemann, Walter, 'Social Criticism and Social Vision in the Deuteronomic Formula of the Judges', *Die Botschaft und die Boten: Festschrift für Hans Walter Wolff zum 70. Geburtstag* (eds. J. Jeremias, L. Perlitt; Neukirchen: Neukirchener Verlag, 1981), pp. 101-14.

Buber, Martin, *The Kingship of God* (3rd edn; tr. R. Scheimann; London: Allen and Unwin, 1967; German, 1956).

—*The Prophetic Faith* (New York: Harper and Row, 1960).

—and Rosenzweig, F., *Die Schrift und ihre Verdeutschung* (Berlin: 1936).

Budde, D. Karl, *Das Buch der Richter* (Freiburg: Mohr, 1897).

Burney, C.F., *The Book of Judges with Introduction and Notes* (London: Rivingtons, 1918).

Clines, D.J.A., 'Theme in Genesis 1–11', *CBQ* 38 (1976), pp. 484-87.

Cohen, A., ed., *The Minor Tractates of the Talmud . . . translated into English with notes, glossary and indices* (2 vols.; London: Soncino, 1965).

Coogan, M.D., 'A Structural and Literary Analysis of the Song of Deborah', *CBQ* 40 (1978), pp. 143-66.

Craigie, P.C., 'A Reconsideration of Shamgar ben Anath (Judg. 3.31 and 5.6)', *JBL* 91 (1972), pp. 239-40.

Crenshaw, James L., 'The Samson Saga: Filial Devotion or Erotic Attachment?', *ZAW* 86 (1974), pp. 470-504.

Cross, F.M., Jr, 'The Structure of the Deuteronomic History', *Perspectives in Jewish Learning* 3 (1968), pp. 9-24.

Crossan, J.D., *The Dark Interval: Towards a Theology of Story* (Niles, Illinois: Argus, 1975).

Crown, A.D., 'A Reinterpretation of Judges IX in the Light of its Humour', *Abr Nahrain* 3 (1961-62), pp. 90-98.

Crüsemann, F., *Der Widerstand gegen das Königtum* (Wissenschaftliche Monographien zum Alten und Neuen Testament, 49; Neukirchen-Vluyn: Neukirchener Verlag, 1978).

Culley, Robert C., 'Structural Analysis: Is it Done with Mirrors?', *Interpretation* 28 (1974), pp. 165-81.

Cundall, A.E., *Judges. An Introduction and Commentary*, in *Judges, Ruth* (Tyndale Old Testament Commentaries; London: Tyndale, 1968).

— 'Judges—An Apology for the Monarchy?', *Expository Times* 81 (1970), pp. 178-81.

Currie, S.D., 'Biblical Studies for a Seminar on Sexuality and the Human Community, I. Judges 19–21', *Austin Seminary Bulletin* 87 (1971), pp. 13-20.

Dahlberg, B.T., 'The Unity of Genesis', *Literary Interpretations of Biblical Narratives, Volume II* (ed. K.R.R. Gros Louis, with J.S. Ackerman; Nashville: Abingdon, 1982), pp. 126-44.

Dahood, Mitchell, 'Scriptio defectiva in Judges 1, 19', *Biblica* 60 (1979), p. 570.

Danby, Herbert, *The Mishnah, translated from the Hebrew with Introduction and brief Explanatory Notes* (Oxford: Oxford University Press, 1933).

Danelius, E., 'Shamgar ben 'Anath', *JNES* 22 (1963), pp. 191-93.

Davidson, E.T.A., 'Hidden Objects and Games in the Book of Judges' (unpublished paper).

Davies, G. Henton, 'Judges VIII 22-23', *VT* 12/2 (1963), pp. 151-57.

Dietrich, Walter, *Prophetie und Geschichte: eine redaktionsgeschichtliche Untersuchung zum deuteronomistischen Geschichtswerk* (FRLANT, 108; Göttingen: Vandenhoeck & Ruprecht, 1977).

Dumbrell, W.J., 'In Those Days There Was No King in Israel; Every Man Did What Was Right in His Own Eyes: The Purpose of the Book of Judges Reconsidered', *JSOT* 25 (1983), pp. 23-33.

Eissfeldt, O., *Die Quellen des Richterbuches* (Leipzig: J.C. Hinrichs, 1925).

Epstein, I., ed., *The Babylonian Talmud; . . . translated into English with notes, glossary and indices* (18 vols; London: Soncino, 1935-52).

—*Hebrew-English edition of the Babylonian Talmud* (13 vols.; London: Soncino, 1963-76).

Exum, Jo Cheryl, 'Aspects of Symmetry and Balance in the Samson Saga', *JSOT* 19 (1981), pp. 3-29.

—'Literary Patterns in the Samson Saga: an Investigation of Rhetorical Style in Biblical Prose' (PhD dissertation; Columbia University, 1976).

—'Promise and Fulfilment: Narrative Art in Judges 13', *JBL* 99 (1980), pp. 43-59.

Fensham, F.C., 'Shamgar ben 'Anath', *JNES* 20 (1961), pp. 197-98.

Fohrer, Georg, *Introduction to the Old Testament* (tr. D. Green; London: SPCK, 1970).

Fokkelman, J.P., *Narrative Art and Poetry in the Books of Samuel, a full interpretation based on stylistic and structural analyses, volume 1, King David (2 Sam. 9–20 and 1 Kings 1–2)* (Assen: Van Gorcum, 1981).

—*Narrative Art in Genesis: Specimens of Stylistic and Structural Analysis* (Amsterdam: Van Gorcum, 1975).

Frei, Hans W., *The Eclipse of Biblical Narrative. A Study in Eighteenth and Nineteenth Century Hermeneutics* (New Haven and London: Yale University Press, 1974).

Gerbrandt, Gerald Eddie, 'Kingship According to the Deuteronomistic History' (ThD dissertation; Union Theological Seminary, Virginia, 1980).

Geus, C.H.J. de, 'Richteren 1.1–2.5', *Vox Theologica* 36 (1966), pp. 32-53.

Ginzberg, Louis, *The Legends of the Jews* (7 vols.; tr. H. Szold; Philadelphia: The Jewish Publication Society of America, 1909-1938).

Globe, A., 'The Literary Structure and Unity of the Song of Deborah', *JBL* 93 (1974), pp. 493-512.

Good, E.M., *Irony in the Old Testament* (2nd edn; Sheffield: Almond Press, 1981).

Gooding, D.W., 'The Composition of the Book of Judges', *Eretz-Israel, Archeological Historical and Geographical Studies, Vol. 16; H.M. Orlinsky Volume* (Jerusalem: Israel Exploration Society, 1982), pp. 70-79.

Gray, J., *Johua, Judges and Ruth* (The Century Bible, New Edition; London: Nelson, 1967).

Greenberg, Moshe, *Understanding Exodus* (Vol. II, part 1 of the Melton Research Centre Project, The Heritage of Biblical Israel; New York: Behrman House, 1969).

Greenstein, Edward L., 'The Riddle of Samson', *Prooftexts* 1/3 (1981), pp. 237-60.

Greimas, A.J., *Du Sens* (Paris: Sevil, 1970).

—*Sémantique structurale* (Paris: Larousse, 1966).

Gros Louis, Kenneth R.R., 'The Book of Judges', *Literary Interpretations of Biblical Narratives* (eds. K. Gros Louis, J. Ackerman, T. Warshaw; Nashville: Abingdon, 1974), pp. 141-62.

Gunn, David M., 'Samson' (unpublished paper).

—*The Story of King David: Genre and Interpretation* (JSOT Supplement Series, 6; Sheffield: JSOT Press, 1978).

Gurewicz, S.B., 'The Bearing of Judges i–ii.5 on the Authorship of the Book of Judges', *Australian Biblical Review* 7 (1959), pp. 37-40.

Homer, *The Iliad*.

Homer, *The Odyssey*.

Jameson, F., 'Marxism and Historicism', *New Literary History* 11/1 (1979), pp. 41-73.

Jellicoe, S., *The Septuagint and Modern Study* (Oxford: Clarendon, 1968).

Jobling, D., *The Sense of Biblical Narrative* (JSOT Supplement Series, 7; Sheffield; JSOT Press, 1978).

Josephus, *Against Apion* (Loeb Classical Library. Josephus, Vol. I; London: 1932).

—*Jewish Antiquities* (Loeb Classical Library, Josephus, Vols. iv-ix; London: 1932).

Jüngling, H.-W., *Richter 19—Ein Plädoyer für das Königtum: Stilistische Analyse der Tendenzerzählung Ri 19, 1-30a; 21, 25* (Analecta Biblica 84; Rome: Biblical Institute Press, 1981).

Kaufmann, Y., *The Biblical Account of the Conquest of Palestine* (tr. M. Dagut; Jerusalem: Magnes, 1953).

—*The Book of Judges* [Hebrew] (Jerusalem: Kiryat Sepher, 1962).

Kautzsch, E., ed., *Gesenius' Hebrew Grammar* (2nd English edn; ed. by A.E. Cowley; Oxford: Clarendon, 1910).

Keil, C.F., and Delitzsch, F., *The Book of Judges* (Commentary on the Old Testament in Ten Volumes, 2; tr. J. Martin; Grand Rapids: Eerdmans, 1973).

Kitchen, K.A., *Ancient Orient and Old Testament* (London: IVP, 1966).

Kittel, R., ed., *Biblia Hebraica* (3rd edn; Stuttgart: Württembergische Bibelanstalt, 1937).

Kline, M.G., *Treaty of the Great King* (Grand Rapids: Eerdmans, 1963).

Kraeling, E.G., 'Difficulties in the Story of Ehud', *JBL* 54 (1935), pp. 205-210.

Lagarde, Paul A. de, *Septuaginta Studien, Teil I* (Göttingen, 1891).

Leach, Edmund R., 'The Legitimacy of Solomon. Some structural aspects of Old Testament history', *Archives Européennes de Sociologie* 7 (1966), pp. 58-101.

Lévi-Strauss, Claude, 'The Structural Study of Myth', *Structural Anthropology* (Garden City, New York: Basic Books, 1963), pp. 202-31.

Licht, J., *Storytelling in the Bible* (Jerusalem: Magnes, 1978).

Lilley, J.P.U., 'A Literary Appreciation of the Book of Judges', *Tyndale Bulletin* 18 (1976), pp. 94-102.

Limburg, J., 'The Root ריב and the Prophetic Lawsuit Speeches', *JBL* 88 (1969), pp. 291-304.

Lindars, Barnabas, 'Deborah's Song: Women in the Old Testament', *BJRL* 65/2 (1983), pp. 158-75.

—'Gideon and Kingship', *Journal of Theological Studies* n.s. 16 (1965), pp. 315-26.

—'The Israelite Tribes in Judges', *Studies in the Historical Books of the Old Testament* (VT Supp. 30; ed. J.A. Emerton; Leiden: Brill, 1979), pp. 95-112.

—'Jotham's Fable—A New Form-critical Analysis', *JTS* n.s. 24 (1973), pp. 355-66.

Malamat, A., 'The Danite Migration and the Pan-Israelite Exodus-Conquest: a Biblical Narrative Pattern', *Biblica* 51 (1970), pp. 1-16.

—'Hazor, "The Head of all those Kingdoms"', *JBL* 79 (1960), pp. 12-19.

—'The War of Gideon and Midian: A Military Approach', *PEQ* (1953), pp. 61-65.

Maly, Eugene, 'The Jotham Fable—Anti-monarchical?', *CBQ* 22 (1960), pp. 299-305.

Martin, James D., *Judges* (Cambridge Bible, Cambridge: Cambridge University Press, 1975).

Mayes, A.D.H., *Deuteronomy* (New Century Bible; London: Oliphants, 1979).

Mendenhall, George E., 'Ancient Oriental and Biblical Law', *Biblical Archaeologist* 17/2 (1954), pp. 26-46.

—'Covenant Forms in Israelite Tradition', *Biblical Archaeologist* 17/3 (1954), pp. 50-76.

Milton, John, *Samson Agonistes*.

Moore, George Foot, *A Critical and Exegetical Commentary on Judges* (2nd edn; International Critical Commentary; Edinburgh: Clark, 1908; 1st edn 1895).

Moran, W.J., 'A Study of the Deuteronomic History', *Biblica* 46 (1965), pp. 223-28.

Muilenburg, J., 'Form Criticism and Beyond', *JBL* 88 (1969), p. 7.

Murray, D.F., 'Narrative Structure and Technique in the Deborah-Barak Story, Judges iv 4-22', *Studies in the Historical Books of the Old Testament* (VT Supp.,

30; ed. J.A. Emerton; Leiden: Brill, 1979), pp. 155-89.

Nathhorst, B., *Formal or Structural Studies of Traditional Tales: the usefulness of some methodological proposals advanced by Vladimir Propp, Alan Dundes, Claude Lévi-Strauss and Edmund Leach* (Stockholm, 1969).

Nelson, Richard D., *The Double Redaction of the Deuteronomistic History* (JSOT Supplement Series, 18; Sheffield: JSOT Press, 1981).

Noth, Martin, 'The Background of Judges 17-18', *Israel's Prophetic Heritage: Essays in honor of James Muilenburg* (eds. B.W. Anderson and W. Harrelson; The Preachers' Library; London: SCM, 1962), pp. 68-85.

—*The Deuteronomistic History* (JSOT Supplement Series, 15; Sheffield, JSOT, 1981). A translation of *Überlieferungsgeschichtliche Studien*, 2nd edn, pp. 1-110.

—*Überlieferungsgeschichtliche Studien* (2nd edition; Tübingen: Max Niemeyer Verlag, 1957). The first edition appeared as *Schriften der Königsberger Gelehrten-Gesellschaft. Geisteswissenschaftliche Klasse, 18* (1943), pp. 43-266.

Patte, D., 'Structural Network in Narrative: The Good Samaritan', *Structuralism, an Interdisciplinary Study* (ed. S. Wittig; Pittsburgh Reprint, 3; Pittsburgh: Pickwick, 1975), pp. 77-98.

Philo, *On the Confusion of Tongues (De Confusione Linguarum)* (Loeb Classical Library. Philo, Vol. IV; tr. F.H. Colson and G. H. Whitaker; London: Heinemann, 1932), pp. 1-119.

—*Questions and Answers on Exodus* (Loeb Classical Library. Philo, Supplement 2: London: Heinemann, 1953).

—*Questions and Answers on Genesis* (Loeb Classical Library. Philo, Supplement 1; London: Heinemann, 1953).

Polzin, Robert M., *Moses and the Deuteronomist. A Literary Study of the Deuteronomic History, Part One: Deuteronomy, Joshua, Judges* (New York: Seabury Press, 1980).

Propp, Vladimir, *Morphology of the Folktale* (2nd edn, revised and edited with a preface by L.A. Wagner, and a new introduction by A. Dundes; Austin and London: University of Texas Press, 1968; original Russian edition, 1928).

Rad, Gerhard von, *Der Heilige Krieg im alten Israel* (4th edn; Göttingen: Vandenhoeck & Ruprecht, 1965).

Radday, Yehuda T., 'Chiasm in Joshua, Judges, and Others', *Linguistica Biblica* 27/28 (1973), pp. 6-13.

Rahlfs, A., *Septuagnta, id est Vetus Testamentum Graece iuxta LXX Interpretes* (2 vols; Stuttgart: 1935).

Richter, Wolfgang, *Die Bearbeitungen des 'Retterbuches' in der deuteronomischen Epoche* (Bonner Biblische Beiträge, 21; Bonn: Peter Hanstein, 1964).

—*Die sogenannten vorprophetischen Burufungsberichte* (Göttingen: Vandenhoeck & Ruprecht, 1970).

—*Traditionsgeschichtliche Untersuchungen zum Richterbuch* (2nd edn; Bonner Biblische Beiträge, 18; Bonn: Peter Hanstein Verlag, 1966).

—'Die Überlieferungen um Jephtah, Ri 10, 7-12,6', *Biblica* 47 (1966), pp. 485-556.

—'Zu den Richtern Israels', *ZAW* 77 (1965), pp. 40-72.

Ricoeur, Paul, 'The Narrative Function', *Semeia* 13 (1978), pp. 177-202.

Rösel, Hartmut N., 'Jephtah und das Problem der Richter', *Biblica* 61 (1980), pp. 251-55.

—'Die "Richter Israels" Rückblick und neuer Ansatz', *Biblische Zeitschrift* 25 (1981), pp. 180-203.

Saussure, Ferdinand de, *Course in General Linguistics* (eds. C. Bally, A Sechehaye; tr. W. Baskin; London: Peter Owen, 1960; first French edition, 1915).

Simpson, C.A., *Composition of Book of Judges* (Oxford: Basil Blackwell, 1957).

Smend, Rudolf, 'Das Gesetz und die Völker: ein Beitrag zur deuteronomistischen Redaktionsgeschichte', *Probleme biblischer Theologie: Gerhard von Rad zum 70. Geburtstag* (ed. H.W. Wolff; München: Chr. Kaiser Verlag, 1971), pp. 494-509.

Soggin, J. Alberto, *Judges: A Commentary* (Old Testament Library; Philadelphia: Westminster, 1981).

Swete, H.B., *An Introduction to the Old Testament in Greek* (Cambridge: Cambridge University Press, 1902).

Thomson, H.C., 'Shophet and Mishpat in the Book of Judges', *Transactions of the Glasgow University Oriental Society* 19 (1961-62), pp. 74-85.

Trible, Phyllis, 'A Meditation in Mourning: The Sacrifice of the Daughter of Jephthah', *Union Seminary Quarterly Review* 31 (1981), pp. 59-73.

Uspensky, Boris, *A Poetics of Composition: The Structure of the Artistic Text and Typology of a Compositional Form* (tr. V. Zavarin, S. Wittig; Berkeley: University of California Press, 1973).

Van Selms, A., 'Judge Shamgar', *VT* 14 (1964), pp. 294-309.

Van Seters, J., 'The Conquest of Sihon's Kingdom: A Literary Examination', *JBL* 91 (1972), pp. 182-97.

—*In Search of History: Historiography in the Ancient World and the Origins of Biblical History* (New Haven and London: 1983).

—'Once Again—The Conquest of Sihon's Kingdom', *JBL* 99 (1980), pp. 117-19.

Vaux, Roland de, *The Early History of Israel, to the Period of the Judges* (tr. D. Smith; London: Darton, Longman and Todd, 1978, originally published in French, 1971).

—'Sur l'Origine Kenite ou Midianite du Yahvisme', *Eretz Israel* 9 (1969), pp. 28-32.

Veijola, Timo, *Die ewige Dynastie. David und die Entstehung seiner Dynastie nach der deuteronomistischen Darstellung* (Annales Academiae Scientiarum Fennicae, Ser. B, Tom. 193; Helsinki: Suomalainen Tiedeakatemia, 1975).

—*Das Königtum in der Beurteilung der deuteronomistischen Historiographie: eine redaktionsgeschichtliche Untersuchung* (Annales Academiae Scientiarum Fennicae, Ser. B, Tom. 198; Helsinki: Suomalainen Tiedeakatemia, 1977).

Vickery, J.B., 'In Strange Ways: The Story of Samson', in *Images of Man and God: Old Testament Short Stories in Literary Focus* (ed. B.O. Long; Sheffield: Almond, 1981), pp. 58-73.

Weinfeld, M., 'The Period of the Conquest and the Judges as seen in the Earlier and the Later Sources', *VT* 17 (1967), pp. 97-113.

Weiser, A., 'Das Deboralied: eine gattungs- und traditionsgeschichtliche Studie', *ZAW* 71 (1959), pp. 67-97.

Westermann, C., *Basic Forms of Prophetic Speech* (Philadelphia: Westminster, 1967).

Wüst, M. 'Die Einschaltungen in die Jiftachgeschichten, Ri 11.13-26', *Biblica* 56 (1975), pp. 464-79.

INDEX

INDEX OF BIBLICAL REFERENCES

INDEX OF AUTHORS

JOURNAL FOR THE STUDY OF THE OLD TESTAMENT
Supplement Series